Disability in Judaism, Christianity, and Islam

Disability in Judaism, Christianity, and Islam

Sacred Texts, Historical Traditions, and Social Analysis

Edited by
Darla Schumm and Michael Stoltzfus

palgrave
macmillan

DISABILITY IN JUDAISM, CHRISTIANITY, AND ISLAM
Copyright © Darla Schumm and Michael Stoltzfus, 2011.

All rights reserved.

First published in 2011 by
PALGRAVE MACMILLAN®
in the United States—a division of St. Martin's Press LLC,
175 Fifth Avenue, New York, NY 10010.

Where this book is distributed in the UK, Europe and the rest of the world,
this is by Palgrave Macmillan, a division of Macmillan Publishers Limited,
registered in England, company number 785998, of Houndmills,
Basingstoke, Hampshire RG21 6XS.

Palgrave Macmillan is the global academic imprint of the above companies
and has companies and representatives throughout the world.

Palgrave® and Macmillan® are registered trademarks in the United States,
the United Kingdom, Europe and other countries.

ISBN: 978–0–230–11972–7

Library of Congress Cataloging-in-Publication Data

    Disability in Judaism, Christianity, and Islam : sacred texts,
historical traditions, and social analysis / edited by Darla Schumm and
Michael Stoltzfus.
      p. cm.
    ISBN 978–0–230–11972–7 (hardback)
     1. Disabilities—Religious aspects. 2. Human body—Religious aspects.
I. Schumm, Darla Y. (Darla Yvonne) II. Stoltzfus, Michael, 1965– III. Title.

BL65.B63D58 2011
200.87—dc22   2011014238

A catalogue record of the book is available from the British Library.

Design by Newgen Imaging Systems (P) Ltd., Chennai, India.

First edition: October 2011

10 9 8 7 6 5 4 3 2 1

Printed in the United States of America.

For Rebecca, William, Jonathan, and Henry

Contents

Section 2   Social and Philosophical Perspectives on Religion and Disability

Acknowledgments

All books have collaborative elements, but this book and its companion volume *Disability and Religious Diversity: Cross-Cultural and Interreligious Perspectives* truly reflect collaboration on many levels. We thank all those who gave their time and talents and contributed chapters to the book. We had a vision for the book that was realized only through the contributions of: Arseli Dokumaci, Bonnie Gracer, Christine James, Jennifer Koosed, Matthew Long, Autumn Molinari, Gerald O'Brien, Elizabeth Sierra, Kristi Upson-Saia, Kirk Van Gilder, Julia Watts Belser, Amy Wilson, and Amos Yong.

Palgrave Macmillan graciously reviewed our original manuscript and recommended that we divide it into two separate volumes. Editor Burke Gerstenschlager and Editorial Assistant Kaylan Connally deftly guided us through the process of preparing two manuscripts for publication. We are grateful to the editorial board of Palgrave Macmillan for their willingness to bring issues of religion and disability to the forefront and publish these books.

Most of what we do would not be possible without the love and support of our families. We thank our parents, Glenn and Geneva Stoltzfus and Clare and Katie Ann Schumm, for their constant care, encouragement, and nurture. Our spouses and children Rebecca Green, William Stoltzfus, Jonathan Harris, and Henry Schumm provide daily inspiration and encouragement and receive our deep gratitude for sustaining us from the beginning to the end of the project.

We thank Elizabeth Smoak, a student assistant at Hollins University, for her help with many details in the editing process. Finally, we are profoundly grateful for the immense contribution Lindsay L. Gray made to the project. She logged countless hours of proofreading, editing, formatting, and then doing it all over, again and again. Lindsay oversaw many of the details involved in compiling and publishing two edited volumes. She kept us on track, and without her work we could have never brought the project to its successful completion.

Editors' Introduction

Darla Schumm and Michael Stoltzfus

The seeds for *Disability in Judaism, Christianity, and Islam: Sacred Texts, Historical Traditions, and Social Analysis* and its companion volume *Disability and Religious Diversity: Cross-Cultural and Interreligious Perspectives* (also published by Palgrave Macmillan) were planted as we conducted research for our first joint scholarly venture examining the intersections between religion and disability and/or chronic illness. We discovered two significant issues during the course of our research. First, while there were numerous resources addressing the intersections between religion and disability from the perspective of a single religious tradition, there were alarmingly few journal articles and no books addressing disability across a variety of religious traditions. Second, the religion and disability literature that did exist was dominated by Christian perspectives. There are several noteworthy books written on religion and disability articulating Jewish and Muslim perspectives, such as *Islam and Disability: Perspectives in Theology and Jurisprudence* by Mohammed Ghaly (2010) and *Judaism and Disability: Portrayals in Ancient Texts from the Tanach through the Bavli* by Judith Abrams (1998), but the vast majority of the literature is Christian based. The growth in religion and disability literature over the past 25 years is notable and encouraging, but gaps in the existent literature reveal a need for broader interreligious and cross-cultural analysis and critique.

In response to the challenges and opportunities posed by a postmodern, pluralistic, global world, our primary goal as contributing editors of these books is to provide a forum that promotes interdisciplinary, cross-cultural, and interreligious dialogue regarding disability and religious diversity. Multicultural education and literature address balancing the particularity of cultural or religious identity with openness to learning from our neighbors who are different. The interplay of the opening and boundary-setting dimensions of religious life is of crucial importance to the flourishing of multicultural societies in general and to the growing field of disability studies in particular. The diverse ways that religions interpret, theorize, and respond to disability and/or chronic illness play an important role in determining how disability is understood and how persons with disabilities are treated or mistreated in a given historical-cultural context. In addition, religious teachings and practices help to establish cultural standards for what is deemed "normal" human physical and mental behavior and in establishing a moral order for the fit and healthy body and mind.

This book and its companion volume began with the editors' desire to create a resource that investigates issues in disability studies from the perspective of religious pluralism. The response to our open call for papers addressing interreligious and cross-cultural perspectives on topics relevant to disability studies produced too much for one volume to contain. After Palgrave Macmillan's gracious offer to publish the collection in two volumes, we were left with the task of organizing the chapters between volumes. When the review process was complete, about half of the remaining chapters addressed disability studies within the frameworks of Judaism, Christianity, or Islam. We therefore decided to dedicate this book largely to those traditions. The religious traditions that explore disability or chronic illness in the companion volume include Baha'i, Celtic Pagan, Wiccan, Native American, Daoist, as well as narrative and comparative pieces that incorporate Catholic and Protestant Christianity, Buddhism, and Islam.

There are many reasons to integrate Jewish, Christian, and Muslim perspectives into a book addressing religion and disability. The most obvious involves their historical, scriptural, and theological continuity. For example, *Allah* is the Arabic word for the God of the Jewish and Christian Bibles. There are many ways of understanding God among Muslims, and there are many ways of understanding God among Christians, but all these are ways of understanding the God of Israel. Christianity began as a Jewish sect. Jesus was born, lived, and died a Jew. Primary sources of the Koran (also spelled Qur'an) are the Jewish and Christian scriptures. The adherents of the religion of Islam consider themselves to be recipients of the same divine guidance that was granted to Jews and Christians.

Jewish, Christian, and Muslim ways of understanding overlap extensively. All proclaim one God. All teach about a common humanity created in the image of the same God and respect for all of humanity. All emphasize the importance of communal values over selfish individualism. All incorporate many of the same central figures, including Adam and Eve, Abraham, and Moses. All struggle with both script and tradition in the light of modern insights. And all face similar challenges when it comes to addressing disability. None of this is meant to gloss over significant differences and tensions that exist between these traditions, but it does help to explain the editors' decision to dedicate one volume to Jewish, Christian, and Islamic perspectives regarding religion and disability.

Disability Studies: Broad Outlines

The essays in this volume do not represent a uniform approach to understanding or responding to disability; nor do they present a monolithic experience of disability and/or chronic illness. Paul Longmore and Lauri Umansky (2001: 4) observe:

> While public policy has sought to fashion *disability* as a generic category and attempted to impose that classification on people with an assortment of conditions, disability has never been a monolithic grouping. There has always been a variety of disability experiences.

One reason that disability studies are so rich and interesting is because "disability" defies definition. It is evident that disability is a pervasive human experience, transcending categories of economic class, race, ethnicity, gender, or religious affiliation. The sheer number of persons with disabilities will only increase as health care improves and becomes more widely available. For example, in 2000, it was estimated that some 64 million or 20 percent of Americans have one or more physical or intellectual disabilities or chronic illnesses; this number is increasing as the population ages (Davis 2002; Harrington n.d.). This makes people with disabilities the largest and most diverse minority group in the United States. Similar statistics are likely representative of the world population as a whole.

Despite evidence demonstrating that disability defies categorization, efforts to compartmentalize people with disabilities abound. One of the more common categories is the medical model, which tends to explain disability as a physical abnormality requiring diagnosis, treatment, and cure. The medical model ascribes disabling conditions to a "lack" of physical ability caused by limitations of culturally defined "normal" bodies. According to this understanding, there are "correct" and "incorrect" ways for the body to function, and all incorrectly functioning bodies should be "fixed." This ignores the reality that many chronically disabling conditions have no established medical protocols for their cure. The medical model posits a typical standard for "whole and healthy" bodies, a perspective that fails to incorporate relevant themes such as cultural exclusion or social accommodation (Garland-Thomson 2005; Longmore and Umansky 2001; Reynolds 2008).

Brent Hardin and Marie Hardin (2005) trace the cultural construction of the standard for "ideal normal bodies" in the medical model of disability through an examination of power and performance in the arena of sports. The advent of sports media in the industrial age created an ideal forum for asserting American capitalist values such as "... respect for authority, individualism, sacrifice 'for the team,' and hard work" (Hardin and Hardin 2005: 4). Autonomy and physical fitness are asserted as the "ideal" American model for the body. Embedded in this perspective is the implicit expectation that through hard work, pain, and dedication, the body is conditioned to its physical peak performance. Thus, the culturally constructed standards of the "ideal normal body" tend to marginalize disabled bodies that do not fit the norm. The medical model perpetuates the assumption that the root problem of disability lies in the disabled individual body rather than in the socioreligious forces that may marginalize and stigmatize persons with disabilities.

While religious attitudes and responses to disability are quite diverse, it is not uncommon for Jewish, Christian, and Islamic perspectives to mimic the medical model by connecting disabling bodily conditions with individual spiritual deficiency. There is a persistent tendency to associate disability with individual sin. Well-meaning people from multiple religious traditions often struggle to offer religious explanations and religious solutions to the "problem" (Reynolds 2008; Simundson 2001). For people with disabilities, such explanations can lead to spiritual anxiety in the private sphere and alienation from religious association in the public sphere. Isolated from the public sphere for physical or intellectual abnormality or difference, such persons likewise find themselves singled out through religious interpretations of that difference, interpretations that might generate stigmatization.

In contrast to the medical and religious models, disability studies scholars posit an alternative understanding of and approach to disability. Disability is not simply summarized by physical limitation; rather, disabling conditions are made more limiting by the marginalization that occurs, for example, when buildings are not accessible or stereotypical attitudes call into question the full humanity of persons with disabilities (Davis 2002; Garland-Thomson 2005; Linton 1998; Wendell 1996). Rosemarie Garland-Thomson explains the difference between the social and medical models of disability as "...a cultural interpretation of human variation [social model] rather than an inherent inferiority, pathology to cure, or undesirable trait to eliminate [medical model]" (Garland-Thomson 2005: 1558). Some disability studies scholars (Morris 1991; Schriempf 2001) argue that the social model tends to minimize genuine physical challenges associated with disabling conditions. Nonetheless, while real physical challenges do exist, issues associated with social attitudes, physical accommodation, and cultural stigmatization should not be ignored.

As Longmore and Umanski (2001) observe, resistance to viewing disability through the lens of the social model mirrors the resistance of the academy to include disability studies as a core component of many college and university curricula outside of the health-care-related disciplines. Disability studies courses are often dismissed as merely promoting identity politics pertinent only to a small group of people. Critics argue that disability studies lack academic rigor and intellectual relevance. Many who otherwise promote inclusion of diverse perspectives into curricular offerings paradoxically minimize the importance of disability perspectives.

> Ironically, supporters of diversity who propose to make teaching and research more comprehensive, more accurate and representative, often marshal the same accusations in opposing the inclusion of disability studies in that project. Some even add the distinctive argument that incorporating disability would "water down" diversity requirements. (Longmore and Umanski 2001: 9)

Therefore, recent movements within the academy to question traditional sources of authority and knowledge are slow to include disability perspectives as important sources for critical analysis and constructive response. In many spheres, disability is not yet considered a pertinent mode of social critique as are race, gender, socioeconomic class, and sexual orientation.

Religious Studies and Disability

Like experiences of disability, religious experiences are pluralistic. There are many forms of religious expression within any given religious tradition and certainly among differing traditions. As a result, religious attitudes and interpretations discussed in this book may not neatly mesh with one another. As is the case with experiences of disability, our goal is not to present uniform interpretations of religious thought and practice; rather, we aim to cultivate dialogue and debate among and within religious traditions about disability. Readers will encounter diverse, even contradictory, perspectives regarding religious experience or textual interpretation in this book.

Echoing the history of disability studies in the academy in general is the introduction of disability as a mode of analysis within religious studies in particular. Douglas Baynton (2001) observes a phenomenon in the field of historical studies that is paralleled in religious studies. Baynton writes, "Disability is everywhere in history, once you begin looking for it, but conspicuously absent in the histories we write" (Baynton 2001: 52). A similar statement is apropos for religious studies; religious communities have always included people with disabilities and many sacred texts reference stories pertinent to disability studies, but the perspectives of people living with disabilities remained largely absent from the academic study of religion until recently.

Several benchmark events laid the groundwork for the study of disability in the arena of religious studies. Hector Avalos notes, "All scholarly disciplines have a landmark event within their history" (Avalos 2007: 91). For disability in religious studies one such "landmark" event occurred on November 20, 1995 (Avalos 2007: 91). This day marked the first meeting of the "Religion and Disability Studies Consultation" at the annual meeting of the American Academy of Religion/Society of Biblical Literature (AAR/SBL) conference and nine years later the SBL held its first session of the "Biblical Scholarship and Disabilities Consultation" (Avalos 2007). The emergence of these two consultations (now official groups or units in both AAR and SBL) ushered in a new era for discussions of disability and religion in the academy.

Another seminal event within the field of religion and disability was the publication of Nancy Eiesland's (1994) pioneering work *The Disabled God: Toward a Libratory Theology of Disability*. Eiesland formulated a theology of disability and invited readers to envision a God different from traditional images of the divine. Eiesland describes her vision of God when she writes:

> ... I had waited for a mighty revelation of God. But my epiphany bore little resemblance to the God I was expecting or the God of my dreams. I saw God in a sip-puff wheelchair, that is, the chair used mostly by quadriplegics enabling them to maneuver by blowing and sucking on a

strawlike device. Not an omnipotent, self-sufficient God, but neither a pitiable, suffering servant. In this moment, I beheld God as a survivor, unpitying and forthright. (Eiesland 1994: 89)

Eiesland created a seismic shift for disability studies within the context of religious studies by opening space for biblical and theological reflection from the vantage point of disability. Since the publication of *The Disabled God,* many scholars have published books and articles on disability and religion and the *Journal of Religion, Disability, and Health* was established as a forum for scholarly debate in religion and disability.[1] Creation of groups in the AAR and SBL for reflection on religion and disability and the debut of scholarly publications in the field of religion and disability were significant milestones for disability studies and religious studies, but as noted above, much more work remains to be done in this burgeoning field. It is our hope that the chapters in this book and its companion volume make a significant contribution to the ever-expanding dialogue about the intersections between religion and disability.

Broad Themes and Book Overview

The organization of this book reflects the type of interreligious and cross-cultural dialogue we hope to model and inspire. This book is divided into two sections: (1) Sacred Texts, Historical Traditions, and Disability and (2) Social and Philosophical Perspectives on Religion and Disability. Each section is prefaced by a brief introduction that highlights key themes and provides previews of the chapters that follow. It is important to note that while each chapter is distinctive and stands on its own as an academic and creative work, basic themes run throughout each section and between sections. Religion and disability are the themes that navigate broad topics associated with textual and historical investigation, social and philosophical analysis, and comparative reflection.

Two questions emerge in many of the chapters in this book: First, how does the story of disability fit in with the story of God in the Jewish, Christian, and Islamic traditions? Second, how might sacred texts and religious traditions challenge discrimination against persons with disabilities while promoting inclusion and justice? The former question incorporates issues pertinent to theodicy concerns: If God is all knowing, powerful, and benevolent, why is there evil and sin in the world? This is an understandable question to ask with respect to disability, but the danger of the question is that it implicitly equates disability with evil and sin. Many authors in this book adopt elements of the social model by suggesting that disability is not a malady to be cured, but simply another form of human variation. Evil is not reducible to the presence of individual disability; and the social attitudes and actions that limit the full humanity of people with disabilities are primarily elements of sinful human interaction. In the final chapter of the book, Amos Yong scrutinizes the philosophy of religion through the lens of disability studies and in doing so tackles the question of theodicy head-on. Yong argues that when put into conversation with disability perspectives, the philosophy of religion can be "transformed into performing justice for all." At the heart of each of the chapters in this book is a desire to disavow connections between disability and individual sin and to promote justice for all, regardless of ability.

Is the experience of disability on par with that of economic oppression, racism, or sexism? Does it represent, in other words, a valid perspective from which to issue calls for social justice and from which to interpret the scriptures of Judaism, Christianity, and Islam? The editors along with many of the authors in this book are convinced that it does. However, as is the case with liberation and feminist perspectives, there must then be attentiveness to a marginalized constituency. The experiences that surround disability, for the disabled persons and their communities, have profound connections to the deepest currents present in the Hebrew Bible, Christian Bible, and Koran. Disability touches directly on the question of a community's identity, on the meaning of transformation, indeed, on the very image people have of God within the Jewish, Christian, and Islamic traditions. Access to full community participation touches on justice, dignity, and what it means to be a child of God in the Jewish-Christian-Islamic contexts. Conversely, exclusion from the community erodes both individual identity and the sense of collective integrity.

All but one of the chapters in Section 1 of the book discuss the way disability is presented and addressed in the sacred texts of Judaism, Christianity, and Islam. In chapters 1 and 2, Julia Watts Belser and Bonnie L. Gracer incorporate Jewish sacred texts and commentaries to critique both ancient and contemporary cultural notions of disability. In chapters 3 and 4, Matthew L. Long and Elizabeth R. Sierra each discuss the marginalization of those afflicted with skin conditions. Long focuses his inquiry on the Muslim community and the Qur'an, while Sierra engages in a comparative analysis gleaned from Jewish, Christian, and Muslim sources. In Chapter 5, Jennifer Koosed and Darla Schumm dissect the use of the metaphor of blindness in the Christian gospel of John. These chapters provide historical-cultural context, assess whether texts foster positive or negative implications for disability studies, explore how particular texts have been applied traditionally, and investigate alternative interpretive meanings. In Chapter 6, Kristi Upson-Saia employs similar tools of exploration while focusing on the writings of St. Augustine, one of the most influential early Christian theologians. The conclusions of the authors in this section are varied, but at the core of all these chapters is a desire to discover how sacred texts and significant historical figures portray disability.

Koosed and Schumm articulate another current running throughout the book when they argue that "metaphors matter." Metaphorical representations of disability often determine how disability is viewed and defined in broader cultural contexts, and often these metaphors wield uncanny power. This is perhaps nowhere more true than in the case of religious metaphors and language. As Koosed and Schumm note in their chapter, womanist Biblical studies scholar Renita Weems (1995) makes a compelling case for the power of metaphors when she argues that metaphors often function to shape and reflect the values of a community. Weems writes, "Metaphors matter because they are sometimes our first lessons in prejudice, bigotry, stereotyping, and in marginalizing others—even if only in our minds. They deserve our scrutiny because they are intrinsic to the way we live and shape reality" (Weems 1995: 107). Gerald V. O'Brien and Autumn Molinari eerily demonstrate the destructive power of religious metaphors in their chapter "Religious Metaphors as a Justification for Eugenic Control: A Historical Analysis." O'Brien and Molinari trace how religious metaphors were used in both the United States and Nazi Germany to support and encourage the use of eugenics in an effort to "control" persons with disabilities. While the aforementioned authors most specifically link religious metaphors with potentially dangerous consequences, underlying all the chapters is the conviction that religious metaphors and language annex power in shaping perceptions of disability.

The argument that "metaphors matter" is matched by a similar assertion that religious views of disability have practical social implications. Arseli Dokumaci, in her chapter "Performance of Muslim Daily Prayer by Physically Disabled Practitioners," examines what, if any, allowances can be made for disabled Muslims when fulfilling one of the five required pillars of practice. Amy T. Wilson and Kirk Van Gilder engage in cross-cultural analysis when they discuss "best practices" for Western Christian missionaries who confront disability (most specifically deafness) through their work in the global south. While the essays in Section 2 most directly analyze the social ramifications of perceptions of disability within religions, underpinning all the analysis in this book is the conviction that religious constructions of disability have real-life consequences.

A final thread weaving through the chapters is what we call the paradox of disability. On the one hand, persons with disabilities are valorized as moral exemplars or "saints" who have much to teach us about gracious suffering, either literally or figuratively. In this context, persons with disabilities are often put on a pedestal and considered "greater-than" as Christine James articulates in Chapter 9. Yet, on the other hand, James notes that persons with disabilities are also often believed to be "lesser-than" insofar as they are perceived to be dependent on others and are uncomfortable reminders of human fragility, mortality, and sin. Whether saint or sinner, both extremes of the dualistic paradox tend to be patronizing to people with disabilities, necessitating critique and broader exploration.

Hopes and Intentions

It is our hope that this book and its companion volume *Disability and Religious Diversity: Cross-Cultural and Interreligious Perspectives* will appeal to a broad audience including members of the disabled community, scholars and students from many disciplines, health-care professionals, social service professionals, and religious practitioners from many traditions. We believe that these books can function as useful tools for college and university courses and as resources for more general audiences interested in the intersection of religion and disability. The books might also help people expand what is sometimes a narrow professional and/or personal frame of reference for viewing and responding to both disability and religion.

The role that disability and religion play in human experience is vast, pervasive, and beyond simplification. The chapters included in this volume portray varied and complex perspectives of Jewish, Christian, and Islamic perspectives. Consensus regarding the experience of disability or the understanding of how these traditions should conceptualize disability is not the goal of this text. Rather, the objective is to foster interreligious and cross-cultural dialogue about religions in an effort to cultivate new and innovative ways to investigate and respond to the expanding field of disability studies.

Our efforts to further promote interreligious conversations between religion and disability studies merely represent the first baby steps in what we hope will be a long and fruitful dialogue. Both of these volumes represent a range of religious diversity; however, to some extent, we miss the mark because Christian voices and perspectives still dominate much of the discussion in this book. Few scholars who work in the areas of Asian religions and disability responded to our call. These realities present ongoing challenges for the fields of religious studies and disability studies. Therefore, we do not view this book and its companion volume as comprehensive representations of religious diversity and disability, but rather as bridges for further dialogue and conversation. If the ensuing years bring broader explorations in cross-cultural and interreligious comparisons of religion and disability, then we can be content with our effort.

Note

1. Examples of books recently published in the field of religion and disability include *Disability and Christian Theology: Embodied Limits and Constructive Possibilities* by Deborah Creamer (2009); *Theology and Down Syndrome: Reimagining Disability in Late Modernity* by Amos Yong (2007); *Vulnerable Communion: A Theology of Disability and Hospitality* by Thomas Reynolds; and *Spirit and the Politics of Disablement* by Sharon Betcher (2007).

References

Abrams, J. Z. (1998). *Judaism and Disability: Portrayals in Ancient Texts from the Tanach through the Bavli.* Washington, DC: Gallaudet University Press.

Avalos, H. (2007). Redemptionism, rejectionism, and historicism as emerging approaches in disability studies. *Perspectives in Religious Studies 34*(1), 91–100.

Baynton, D. (2001). Disability and the justification of inequality in American history. In P. Longmore & L. Umansky (Eds.), *The New Disability History: American Perspectives* (pp. 33–57). New York, NY: New York University Press.

Betcher, S. V. (2007). *Spirit and the Politics of Disablement.* Minneapolis, MN: Fortress Press.

Creamer, D. B. (2009). *Disability and Christian Theology: Embodied Limits and Constructive Possibilities.* New York, NY: Oxford University Press.

Davis, L. (2002). *Bending over Backwards: Disability, Dismodernism & Other Difficult Positions.* New York, NY: New York University Press.

Eiesland, N. L. (1994). *The Disabled God: Toward a Liberatory Theology of Disability.* Nashville, TN: Abingdon Press.

Garland-Thomson, R. (2005). Feminist disability studies. *Signs: Journal of Women in Culture and Society 30*(2), 1558–1587.

Ghaly, M. M. I. (2010). *Islam and Disability: Perspectives in Theology and Jurisprudence*. London, UK: Routledge.

Hardin, B., & Hardin M. (2005). Performances or participation…pluralism or hegemony? Images of disability and gender in *Sports 'n Spokes* magazine. *Disability Studies Quarterly 25*(4), 1–16.

Harrington, C. (n.d.). Disability Statistics Center. Retrieved from http://dsc.ucsf.edu/main.php

Linton, S. (1998). *Claiming Disability: Knowledge and Identity*. New York, NY: New York University Press.

Longmore, P., & Umansky, L. (Eds). (2001). *The New Disability History: American Perspectives*. New York, NY: New York University Press.

Morris, J. (1991). *Pride Against Prejudice: Transforming Attitudes to Disability*. London, UK: The Women's Press, Ltd.

Reynolds, T. E. (2008). *Vulnerable Communion: A Theology of Disability and Hospitality*. Grand Rapids, MI: Brazos Press.

Schriempf, A. (2001). (Re)fusing the amputated body: An interactionist bridge for feminism and disability. *Hypatia 16*(4), 56–72.

Simundson, D. J. (2001). *Faith Under Fire: How the Bible Speaks to Us in Times of Suffering*. Lima, OH: Academic Renewal Press.

Weems, R. J. (1995). *Battered Love: Marriage, Sex, and Violence in the Hebrew Prophets*. Minneapolis, MN: Fortress Press.

Wendell, S. (1996). *The Rejected Body: Feminist Philosophical Reflections on Disability*. New York, NY: Routledge.

Yong, A. (2007). *Theology and Down Syndrome: Reimagining Disability in Late Modernity*. Waco, TX: Baylor University Press.

SECTION 1

Sacred Texts, Historical Traditions, and Disability

The Islamic tradition has used the phrase "people of the book," to describe Jews, Christians, and Muslims. These three religions tend to prioritize their respective sacred texts as authoritative sources regarding questions of tradition, membership within the community, belief, ethical conduct, and social customs. As such, the sacred texts of Judaism, Christianity, and Islam are powerful determinants in shaping how religious discourse functions to alienate, welcome, or categorize people with disabilities or chronic illnesses. What do the sacred texts of these traditions reveal about disability? How have the sacred texts shaped belief and practice in Judaism, Christianity, and Islam regarding disability? How have the historical traditions of these three religions interpreted and applied understandings of disability as a result of textual hermeneutical investigations? These are some of the questions that the chapters in Section 1 of the book begin to address. Hermeneutical exploration reveals many possibilities, and the essays in Section 1 offer multiple ways of interpreting how Jewish sacred texts, the Christian Bible, and the Qur'an (and other Islamic historical writings) portray disability.

Hector Avalos (2007) provides a helpful framework for understanding the various hermeneutical approaches employed by the authors. Avalos identifies three emergent trends for examining disability within the context of biblical studies: redemptionism, rejectionism, and historicism. "Redemptionism" attempts to retrieve redeeming value in sacred texts through a process of recontextualization, even when the text communicates negative messages about disability. If the text conveys positive messages about disability, the redemptionist approach then turns toward "rescuing" the text from modern interpretations that gloss over, ignore, or misrepresent positive depictions of disability. Julia Watts Belser, Bonnie Gracer, and Kristi Upson-Saia incorporate elements of the redemptionist approach in their respective chapters. Watts Belser and Gracer examine sacred Jewish texts, while Upson-Saia explores the writing and teachings of St. Augustine. In the shadow of each author's analysis is the awareness that the texts they scrutinize have perpetuated negative attitudes about people with disabilities. Important questions addressed in these chapters include the following: How are people with disabilities represented in the texts? How have the texts been interpreted and used historically? How might contemporary scholars reinterpret the texts in light of the themes and issues highlighted in disability studies literature?

"Rejectionism" contrasts with redemptionism by suggesting that if negative portrayals of disability exist in sacred texts, then those portrayals should be criticized and rejected. Underpinning the rejectionist approach is the question: How much should religious traditions rely on ancient texts for establishing modern standards and norms? In Chapter 5, Jennifer L. Koosed and Darla Schumm incorporate elements of the rejectionist approach when they warn readers that uncritical acceptance of biblical metaphors can yield dangerous and harmful consequences. While Koosed and Schumm do not entirely repudiate the biblical texts they explore, they do not rule out rejectionism as a viable possibility in some circumstances.

The "historicist" approach interrogates historical depictions and interpretations of disability in sacred texts, but is not explicitly concerned with the ramifications for modern readers. Matthew L. Long and Elizabeth R. Sierra each scour historical texts for descriptions and analyze how persons with skin diseases were perceived and treated in their respective communities. Sierra broadens the historicist approach by discussing some of the modern implications of her historical analysis.

Julia Watts Belser's chapter opens the book by examining how the Talmud can be used to critique cultural notions of disability. Watts Belser sets contemporary disability theorists in conversation with textual representations of disability in ancient rabbinic tales and legends in order to articulate the ways in which disability functions as metaphor, mirror, and contested category in rabbinic representation. The chapter demonstrates how the Babylonian Talmud, a complex sixth-century literary and legal text, constructs disability as an ambiguous cultural sign that allows the rabbis to use disabled figures to underscore the instability of the body. Watts Belser argues that the Talmud might be interpreted as locating the problem of disability primarily in the eye of the beholder by making use of what contemporary disability studies have termed "the stare" or intrusive gaze of a viewer, which often objectifies the person being stared at.

In Chapter 2, Bonnie L. Gracer examines deafness in Jewish antiquity as expressed in the Mishnah, a foundational document of rabbinic Judaism. Gracer surveys ancient Greek and Roman attitudes toward disability and deafness in order to establish the context within which the Mishnah was formulated, and to assess whether, and to what extent, Greco-Roman beliefs may have influenced Jewish law on matters pertaining to deafness. Particular focus is given to (a) infanticide and gratitude as two opposing responses to disability in antiquity and (b) the common belief that hearing and speech are precursors to intelligence. Gracer surveys the Mishnah in order to elaborate on these points and discuss their implications for the participation of deaf people in Judaism.

In Chapter 3, Matthew L. Long offers a textual and historical exploration of leprosy in the early Muslim community. The different Arabic terminology related to the English terms "leper" and "leprosy" is analyzed along with a number of primary sources of Islamic literature including the Qur'an, the Hadith, and biographies of Muhammad and his companions. Long investigates whether or not the Muslim community made a distinction between different forms of leprosy and whether Muhammad and his companions reacted differently based upon the type of leprosy. Evidence from Arabic sources demonstrates that lepers were treated with great trepidation during Muhammad's lifetime.

In Chapter 4, Elizabeth R. Sierra offers a comparative historical inquiry into Jewish-Christian-Islamic conceptions of uncleanness, suffering, and healing regarding vitiligo, a noninfectious, gradually progressive dermatological condition, and an examination of bias toward people living with vitiliginous skin. Sierra documents how people with vitiligo have long endured similar treatment as people with leprosy, their unevenly whitening skins viewed as a marker of sin, a sign of divine retribution, and cause for exile in Jewish, Christian, and Islamic societies. Sierra offers a splendid inquiry into the historical religious aspects of the social construction of bias against people with vitiligo, including the role that multiple religious traditions have played in misinformed stigmatization of vulnerable people and its ongoing modern implications.

In Chapter 5, Jennifer L. Koosed and Darla Schumm argue that the literal and metaphorical depictions of broken bodies in the Christian gospel of John function to not only exclude persons with disabilities but also foster anti-Semitic and anti-Jewish attitudes among Christians. Through a focus on the trope of blindness, Koosed and Schumm maintain that the gospel writer uses double entendre to connect two meanings of blindness: blindness as a physical state (the literal meaning) and blindness as a spiritual state (the metaphorical meaning). The authors issue strong warnings when they argue that "metaphors matter" and can often serve as powerful shapers of community values and beliefs. Koosed and Schumm conclude the chapter with an examination of how the gospel does at times disrupt its own characterizations of broken bodies when discussing the resurrected body of Christ.

In the final chapter of Section 1, Kristi Upson-Saia utilizes select writings from Augustine to challenge representations of disabled bodies in antiquity in general and early Christian interpretations of scarred or deformed bodies in particular. Contemporary disability theorists often find little worth salvaging in ancient Greek and Roman literature because disabled characters were stereotypically either characterized as weak and wicked or merely used as pawns to praise the healers who "save" disabled persons from their abnormal bodily disfigurement. Upson-Saia convincingly articulates that Augustine calls into question some of the conventionally wholesale denigration of all bodily deformities pervading the literature of his time. Upson-Saia explores the ways in which Augustine incorporates the scars and wounds of Jesus and the martyrs to be part of Christians' perfected spiritual identity and worthy of the heavenly realm associated with resurrected bodies. Along the way, she also explores the aesthetics of perfected Christian bodies and of the heavenly space.

Reference

Avalos, H. (2007). Redemptionism, rejectionism, and historicism as emerging approaches in disability studies. *Perspectives in Religious Studies 34*(1), 91–100.

CHAPTER 1

Reading Talmudic Bodies: Disability, Narrative, and the Gaze in Rabbinic Judaism

Julia Watts Belser

Within literature and religious texts, disability often functions as both metaphor and mirror—allowing readers to examine critically how cultures view bodies, the limits of normalcy, and the spectacle of difference. The Babylonian Talmud, a wide-ranging and complex literary and legal text redacted in the sixth century CE, represents the flourishing of rabbinic Jewish culture. The Talmud is a primary and central source for the development of Jewish law—and it remains essential in contemporary Jewish thought. My essay examines textual representations of disability in rabbinic legal texts and legends to argue that the classical rabbis used disabled figures to underscore the instability of the body and to grapple with the experience of physicality, frailty, and embodiment. By setting contemporary disability theorists in conversation with these ancient texts, I show that the Babylonian Talmud expresses intense interest in what disability studies has termed "the stare"—the intrusive gaze of a viewer, which often objectifies and disables the person being stared at. In its interpretation of the Leviticus (21: 16–23) restrictions on priestly bodily blemishes, the Talmud locates the problem of disability primarily in the eye of the beholder.[1]

Numerous passages within the Babylonian Talmud rest on assumptions about disability that are roundly critiqued by contemporary disability activists: links between disability and sin, equations of physical suffering and divine punishment or curse, and assessments of disabled figures as "spoiled" sages or insufficient marital prospects. Yet Talmud's portrayal of the disabling gaze has the potential to articulate a subtle self-critique of these cultural and theological assumptions, as it destabilizes the surface judgments people make about the meaning of embodied identity. In the second half of my essay, I suggest that—just as a disability activist or performance artist can sometimes draw the stare in order to reframe and refashion the meaning of disability—the Babylonian Talmud includes key narratives centered on disability that call attention to these dynamics of the gaze. Through their intense interest in the act of looking and knowing, I argue that a number of talmudic texts feature what Rosemary Garland-Thomson (2000) has called "stare-and-tell" rituals, performative moments that can raise provocative questions that contest received assumptions about disability. Through these texts, the Talmud constructs disability as an ambiguous cultural sign that allows the rabbis to interrogate the significance of physicality, the power of the gaze, and the ultimate inscrutability of bodies that refuse to surrender to a simple, surface reading.

Ethical Ideals and Priestly (Im)Perfections

The Hebrew Bible provides an important ethical foundation for affirming the humanity and dignity of people with disabilities. As Elliot Dorff (2007) emphasizes, the Hebrew Bible traditions represent a significant counterpoint to the views on disability espoused by Plato and Aristotle, both of whom advocated infanticide for babies born with disabilities.[2]

In the command to not insult the deaf nor place a stumbling block before the blind (Lev. 19: 14), for example, the Hebrew Bible articulates a profound obligation to treat disabled people fairly. At the outset of his study of disability in Jewish law, Tzvi Marx (2002) asserts that compassion for people with disabilities permeates the heart of the Jewish tradition and argues that the biblical foundations of Judaism bespeak a "sensitive, humane, and dignified attitude toward all persons, regardless of individual differences." Yet Marx himself acknowledges the dissonance within Jewish tradition that prompted his study, as he aims to reconcile the concern and kindness toward people with disabilities that coexists alongside "instances of apparent indifference, even callousness" (Tzvi Marx 2002: 1).

Critical assessments by disability studies scholars have highlighted key issues of power and representation in the biblical text that privilege the able-bodied and marginalize people with disabilities. The very premise of "compassion for" people with disabilities reinforces a mode of relationship that is marked by paternalism, charity, and pity. As Rebecca Raphael (2008) has pointed out, the biblical legal traditions that protect the well-being of people with disabilities—despite their beneficent intent—represent the people addressed by the commandments as able-bodied and presume little or no agency on the part of the blind or the deaf themselves (Rebecca Raphael 2008: 22). Olyan has examined how the biblical text's use of the terms "good" (*tov*) and "bad" (*ra'*) to signify beauty and ugliness has profound implications for the wide-ranging stigmatization of people with disabilities in the biblical tradition (Olyan 2008: 22). Raphael (2008), Olyan (2008), and Abrams (1998) have all called attention to the use of disability as a negative metaphor, particularly the way that a number of prophetic utopian visions exalt God's redemptive and transformative power by figuring people with disabilities as weak, disempowered, and awaiting eschatological healing. In many cases, the prophet's ideal, longed-for future erases the very presence or possibility of disability.

Within the Hebrew Bible, the "problem" of disabled bodies surfaces dramatically with regard to the idealized body of the priesthood. In the discourse of the Priestly sources, priests represent physical exemplars of holiness within the context of divine service and any detraction from the priests' physical form represents a danger for both priest and community (Abrams 1998). The central text for formulating the priestly rubric of physical perfection appears in Leviticus (21: 16–23):

> The Lord spoke further to Moses: Speak to Aaron and say: No man of your offspring throughout the ages who has a defect (*mum*) shall be qualified to offer the food of his God. No one at all who has a defect shall be qualified: no man who is blind, or lame, or has a limb too short or too long; no man who has a broken leg or a broken arm; or who is a hunchback, or a dwarf, or who has a growth in his eye, or who has a boil-scar, or scurvy, or crushed testes.
>
> No man among the offspring of Aaron the priest who has a defect shall be qualified to offer the Lord's gift; having a defect, he shall not be qualified to offer the food of his God. He may eat of the food of his God, of the most holy as well as of the holy; but he shall not enter behind the curtain or come near the altar, for he has a defect. He shall not profane these places sacred to Me, for I the Lord have sanctified them.

The priest with a blemish does not lose his status as a priest and is still eligible to eat food that has been brought as an offering to God. He still has greater access to holiness and holy food than nonpriestly Israelites. Yet relative to other priests, he is stigmatized through his loss of access

to the holiest places and his exclusion from the act of divine service—
the most esteemed responsibilities of the priesthood. By virtue of his
blemish, he becomes capable of profaning that which God has sanctified and therefore represents an ever-present threat to the holiness of the
sanctuary (Olyan 2008: 31).

The precise criteria that the Priestly sources consider in constructing
the category of "blemish" remains elusive. Milgrom (2000) emphasizes
that appearance is a major consideration in determining a prohibited
blemish. An appearance-based schema might explain the fact that deafness, mental disability, or the inability to speak go unmentioned, yet it
hardly accounts for the exclusion of a blind priest, unless one follows
the awkward suggestion that the blind person must actually be missing an eye. In any event, the premise that the Priestly writer aims to
exclude "visible flaws" does not explain *why* such conditions are considered unacceptable among priests performing the divine service. Instead,
it reinforces an ableist assumption that such conditions are obviously
undesirable. In his study of biblical defect paradigms, Olyan concludes
that while no single criterion encompasses all the conditions listed, most
of the priestly defects are "visible to the eye, long lasting or permanent
in nature, and characterized by physical dysfunction, and more than a
few share asymmetry as a quality" (Olyan 2008: 30). He argues that the
biblical concepts of the blemish are contrasted against native descriptions of beauty and wholeness, so that blemished status equates ugliness
(Olyan 2000: 103).

Leviticus (21: 16–23) focuses attention on the "marred" visual form
of the priest, in the sanctified space of the divine domain. Drawing
upon Hector Avalos's (2007) sensory analysis of the Deuteronomist's
tendency to denigrate the visual and emphasize the auditory, Rebecca
Raphael (2008) argues for the contrasting significance of the visual
and spatial dimensions in the priestly sources. The priestly writer's
interest in the visual plays a key role in the construction of the appropriate priestly body. Raphael argues that "in a cult that eschewed
visual iconography, the visible representatives of God would be the
sacred precincts and the priests" (Rebecca Raphael 2008: 39). The
specific form of the priestly bodies entrusted with God's service provide a kind of visual signifier to mark the unseen body of God.[3] In
her view, the contours of the permitted priestly body are characterized by symmetry and order, a smooth and unruptured surface, and
clear, unbroken boundaries. Amidst the strong visual culture of the
priestly sources, the "unblemished" priest who performs the divine
service takes up a priestly responsibility to represent, in some fashion,

the divine presence and to "stand in" for the unseen, perfect body of God. The priestly source perceives "blemishes" as conditions that impair a priest's ability to see and be seen before God and community. Later rabbinic texts augment this tension between visible and invisible forms, intensifying the dynamic interplay between the seen and the un/seeable.

Staring and Seeing: The Problem of Priestly (Im)Perfection

After the destruction of the Second Temple by the Romans in 70 CE, the rabbinic movement articulated a system of Jewish law and practice that was centered upon the study house, the home, and the synagogue—recasting biblical texts that assume a now obsolete sacrificial system.[4] The rabbis developed *midrash,* a method of biblical reading that derived details of law and practice out of biblical verses, and which featured creative homiletic and theological readings rooted in biblical narrative. In this essay, I focus on sources from two key rabbinic texts: the Mishnah and the Babylonian Talmud. The Mishnah is an early postbiblical text of Jewish law, redacted circa 200 CE, consisting of relatively concise debates between various rabbis around particular topics in the performance of Jewish commandments and legal obligations. The oral traditions of commentary and debate that greatly expanded the Mishnah were eventually canonized into two different Talmuds. The earlier, shorter Palestinian Talmud is usually dated to the fourth century CE. The more complex and expansive Babylonian Talmud, also known as the Bavli, was likely redacted in the fifth or sixth centuries. For later generations, the Bavli represented the *magnum opus* of rabbinic scholarship. Its stories, legal dicta, and elaborate argumentation have become a central pillar of Jewish life.

In her foundational study *Judaism and Disability: Portrayals in Ancient Texts from the Tanach through the Bavli,* Abrams (1998) emphasizes that disability in ancient Jewish texts shifted its meaning in response to changing religious ideologies and practice. While the levitical texts reflect a priestly culture that celebrated the impeccable lineage and physical perfection of a few priestly bodies who were able to withstand the rigors of temple service, the rabbinic culture that emerged after the destruction of the Second Temple valorized understanding and discernment (*da'at*) within the framework of an intensely oral culture. Accordingly, while rabbinic Jewish texts retain some of the priestly concerns with physical "blemishes," the most significant disabilities for the rabbis were those that compromised a Jew's capacity to understand and discern Torah and Jewish law—and to learn and transmit that law and tradition in its

oral context. The sages feared and stigmatized deafness, speech disabilities, intellectual disabilities, and mental illness, which they perceived as
rendering a person unable to participate in the system of holiness and
sanctity that they had crafted. While physical disabilities and blindness
do figure as impairments within the rabbinic system, limitations in the
realm of moving and seeing were less disabling in a rabbinic context.
Although they did proscribe a Jew's abilities to fulfill certain obligations
and thereby limited a person's full capacity for participation within the
rabbinic framework of divine service, these disabilities did not place the
Jew outside the very framework of rabbinic religiosity.

Following the destruction of the Temple, the synagogue became a
key site for recasting obligations that had once been fulfilled through
Temple service, with communal prayer services fixed by the rabbis to
evoke and substitute for the biblically mandated cycle of sacrifices. The
priestly blessing ritual was transposed from the Temple to the synagogue, and the ritual form served to stress the continuity between both
sites—as well as acknowledging the discontinuities of destruction
(Kimelman 2006: 599).[5] During the days of the Temple, the priests
would recite the biblical blessing in Numbers (6: 2–7) daily, in a special ritual upon a platform in the Temple, as a means of blessing the
people. After the destruction of the Temple, the ritual blessing moved
to the synagogue—and when the prayer leader came to the appropriate
place in the liturgy, those in the congregation who descended from the
ancient priesthood (the *kohanim*) would come forward to perform the
ritual blessing. In preparation, they would remove their shoes and have
their hands washed by the second rank of the priesthood, the Levites.
Then, at the prayer leader's invitation, the *kohanim* would stand before
the ark, raise their hands, and recite the blessing over the congregation.
(Jacobs 1997: 84–85)

Yet unlike the Priestly writers' requirements of strict physical perfection for Temple service, the performance of the priestly blessing in the
synagogue proved to be more amenable to a certain degree of bodily
variation. Mishnah Megillah (4: 7) takes up the issue of "blemished"
priests, as it discusses the synagogue blessing ritual:

> A priest whose hands are blemished may not lift up his hands. Rabbi
> Yehudah says: Also one whose hands are stained by woad or madder may
> not lift up his hands because the people might gaze at him.

This text uses the same term, "blemish (*mum*)," that recurs throughout
Leviticus (21: 16–23), but where the biblical text operated with an expanded

list of prohibited blemishes, the Mishnah asserts that the only significant blemish in post-Temple times was that which appeared on priests' hands. The classical sources emphasize the significance of the priests' hands and their proper positioning; the midrash in Pesikta de-Rav Kahana describes God as sending blessing through the openings formed by the priests' fingers.[6] As the locus of great sanctity, the hands are figured as essential to the process of blessing—and dangerous to look upon. In Ḥagigah 15a, the Talmud states that gazing at the hands of the priest will cause a person's eyes to become dim, while the medieval commentator Rashi explains that this is due to the divine presence (the Shekhinah) that rests upon the priests' hands (Jacobs 1997). The Tosafot, later medieval commentators, disagreed with Rashi's reasoning, arguing that looking at the priests might distract a person's attention from the blessing itself (Spiegel 2000). Customarily, the priests draw their prayer shawls over their heads and hands while blessing, in order to shield their bodies—and perhaps the Divine—from the congregation's gaze.

The text of the Mishnah focuses on the hands, describing the entire ritual with the phrase "lifting up the hands." In keeping with the centrality of the hands, it prohibits priests with "blemished" or stained hands from performing the blessing, but mentions no other causes for exclusion. Yet the Mishnah's final statement introduces an important qualification into the nature of this prohibition. Priests with discolored hands—presumably due to their work as dyers—are also prohibited from blessing, lest the people stare at them. In her article "Staring Back: Self-Representations of Disabled Performance Artists," Garland-Thomson discusses the social dynamics through which stares mark and register difference, stigmatize the person who is stared at, and demand a story of how and why a person became disabled. She writes, "In the social context of an ableist society, the disabled body summons the stare, and the stare mandates the story.... This stare-and-tell ritual constitutes disability identity in the social realm" (Garland-Thomson 2000: 335). Garland-Thomson emphasizes that, in a social sense, staring functions as a kind of ritual exclusion that itself helps create disability. Disability, she argues, "is not simply a natural state of bodily inferiority and inadequacy. Rather, disability is a culturally fabricated narrative of the body, similar to what we understand as the fictions of race and gender" (Garland-Thomson 2000: 335).

Garland Thomson's insights illuminate a number of issues present within the Mishnah. The Mishnah acknowledges and fears that priestly difference will "summon the stare." The Mishnah's text also makes manifest the social construction of disability, the way the dynamic of staring forges a stigmatized and excluded body. In Mishnah's second case, the excluded priestly body is manifestly not marked a physical disability, but a mark of difference based on profession or circumstance. By including stained hands in its prohibition, the Mishnah introduces a wedge in the usual ableist assumption that "problem" posed by disability is the obvious undesirability of a misshapen or malformed body. Here, there is no body problem, per se. The stained hands are working hands, gainfully employed and fully able. Yet they are still prohibited, because they are marked and read as different. By explicitly stating the prohibition in terms of the gaze that unusual hands might provoke, the Mishnah implies that the "problem" has shifted from the priests' hands to the lingering eye of the congregation. Difference, the Mishnah argues, will evoke the stare—and the stare cannot be allowed. The priestly blessing in the synagogue is a moment of ritual and religious performance, but it is a performance in which the bodies of the priests aim to be invisible, to *avoid* the gaze of those in the gallery. The priest body is imagined as a kind of negative space, one that avoids engaging the viewer. Whether because the blessing occasions a potent manifestation of the divine presence or because the priestly body might distract viewers from their reception of the blessing, the priests who transmit God's blessing strive to elude the eye.

Familiarity Defuses the Stare: Priestly Blemishes in the Bavli

In its treatment of the Mishnah, the Babylonian Talmud intensifies Mishnah's interest in the dynamics of the gaze and further emphasizes the way that viewers' perceptions constitute disability in the social and religious realm. Bavli Megillah 24b begins by restating a tradition from the Tosefta, another early rabbinic text similar to the Mishnah, which prohibits a priest from performing the priestly blessing ritual in the synagogue if he has a "blemish" on his face, his hands, or his feet:

> It is taught: The blemishes of which they spoke are on his face, his hands, and his feet. Rabbi Yehoshua ben Levi said: One with skin disease on his hands shall not lift up his hands. Likewise, it is taught: One with skin disease on his hands shall not lift up his hands [and one whose hands are] curved or crooked shall not lift up his hands.

Rabbi Yehoshua prohibits a priest with visible skin disease from raising his hands in blessing, and the text likewise excludes a priest whose hands are curved or crooked. Yet while the text opens with a clear enumeration of apparent physical disabilities or illnesses that the sages used to exclude a priest from offering the blessing, the next speaker introduces a significantly different rubric for exclusion:

> Rav Ashi said: One from Haifa or Beshan shall not lift up his hands. Likewise, it is taught: People from Beit Sh'an or Haifa or Tib'onin shall not descend before the ark because they recite [the letter] *aleph* as [the letter] *ayin* and the *ayins* as *alephs*.

Rav Ashi disqualifies priests from a particular area from raising up their hands in blessing, because their speech patterns alter the sound of the recited blessing.[7] While his principle might be interpreted to render individuals with speech disabilities suspect, Rav Ashi's concern is manifestly *not* with speech disability per se. He excludes priests from entire regions and towns based upon a regional accent, not individual speakers with slurred or indistinct speech. Here, Rav Ashi treats local dialect and social status as an excluding condition, forbidding the platform to priests whose language marks and manifests their difference.

The passage that follows devolves into ad hominim attacks between sages who each find ample cause to exclude one another from priestly service, had either of them been eligible to perform the blessing ritual:

> Rabbi Ḥiyya said to Rabbi Shimon bar Rabbi: Had you been a Levite, you would have been unfit for the priests' platform on account of your rough voice. He went and told his father. [His father] said to him: Go and say to [Rabbi Ḥiyya], "When you come to the verse *I will wait for the Lord,* will we not find you a blasphemer and a reviler?"

When Rabbi Ḥiyya excludes Rabbi Shimon bar Rabbi from the priestly platform on account of the flaws in his voice, he uses the term *paṣul*—not the same word as appears in Leviticus 21, but one that likewise means "blemished" or "invalid"—to declare him unfit for ascending to the podium. Rabbi Shimon retorts with a slur that highlights Rabbi Ḥiyya's apparent inability to correctly articulate a certain guttural sound, so that he reads a verse that actually says "I will wait *[ḥikiti]* for the Lord all my days" as "I will smite *[hikiti]* the Lord!" From a disability studies perspective, this passage highlights the socially constructed nature of disability, the way in which disability is not simply a physical "fact" of a blemished body. Instead, the viewer's gaze actively creates the social experience of disability and exclusion on account of various social, cultural, physical traits that the viewer interprets as a source of stigma.

The final portion of Bavli's discussion of the priestly blessing highlights the social factors that allow the sages to allow certain priests to recite the blessing, even though they seem to be clearly excluded by the criteria it has just described. The Babylonian Talmud presents three cases where a category of priests is forbidden from blessing. In each situation, the anonymous "editorial" voice of the Talmud argues against the prohibition, citing a priest whose example counters the rule just stated:

> Rav Ḥuna said: A man with bleary eyes shall not lift up his hands. But there was a man like this in Rav Ḥuna's neighborhood—and he spread his hands! He was familiar in his town. Likewise it was taught: A man with bleary eyes shall not lift up his hands, but if he is familiar in his town it is permitted.
>
> Rabbi Yoḥanan said: A man who is blind in one eye may not lift up his hands. But there was a man like this in Rabbi Yoḥanan's neighborhood—and he spread his hands! He was familiar in his town.
>
> Likewise it was taught: A man who is blind in one eye may not lift up his hands, but if he is familiar in his town it is permitted. Rabbi Yehudah said: He whose hands have stains shall not lift up his hands. It was taught: If most of the people of the town work in that way, it is permitted.

In each case, the anonymous editorial voice resolves the contradiction by affirming the general principle, but asserting that if a person was known in a particular town (or if the condition of their hands is commonplace), they are permitted to bless. Here, the Bavli emphasizes that the disabled body itself is not the source of the problem, but the community's disabling gaze. But familiarity defuses the stare. The people will not look at one they already know. The Bavli fixes the social problem of disability in the eyes of those who stare, whose gaze manufactures stigma. Its discourse of exclusion forces the disabled person to bear the burden of those stares—it excludes, after all, the one who is stared at, not the ones who stare. But it emphasizes that the primary problem with disabled priests lies not in the priestly body itself, but in the social mis/seeing that body occasions. A disabled priest who is known to the congregation need not be excluded from the ritual of blessing, because the community's gaze will not stumble over his familiar form.[8]

Normalcy and Deviance: The Rabbinic Categorization of Disability

While rabbinic texts never articulate a single category of "the disabled," rabbinic legal thought commonly responds to disability by means of naming and categorizing individuals who are exempt from the performance of commandments (*miẓvot*). In many cases, women, slaves, the young, the deaf, the blind, and those with intellectual or physical disabilities are marked as exempt from certain legal obligations. The language of exemption has often been explained as a kind of "accommodation" to the impairments of the population in question. As Abrams (1998) shows, the Palestinian Talmud's discussion of this passage provides explicit rationales for the exclusion in both exegetical and practical terms. A man who cannot walk is released from the obligation to make pilgrimage, acknowledging that his disability presents an obstacle in the fulfillment of this commandment. While the logic of exemption may seem "sensible" or "compassionate" in the case of disability, the culture-bound specificity of exemptions is more evident in the discourse of exemptions made on the basis of gender. In many strata of rabbinic texts, women are exempt from positive, time-bound commandments, a ruling often explained by commentators as a reflection of the competing claims that children and family life place upon a woman's time. According to this logic, a woman is freed from time-sensitive commandments out of an awareness that she might have a prior obligation to nurse an infant or care for children. Hauptman (1998) has provided a compelling analysis of the insufficiency of this and other apologetic explanations. In cases of gender and physical difference, the presumed "facts" of impairment are scripted upon people's bodies and used to disable them. In rabbinic culture, exemption translates into exclusion. The rabbis frequently prohibited a person who was exempt from undertaking even a *voluntary* performance of a particular action. The rabbinic discourse of exemption allows the elite group to structure and circumscribe the possibilities available to those they have exempted. In rabbinic society, to be exempt from a commandment represented a significant disability. Because the exempt/excluded have lost access to a particular means of fulfilling an obligation to God, they are religiously diminished and rhetorically distanced from the Holy.

Through their emphasis on the proper categorization of bodies with regard to legal obligations, rabbinic texts explicitly construct an insider group that represents a normalized, collective body. Regarding the obligation to make pilgrimage and bring the festival (*ḥagigah*) and appearance (*re'iyah*) offerings to the Jerusalem Temple, M.Ḥagigah (1: 1) states:

All are obligated regarding the appearance offering (*re'iyah*), except for the deaf-mute, the intellectually disabled, the young, the gender-indeterminate, the androgynous, women, slaves who have not been set free, the lame, the blind, the sick, the old, and anyone who is not able to ascend upon his feet. Who is young? One who is not able to ride upon the shoulders of his father to ascend to Jerusalem to the Temple Mount—these are the words of the House of Shammai. The House of Hillel says: One who is not able to grasp his father's hand and ascend to Jerusalem to the Temple Mount, as it says: *Three walking-pilgrimages (shaloshregalim)* (Exodus 23: 17). The House of Shammai says: the appearance offering is two silvers and the festival offering is one silver. The House of Hillel says: the appearance offering is one silver and the festival offering is two silvers.

This Mishnah begins by introducing a collective category, *all*, who are obligated to appear before God, bearing a particular offering, at the appropriate times of pilgrimage. The text constructs the "normal" group by explicitly constituting the categories that are *not* included in the performance of pilgrimage, those who need not appear before God or bring an offering. The bulk of the mishnaic text centers upon deviance, naming and periodically elaborating upon the particular categories it deems outside the whole. By the conclusion of the list, the category "all" has shrunk considerably: free, healthy, men of stable gender status, who can hear, speak, reason, walk, and see, and who are neither too young nor too old. In a classic normalizing move, this subset of the population never receives its own name. Instead, it passes as the collective—the normalized body of *all* of us—while others are rhetorically demarcated and separated out.

The Bavli begins its discussion of the Mishnah by examining the conceptual limits of Mishnah's categories. The anonymous voice of the Bavli subjects the language of the Mishnah to minute analysis, centering on the first term: *hakol* (all).[9] As the Bavli asks why the mishnaic text has chosen to begin with this collective term, its discourse assumes that *hakol* must include a hitherto unspecified group. The text surfaces three possibilities, each of which meet with objections:

Why use the term *hakol* (all)? It comes to include one who is half slave and half free. But if like Ravina, one says: One who is half slave and half free is exempt from the appearance offering, why use *hakol*? It comes to include one who is lame on the first day, but who has straightened up on the second day. That works for one who says he may make payment on this [second day] for this [first day]. But what about one who says all must pay on the first day? It comes to include someone who is blind in one eye. But what about that which has been taught? Yoḥanan ben

Dahav'ai says in the name of Rabbi Yehudah: A person blind in one eye is exempt from the appearance offering, as it is written (Exodus 23: 17): *He will be seen (yera'eh)*. He will see *(yir'eh)*—just as he comes to look, so shall he come to be looked upon. One who sees with two eyes will be seen with two eyes .... (bHagigah 2a)

As is quite common in talmudic reasoning, the Bavli constructs an individual who falls on the borderlines of the categories the Mishnah has outlined: a man born to a slave and free person, a man who is lame on the first day but able to walk smoothly on the second day, and a man who has sight in a single eye. By crafting these somewhat improbable hypotheticals as test cases, the Bavli uses liminal figures to probe the boundaries of mishnaic law.[10] As each case is considered, the Bavli acknowledges the potential for inclusion but retorts with a legal scenario that excludes the liminal individual.

The Bavli's questions simultaneously underscore the fragility of Mishnah's categories, while ultimately protecting the normative category *all* from incursion. While the half-slave might appear to straddle Mishnah's categorical system, the question of his appearance offering has already been rendered moot by Ravina's ruling. The man who cannot walk on the first day of the festival might theoretically make his offering on the second day, but this example holds only if one assumes the appearance offering can be paid upon the second day of the festival. The man who has sight in only one eye seems the most eligible for inclusion, for he *can* see. Yet the Bavli responds by declaring his vision insufficient for the task, opening up a theological reflection on the significance of seeing and being seen that will recur throughout Bavli Hagigah. Rabbi Yehudah's statement reflects a common type of rabbinic midrash, a homiletical rereading of a biblical verse or phrase. In Exodus (23: 17), "Three times a year, all your males shall appear before the sovereign, the Lord," the word "appear" (yira'eh) could be read as "see" (yir'eh) via a minor change in vowels. In the printed biblical text, which consists of consonants alone, the two words are interchangeable. Thus, Rabbi Yehudah asserts an intricate and intimate connection between seeing and being seen. Just as one goes to the Temple with the expectation of being fully seen by God, so too a man must be able to wholly see. The midrash asserts an interplay of holy and human sight, so that the two eyes of the human party evoke the gaze of God.

What is particularly striking about the midrash, however, is the unsupplied "object" of the man's seeing. We might complete Rabbi Yehudah's midrashic referent so that it reads, "Just as he comes to look *upon God,* so *God* will come to look upon him." Abrams (1998) has argued that the pilgrimage itself provides a moment for God's visual inspection of the Israelite people, thereby justifying for the rabbis the exclusion of those with disabilities—since "all Israelites who appeared at the Temple for God's inspection would be required to be as close to the priestly ideal as possible" (Abrams 1998: 51). In parallel, then, the midrash also evokes and idealizes a narrative possibility of gazing upon God. Despite the common assumption that Jewish texts have always denied the visual apprehension of the divine form, Boyarin (2003) argues that rabbinic literature often valorizes the desire for and possibility of a vision of God and a visual revelation. Whether or not the rabbis actually imagined the possibility of a Temple-based theophany for individual pilgrims, Rabbi Yehudah's midrash situates the "appearance" offering as a moment where the Seer who is customarily unseeable actually becomes seen—but only if the divine gaze is appropriately met by the human.

Seeing and Being Seen: The Blind Sage

The theme of seeing and being seen recurs throughout the first portion of Bavli Ḥagigah and manifests again explicitly in a narrative that describes two rabbis who come to meet a colleague of theirs who is blind:

> Rabbi and Rabbi Ḥiyya were on the road. When they reached a certain town they said, "Is there a sage here? Let us go and greet him!" The people said to them: "There is a sage here and he is blind." Rabbi Ḥiyya said to Rabbi: "You, sit. I will go and greet him so that you don't degrade your exalted status." But he prevailed over him and they went together. When they were taking their leave [of the blind sage], he said to them: You have received the one who is seen, but who does not see. May you merit to be received by the One who sees, but who is not seen." Rabbi said to Rabbi Ḥiyya: "If I had followed your advice, you would have kept me from this blessing!" (Ḥagigah 5b)

In this tale, Rabbi and Rabbi Ḥiyya are on the road, and when they come to a town, they decide to pay their respects to any fellow rabbis who live there. When they ask the people, they discover that the local sage is blind. This revelation prompts Rabbi Ḥiyya to instruct his more illustrious colleague Rabbi, the chief rabbi of his day, to avoid the meeting. Rabbi Ḥiyya's remark indicates his dismissive reading of the blind sage, clearly one less worthy than he and Rabbi. Yet his instruction to Rabbi to "sit...so that you don't degrade your exalted status" also suggests something perversely powerful about the blind man. His very being has the capacity to "degrade" Rabbi's exalted position.

While Rabbi Ḥiyya clearly gives voice to the profound stigma associated with blindness, the narrative nonetheless "pushes back" against its own assumptions. Rabbi does not accept Ḥiyya's view; the two of them argue off-stage; Rabbi prevails, and they both go together to meet the blind rabbi. At the conclusion of the story, the blind rabbi offers both his visitors a blessing, by which the text affords him the socially powerful stance of bestowing God's blessing upon his guests. The content of his blessing likewise privileges his own place—and vindicates Rabbi's decision to greet him. The blind rabbi's blessing sketches a correspondence between his own being and God. Because the rabbis have received the blind man "who is seen, but who does not see," he blesses them that they likewise be received by God, "the One who sees, but who is not seen." In a familiar move, the talmudic story uses the blind man as metaphor. Just as he stands before them, so the rabbis stand as blind men before God: seen, but unable to see. Yet by situating the metaphor within the mouth of the blind man, the Talmud rhetorically affirms the agency of the blind man—the one who blesses on behalf of the ultimate unseen Seer. It crafts a kinship between the blind man and God, situating holiness in the tension between the visible and the invisible, the effective and the averted gaze. In contrast to Rabbi Yehudah's midrash in bḤagigah 2a, the man who cannot see becomes the one who effectively transmits the blessing of an unseen God to the sighted sages.

Reading the Suffering Body: The Contested Meanings of Naḥum of Gamzo

Rabbinic uncertainty regarding the dynamics of seeing and being seen centers on the contested meaning of disability that structure the talmudic narrative of Naḥum of Gamzo, a rabbi who curses himself and becomes disabled—and whose disability becomes the subject of his students' perplexed gaze. In the Palestinian Talmud's version of this story, the wealthy Naḥum encounters a suffering man who asks him for charity. Naḥum does not feed him right away, but promises to give him something when he returns from his journey. When Naḥum returns, he finds that the man has died—and he curses himself to suffer physical punishments for his failure to act in a timely fashion. At the end of the Palestinian narrative, a chastened Naḥum is visited by Rabbi Aqiva, who laments that he sees the sage in such degradation. Naḥum retorts that *he* is sorry that Rabbi Aqiva is not suffering in a similar fashion.

When his visitor expresses surprise at the curse, Naḥum asks him why he rebels against divine punishment—and presumably, why he would forfeit the atonement that such suffering brings. Abrams (1998) analyzes the Palestinian narrative in its larger context, demonstrating how it reveals the principle of measure for measure punishment and the idea of atonement through suffering.

By contrast, Bavli's version of this story emphasizes a strikingly different message—one that troubles the idea that a body can be easily interpreted and its meaning entirely understood. Borrowing Garland-Thomson's model (2000), I argue that Naḥum functions as a kind of disability performance artist—whose disabled body becomes "center stage" precisely so that the performer can draw the objectifying stare and critique its power. In the priestly texts we have examined, I argued that the dynamics of the priestly blessing frame the gaze as particularly dangerous—and thus, the unfamiliar form of the disabled priest becomes a potential "snare" to the congregation, whose stares might be drawn toward his body. Unlike the priests, who are expected to elude the eye, Bavli's Naḥum *wants* his body to be seen—because the Bavli aims to *use* his body to critique his students' assumptions.

In Garland-Thomson's assessment, disability performance art involves a disabled artist who intentionally elicits the gaze of the audience and uses the disabled body as medium and content of performance. Garland-Thomson examines the work of disability performance artist Mary Duffy, a woman born without arms who poses nude as the classical figure of Venus de Milo, demonstrating how Duffy's performance "stages the dynamic of two opposing modes of looking: staring at the freakishly different body and gazing at the female body as a beautiful work of art." Duffy's performance intentionally "elicits a confusing combination of the rapt gaze and the intrusive stare." Duffy's artistry makes plain the way "the templates culture has supplied her audience are inadequate to make sense of her body. Framed as a work of art, her body is paradox incarnate, leaving her viewers' sense of the order of things in ruins. Hers is the art that transforms consciousness, that grants a new way of seeing the known world" (Garland-Thomson 2000: 336). Garland-Thomson describes how artists such as Duffy manipulate the "stare-and-tell ritual," which is usually used to construct and constitute the otherness of disabled bodies, in order to "critique the politics of appearance" and control the terms of encounter between herself and those who stare at her.

Naḥum of Gamzo, if we can even speak of him as a "historical" figure, is an unlikely man to recast as a disability activist. First, Naḥum's tale makes explicit a number of problematic assertions regarding the significance and meaning of disability, particularly the idea of disability as punishment for transgressions or the idea of suffering as a means of generating atonement. Modern disability activists look in vain for a clear and certain refutation of these theological ideas, which have cast a long and pervasive shadow through the history of Jewish and Christian thought regarding disability. Second, the element of *self-representation,* which is so critical to contemporary disability performance art, is lost in the literary form of the Babylonian Talmud. Nahum is a character in someone else's drama; his tale is crafted by tellers and retellers for their own purposes. Yet even though we cannot reconstruct how a historical figure like Nahum might have told his *own* tale, Bavli's redactors retell and make use of his tale in a way that bears striking similarity to the aims of contemporary disability performance artists.

The Bavli initially describes Nahum through explicit physical suffering—depicting a body and being brought to the outer bounds of experience. In our initial encounter with the sage, Nahum's body is centered, constructing the whole of his textual reality. Even his bed, the site in which he lies—is assailed by ants against which the man would be helpless:

> They said regarding Nahum, the man of Gamzo, that he was blind in both eyes, withered in both hands, and lame in both legs, that his entire body was filled with sores, and that his bed stood in four basins of water lest the ants ascend upon it.
>
> Once, he was lying in bed in a rickety house and his disciples sought to remove him from it. He said to them: "Take out the vessels and afterward, take out the bed, for the whole while that my bed is within this house, you can be assured that the house will not collapse." They took out the vessels, and afterward, they took out his bed. Immediately, the house collapsed. (bTa'anit 21a)

The rickety house in which Nahum rests is actually the narrative hook that links this story to the tales that precede it in the Bavli. This story appears in the midst of a series of "collapse" tales—where we see rabbis stabilize rickety buildings and prevent houses from falling down through the power of their merit that is manifest in their bodies. In rabbinic consciousness, collapsing houses are not simply the result of poor building or ordinary misfortune. Rather, the rabbis read collapse as a reflection of more profound instability, a sign that God has torn down and that the built can no longer stand. As Stein (2008) has argued, these stories are deeply symbolic of the larger rabbinic project. The rabbis are writing in the shadow of the ultimate collapse, the destruction of the Temple. In this world of collapsing structures, the rabbis imagine their most illustrious compatriots as the physical pillars of Torah that must strive to shore up the crumbling world and keep the house from caving in.

In our narrative, Naḥum evokes this motif—becoming the rabbinic strongman who can sustain the rickety house. Yet the text juxtaposes his manifest power to prevent collapse and the moral strength that action implies with a body that his disciples read as marked by weakness and suffering wrought by God. The narrative continues with a telling question: His disciples said to him: "Teacher! Since you are a completely righteous man [ẓadiqgamur], why has all this come upon you?" The disciples' question situates them in the midst of two conflicting cultural templates. On the one hand, Naḥum's status as a righteous man has just been confirmed by the house that crumbled as soon as his sustaining body was withdrawn. On the other hand, his disabilities reflect a sign of divine disfavor. To evoke Garland-Thomson's language again, the Bavli has staged the story to juxtapose these two opposing modes of seeing: the strong-man as righteous, powerful body and the disabled-man as suffering for his sins. The disciples cannot reconcile the tension of the story—that the profoundly disabled body of their teacher, which cannot even slap away the ants, has the power to hold up houses. The negative moral valence that the disciples associated with Naḥum's bodily loss collides with the intense sustaining power of Naḥum's body. The affliction they read into their teacher's physical experience is belied by the house that does not fall.

The Bavli structures Naḥum's own response to heighten the conflict the disciples experience, rather than ameliorating it. Like Duffy, whose performance is designed to accentuate her body and force the viewer to mediate between perceptions of the "freakish" and the "beautiful," the Bavli draws its readers into the tension:

> He said to them: "I did it to myself. Once, I was journeying to the house of my father-in-law and I had with me three laden donkeys, one with food, one with wine, and one with all sorts of fine things. A man appeared before me and said to me: "Teacher, sustain me!" I said to him: "Wait until I unload my donkey." After I unloaded, I returned and I found that he had died.[11]

I threw myself down upon him and I said: "My eyes which did not have mercy on your eyes, may they become blind. My hands, which did not have mercy upon your hands, let them wither. My feet, which did not have mercy upon you feet, let them become lame." But my mind was not set to rest until I said, "May my entire body become covered with sores."

The Bavli may intend to chastise Naḥum for being too slow to aid the starving man. The manuscript traditions differ about whether Naḥum stopped immediately to unload his donkey but found the man dead before he could get food into his mouth, or whether he kept onto his destination and only later came back to help the poor man. Regardless of whether the reader is meant to blame Naḥum, the sage clearly blames himself. When his students ask why this suffering has come upon him, Naḥum emphasizes his own agency: "I did it to myself." After the man dies, Naḥum curses himself—using performative speech to change the very nature of his body. He makes himself into a man who *cannot* see suffering, or stretch out his hand to his fellow, or run to help another. He rues so profoundly his own inability to sustain the poor man that he speaks sores into being—marking himself as a man who knows great pain. He cures the grave turmoil of his mind through a self-imposed weakening of his body. The intentional disabling of his body perversely affirms his own power. When Naḥum says, "I did it to myself," he has articulated his own moral force and his own righteousness through the very signs his disciples read as moral weakness.

Finally, the Bavli closes the narrative with a final exchange of dialogue that emphasizes the power of perception.

Rabbi Aqiva said: "Woe to me that I have seen you in such straits." He said to him: "Woe to me if you had not seen me in such straits."

The popular Vilna edition of the Bavli revises these final lines so that the dialogue is spoken by Naḥum's students—a shift that makes the exchange more comprehensible in its present context. But the manuscripts versions testify conclusively that Naḥum's tale ends in an encounter with Rabbi Aqiva, thus evoking and explicitly revising a scene that closed the Palestinian version of the story. In the Palestinian version, Naḥum asks Rabbi Aqiva why he refuses to accept divine punishment, thereby reiterating a theology that suffering (and disability) serves as a means of atonement for sin (Abrams 1998: 97). In the Bavli, however, Naḥum does not wish suffering on Rabbi Aqiva and he offers no teaching about accepting suffering as divine punishment. Bavli's Naḥum never describes suffering as *God's* punishment. Instead, Naḥum claims the power to refashion his own self. The intentional disabling of his body perversely affirms his own power. Naḥum has articulated his own moral force, his own righteousness through the very signs his disciples read as moral weakness.

Naḥum claims his remade body as a site of profound power and acute sensitivity. His body, which seemed irreconcilable with his status as righteous man, becomes the site of empathetic suffering. The Bavli never fully resolves the collision of meanings it situates in Naḥum's tale. Instead, it stresses these very disjunctures between perception and meaning, in order to critique a too-certain reading of the significance of a body. Through the eyes of Naḥum's students, who must grapple with the meaning of their teacher's disability, the redactors wrestle with the complex ways the disabled body is seen and perceived—ultimately creating a powerful gap between the "onlookers" and the disabled man himself. Through Naḥum's tale, the Bavli constructs disability as an ambiguous cultural sign and affirms the ultimate inscrutability of bodies that refuse to surrender to a simple, surface gaze.

In their discussion of disability, Bavli's redactors problematize the idea of disability as a static bodily condition. Instead, they envision disability as an experience fashioned through dynamic interplay: between a particular body and the gaze of onlookers who see and signify difference. Where Leviticus 21 presented "blemish" as a fault with the priestly body, Mishnah and Bavli Megillah situate disability as a problem of the communal gaze. Although the Bavli never dismantles the theoretical expectation of priestly perfection, it nonetheless determines the actual permissibility of a priest's blessing based on the way the community regards him. Likewise, though Mishnah Ḥagigah exempts people with disabilities from the obligation of pilgrimage, Bavli's narrative treatment of "seeing and being seen before God" formally upholds Mishnah's exclusion, while positioning a blind sage as a powerful channel for conveying the unseen God's blessing. Finally, through Naḥum of Gamzo, the Bavli highlights the collision of cultural meanings Naḥum's pious disciples experience when they see their teacher's disabled body. By staging the gaze in a way that problematizes the association between disability and sin, Bavli's redactors reject the very idea that a body conveys clear and certain moral meaning—and instead treat the disabled body as a supple instrument that can refract and refashion the community's vision.

Notes

I express my gratitude and appreciation to Ruth Haber, my ḥevruta, for stimulating conversation about many of the talmudic passages treated in this essay.

1. My chapter will center on the issue of priestly blemishes in the context of the priestly blessing, particularly as it was relocated by the rabbis from the Temple complex to the synagogue, following the destruction of the Second Temple. Rabbinic interpretation of animal and priestly blemishes in the actual context of the Temple service are also discussed extensively in another tractate of the Bavli, Bekhorot. See Rabinowitz (2007).
2. For an excellent discussion of ancient Greek infanticide and the ways in which it was (but was not *always*) associated with disability, see Martha L. Rose (2003: 7). Rose points out that "the lurid image of the Greeks unreflectively killing all their imperfect young is an unfounded conclusion of nineteenth-century scholars.
3. Raphael (2008) also advances a compelling analysis of the way in which Deuteronomist's strong preference for aural revelation and denigration of the visual intersects with the text's portrayal of idols as "disabled" gods whose ability to be seen but not heard reflects and reinforces their powerlessness.
4. For an excellent introduction to the cultural and social transformations associated with this period in Greco-Roman Palestine, see Meyers (2002).
5. Key alterations in the priestly blessing ritual are discussed in Mishnah Sotah (7: 6).
6. *Pesikta de-RavKahana, Parshat ha-Hodesh,* 8 (Mandelbaum ed.: 91), cited and discussed in Spiegel (2000).
7. Hauptman notes that this particular mispronunciation would result in changes in the meanings of words, thus rendering the blessing invalid (Hauptman 1988: 128).
8. This principle was reaffirmed by the Shulḥan Arukh, a Jewish law code composed in the sixteenth century by Rabbi Joseph Caro, which is still considered one of the primary Jewish law codes for the formulation of halakhah (Abrams 1998: 201; Shulhan Aruch, Orach Chayyim, 128: 30).
9. I have translated *hakol* as "all," but the Hebrew is actually a definite noun: "the all" or "the collectivity."
10. As Abrams (1998) has observed, talmudic discussions about disability serve as "logical or exegetical exercises" that emerge out of a rabbinic desire to carry legal reasoning to its fullest conclusions. Leslie Gordon (2006) has addressed the tokenizing nature of this tendency, from a disability studies perspective.
11. The popular printed edition (the Vilna) and another late printing (the Pesaro) have an alternate reading here that implies that Naḥum unloaded his donkey

in order to sustain the man: "Wait until I unload [something] from my donkey. But I had not finished unloading my donkey before his soul went forth." I have translated the text in accordance with the majority of the manuscripts, which suggest that Naḥum continued on—and later returned—to find that the man had died.

References

Abrams, J. (1998). *Judaism and Disability: Portrayals in Ancient Texts from the Tanach through the Bavli.* Washington, DC: Gallaudet University Press.

Avalos, H. (2007). Introducing sensory criticism in biblical studies: Audiocentricity and visiocentricity. In H. Avalos, S. Melcher, and J. Schipper (Eds.), *This Abled Body: Rethinking Disabilities in Biblical Studies.* Semeia Studies 55. Atlanta, GA: Society for Biblical Literature.

Boyarin, D. (2003). The eye in the Torah: Occular desire in midrashic hermeneutic. In *Sparks of the Logos: Essays in Rabbinic Hermeneutics.* Boston, MA: Brill.

Dorff, E. (2007). Mishneh ha-briyyot: A new Jewish approach to disabilities. In W. Cutter (Ed.), *Healing in the Jewish Imagination.* Woodstock, VT: Jewish Lights Publishing.

Garland-Thomson, R. (2000). Staring back: Self-representations of disabled performance artists. *American Quarterly 52*(2), 334–338.

Gordon, L. (2006). *Theheresh and the Rabbis: A Question of Intelligence.* M.A. Thesis. Graduate Theological Union.

Hauptman, J. (1988). *Development of the Talmudicsugya.* Lanham, MD: University Press of America.

Hauptman, J. (1998). *Rereading the Rabbis: A Woman's Voice.* Boulder, CO: Westview Press.

Jacobs, L. (1997). The body in Jewish worship. In S. Coakley (Ed.), *Religion and the Body.* New York, NY: Cambridge University Press.

Kimelman, R. (2006). Rabbinic prayer in late antiquity. In S. Katz (Ed.), *The Cambridge History of Judaism 4.* New York, NY: Cambridge University Press.

Marx, T. C. (2002). *Disability in Jewish Law.* New York, NY: Routledge.

Meyers, E. (2002). Jewish culture in Greco-Roman Palestine. In D. Biale (Ed.), *Cultures of the Jews: Mediterranean Origins.* New York, NY: Schocken Books.

Milgrom, J. (2000). *Leviticus 17-22: A New Translation with Introduction and Commentary.* The Anchor Bible. New York, NY: Doubleday.

Olyan, S. (2000). *Rites and Rank: Hierarchy in Biblical Representations of Cult.* Princeton, NJ: Princeton University Press.

Olyan, S. (2008). *Disability in the Hebrew Bible: Interpreting Mental and Physical Differences.* New York, NY: Cambridge University Press.

OlyanRabinowitz, L. I. (2007). Blemish. In M. Berenbaum & F. Skolnik (Eds.), *Encyclopaedia Judaica, 3,* 2nd ed. (pp. 749–750). Detroit: Macmillan Reference USA.

Raphael, R. (2008). *Biblical Corpora: Representations of Disability in Hebrew Bible Literature.* New York, NY: T&T Clark.

Rose, M. L. (2003). *The Staff of Oedipus: Transforming Disability in Ancient Greece.* Ann Arbor, MI: University of Michigan Press.

Spiegel, J. (2000). Why do we not look at the priests? *Parashat Naso 5760/10 June 2000.* Bar Ilan University. http://www.biu.ac.il/JH/Parasha/eng/naso/spi.html

Stein, D. (2008). Collapsing structures: Discourse and the destruction of the temple in the Babylonian Talmud. *Jewish Quarterly Review 98*(1), 1–29.

CHAPTER 2

What the Rabbis Heard: Deafness in the Mishnah[1]

Bonnie L. Gracer

This chapter examines deafness in Jewish antiquity as expressed in the Mishnah, the foundation document of rabbinic Judaism. Ancient Greek and Roman attitudes toward disability and deafness are surveyed in order to establish the context within which the Mishnah was formulated, and to assess whether, and to what extent, Greco-Roman beliefs may have influenced the rabbis and Jewish law on matters pertaining to deafness.

Particular focus is given to (a) infanticide and gratitude as two opposing responses to disability in antiquity and (b) the common belief that hearing and speech are precursors to intelligence. The major findings of this chapter are that while the rabbis of the Mishnah did not adopt the Greco-Roman practice of infanticide in response to the birth of a child with a disability, they did incorporate Greco-Roman beliefs about the connections between hearing, speech, and intelligence into Jewish law. This chapter surveys the Mishnah in order to elaborate on these points and discuss their implications for the participation of deaf people in Jewish life.

Disability: A Time to Kill, a Time to Bless

This section explores two distinct responses to disability in ancient times: murder, and gratitude.

Ancient Greece and Rome

In Ancient Greece, infanticide was an accepted response to the birth of a child with a disability. Hippocrates raised the question, "which children should be raised?"[2] The responses of Plato (c. 427–347 BCE) and Aristotle (384–322 BCE) make it clear that people with disabilities were not those slated to live. Plato stated, for example:

> This then is the kind of medical and judicial provision for which you will legislate in your state. It will provide treatment for those of your citizens whose physical and psychological constitution is good; as for the others, it will leave the unhealthy to die, and those whose psychological constitution is incurably corrupt it will put to death. That seems to be the best thing for both the individual sufferer and for society. (*The Republic*, Book III: 409e–410a)

Aristotle was in full agreement: "With regard to the choice between abandoning an infant or rearing it, let there be a law that no crippled child be reared" (*Politics*, 7, 1335b: 19–21).

Plato and Plutarch go so far as to provide detail on the process of making the decision about who should live and who should die. Plato stated: "... we must look at our offspring from every angle to make sure we are not taken in by a lifeless phantom not worth the rearing" (Theaetetus, 160E–161A, as quoted in Martha L. Edwards, 1996: 82). Plutarch maintained that the decision lay with the tribal elders rather than with the father (*Lives*, Vol. I., Lycurgus: 16). The mother, apparently, was not part of the decision-making process.

In Rome (c. 450–449 BCE), contemporary Roman custom was codified in a legal document known as the Twelve Tables. Although certain parts of the Twelve Tables became antiquated, they never were repealed. They remained, at least in theory, the foundation of Roman law for the next 1,000 years.[3] The Twelve Tables granted the male head of the family (the paterfamilias) exclusive power over his sons and daughters, including power over life and death.[4] Table IV of the Twelve Tables states: "kill quickly... a dreadfully deformed child" (Lewis and Reinhold 1990: 110).[5] The life and death power of the *paterfamilas* disappeared by the second century CE, and by the third century CE abandoning a child was considered murder (Carcopino 1960: 77).

Ancient Judaism

In contrast to the evidence of infanticide as a response to disability in ancient Greece and Rome, the Mishnah records no debates on whether people with disabilities should be allowed to live; infanticide is never even raised as a possibility. Quite the contrary, the rabbis cherish life and see human variety as evidence of God's greatness. This is evident in the Mishnah and later rabbinic literature. For example, M. Sanhedrin (4: 5) states:

> ... whoever destroys a single soul..., Scripture accounts it as if he had destroyed a full world; and whoever saves one soul..., Scripture accounts it as if he had saved a full world...declare the greatness of the Holy One...for man stamps out many coins with one die, and they are all alike, but the King of Kings, the Holy One...stamped each man with the seal of Adam, and not one of them is like his fellow.[6]
>
> The Mishnah also states: "One is obliged to bless for the evil just as one blesses for the good ....Whatever treatment God metes out to you, thank Him very, very much" (M. Berakhot, 9: 5). Moses Maimonides (1135–1204) later explains (in his commentary on this Mishnah): "There are many things that seem good initially, but turn out evil in the end. Hence the wise man is not confounded when great troubles befall him, since he does not know what will eventuate." (Kehati commentary to M. Berakhot 9: 5).
>
> But how does all of this relate to disability? Other than not killing children with disabilities, how is society to respond, according to the Tannaim? They are to respond with gratitude and blessing. This is evident in two blessings of rabbinic origin: the "True Judge" blessing and the "varied creatures" blessing. M. Brachot 9: 2 directs: "On hearing bad tidings, (one) says: 'Blessed is the True Judge.'" The Tosefta[7] clarifies the application of this blessing to disability: "[One who sees] an amputee, or a lame person, or a blind person, or a person afflicted with boils, says, 'Blessed [are you Lord our God, Ruler of the Universe], the True Judge.'" (T. Berakhot 6: 3)[8]

As for varied creatures, the Tosefta also directs:

> One who sees an Ethiopian, or an albino, or a [man] red-spotted in the face, or [a man] white spotted in the face, or a hunchback, or a dwarf (or a *cheresh* or a *shoteh* or a drunk person) says, "Blessed [are you Lord our God, Ruler of the Universe who creates such] varied creatures." (T. Berakhot, 9: 1)

The Jerusalem Talmud, a later rabbinic elaboration on the Mishnah, discusses the differences between the "True Judge" and "varied creatures" blessings:

> This teaching [to say the blessing, "the True Judge"] applies [to those who see persons with disabilities who were born] whole and later were

changed. But if [one sees a person who] was born that way he says, "Blessed [are you Lord our God, Ruler of the Universe who creates such] varied creatures." (Y. Berakhot, 9: 1)[9]

Judith Abrams concludes, "If one is born without disabilities and they later develop, then the disabilities are a judgment from God. Those born with disabilities, however, are simply among God's varied creatures" (Abrams 1998: 119). In either case, it is evident that both the Tannaim and the later rabbis considered encountering persons with disabilities as occasions to bless and thank God, not as occasions to kill.

Speech, Hearing, and Intelligence

Oral debate and dialogue were core activities at the heart of the ancient world. In the Greco-Roman world, this was manifest, for example, in Plato's Socratic Dialogues (and the Socratic method of teaching by questioning), in the emphasis on both tragic and comic plays,[10] and in the speeches, debate, and discussion in the Roman Senate. In ancient Judaism, rabbinic law was passed down from one generation to the next by means of oral and aural transmission of knowledge. Indeed, "Torah *sh'be al peh*" Torah from the mouth, or Oral Torah[11]—transformed Judaism from a biblical to a rabbinic religion.

Words were critical to ancient society.[12] What, then, did the ancients understand about deafness and deaf people?

Ancient Greece and Rome

Martha Edwards (1995), in her extensive discussion of disability in ancient Greece, notes:

> Language was the hallmark of human achievement, so muteness went beyond a physical condition. An inability to speak went hand in hand with an inability to reason, hand in hand with stupidity. Plato (Theaetetus 206d) has Socrates say that anyone can show what he thinks about anything, unless he is speechless or deaf from birth. (Edwards 1995: 101)

Aristotle made profound connections between hearing, speech, and intelligence.[13] In a statement that was to have profound implications for the education of deaf individuals henceforth, Aristotle stated:

> ... it is hearing that contributes most to the growth of intelligence. For rational discourse is a cause of instruction in virtue of its being audible

....Accordingly, of persons destitute from birth of either sense, the blind are more intelligent than the deaf and dumb. (*Sense and Sensibilia*, 436b.16, 437a.15)

Aristotle also asserted that "Men that are born deaf are in all cases also dumb[14]; that is, they can make vocal sounds, but they cannot speak" (*History of Animals*, Book IV, 9, 536b.4). Benderly (1980), describing this statement as "widely mistranslated," notes: "Because many took 'speechless' to mean 'stupid,' the authority whose word ruled Western thought for over a thousand years appeared to state that the congenitally deaf were necessarily congenital morons" (Benderly 1980: 107).

The passionate emotion in Benderly's writing is common in the history of deafness and no wonder. The link between hearing, speech, intelligence, and the ability to learn has had staggering educational consequences.[15] Radutsky reports, for example,

...the Romans did not consider deafness a separate phenomenon from mutism and...consequently, many believed all deaf people were incapable of being educated. Ancient Roman law, in fact, classified deaf people as "mentecattifuriosi" which may be translated roughly as raving maniacs and claimed them uneducable. (Radutsky 1993: 239)[16]

The Roman writer Pliny the Elder (23–79 CE), in Natural History, writes: "There are no persons born deaf who are not also dumb."[17] As Benderly has noted, confusion over the terms "dumb," "stupid," and "mute" has had serious repercussions for deaf people throughout history.

Ancient Judaism

The Tannaim appear to have incorporated Aristotelian connections between hearing, speech, and intelligence into Jewish tradition. The Mishnah sets forth two types of categories through which to examine deafness. The first is a larger category, into which deaf people fit, and the second is a series of smaller, more deafness-specific categories. The larger category is grouped as "*cheresh, shotehvekatan*"—"a deaf mute, a mentally defective person, and a minor." This category is noteworthy in its apparent linking of deafness and muteness[18] with cognitive abilities and moral reasoning. The more specific categories include "deaf mute" (M. Terumoth 1: 1); "deaf and can speak" (M. Terumoth 1: 2); one who has "become a deaf mute" (M. Sotah 4: 5; M. Yevamoth 14: 1); a "deaf mute who recovered his senses" (M. Gittin, 2: 6); a "deaf mute" who "recovered his speech" (M. Baba Kamma 4: 4); and "deaf" (M. Sanhedrin 8: 4).

These categories are noteworthy in two respects. First, their focus on "senses" and speech suggests parallels to Aristotelian thought and demonstrates the importance of hearing and speech to the Tannaim. Second, the categories demonstrate a recognition of human difference—including differing abilities and modes of communication in deaf people.

The major concern of the rabbis seems to have been whether a deaf person (*cheresh*) could develop *da'at*—knowledge, intelligence, morality, reasoning abilities (Abrams 1998). It is here that Aristotle's pronouncements regarding the connections between speech, hearing, and intelligence seem to be paralleled: voice is connected to soul and imagination; audition is connected to rational discourse; hearing is connected to intelligence.

Both with respect to participation in society and responsibility for wrongdoing, these beliefs had serious, real-life consequences. On the one hand, social and religious opportunities were limited for deaf people. M. Arachin (1: 1) states, for example, " . . . a deaf mute, a mentally defective person, and a minor" may not vow or dedicate the worth of another, because they possess no understanding (*da'at*) (to formulate vows or to make assessments). On the other hand, deaf people appear to have been treated leniently with respect to criminal justice situations. For example, the Mishnah describes situations where able-bodied persons were held responsible and punished for damage or wrongdoing, but deaf persons were not. M. Baba Kamma (8: 4) states, "It is a bad thing [for anyone] to knock against a deaf mute, a mentally defective person, or a minor, since he that wounds them is liable, whereas if they wound others they are not liable." And according to M. Baba Kamma (4: 4),

> If an ox of a person of sound senses gored an ox of a deaf-mute, or a mentally defective person, or a minor, he is liable; but if one belonging to a deaf mute, or a mentally defective person, or a minor gored an ox of one of sound senses, he is exempt.

Deaf people, it seems, could injure others (or let their animals injure others) and get away with it.[19] Why? The rabbis, like Aristotle, seem to have linked deafness with some sort of moral or cognitive deficiency. Rabbinic pedagogy relied heavily on verbal communication. Prime activities included verbal arguing, discussing, and questioning. Without the ability to participate in the discussions and arguments, deaf people may have been seen as having no way to develop or communicate *halachic* or other reasoning skills.[20]

The link between deafness (cherish) and intelligence-understanding (da'at) for the rabbis, as for Aristotle, appears to have been speech. M. Terumoth 1:1 and 1:2, when examined together, illuminate this point. M. Terumoth 1:1 states,

> There are five who may not separate the priest's share of the produce, and if they do so their separation is not valid... a deaf-mute (*cheresh*), an insane person (*shoteh*), and a minor (*katan*) .... [21]

Compare this to M. Terumoth 1:2:

> A deaf person such as can speak but cannot hear (*cheresh ha m'daberv'ainoshomayah lo*) should not separate...but if he did so his separated priest's share is valid.

In M. Terumoth 1: 1, the *cheresh* has no chance of his separation being valid. In M. Terumoth 1: 2, he does. The *cheresh* in 1: 1 "may not" separate. The *cheresh* in 1: 2 "should not" separate. Legally, this may have been a major distinction. In 1: 1, if a *cheresh* separated, anyway the separation still was not valid. In 1: 2, it was. And what was the only difference between the deaf people in the two Mishnaic traditions? Speech. As if to answer any remaining question, M. Terumoth (1: 2) continues: "The *cheresh* of whom the Sages have spoken in all cases is one who can neither hear nor speak."

Even without the linking of hearing and intelligence, the simple ability to hear and speak clearly had important implications for participation and leadership in rabbinic society. Take, for example, the religious obligation to recite the "Shema," a defining prayer in the Jewish liturgy. The Hebrew word "Shema" typically is translated as "hear." The first line of the prayer reads: "Hear O Israel, the Lord is our God, the Lord is One."[22] The Mishnah records the following debate:

> If someone read the Shema but did not hear it, he fulfills his obligation. Rabbi Yose said, He has not fulfilled his obligation. (M. Berakhot 2: 3)

Pinchas Kehati (a recent commentator), noting that "R.Yose's ruling is the norm," explains: "[He has not fulfilled his obligation] ... to read the

Shema, since the verse reads, 'Hear' ... make audible to your ear what your mouth has to say (Gemara)." However, it is worth noting that an alternate translation of the word "shema" is "understand." The first Tanna, Kehati explains, "interprets Shema to mean 'understand' (as in 2 Kings 18: 26 tr), hence, 'Shema In any language that you understand.' It is permissible, then, for one to recite the Shema in any language he understands."[23] The Mishnah continues:

> If one read the Shema without enunciating the letters properly, R. Yose says, He has fulfilled his obligation. Rabbi Yehudah says, He has not fulfilled his obligation. (M. Berakhot 2: 3)

In this instance, R. Yose's ruling also prevails. However, Kehati notes that " ... ab initio one is required to pronounce the letters precisely and to take care not to run two identical or similar letters into one .... "[24] While people with hearing and/or speech impairments are not explicitly discussed in this Mishnah, questions certainly arise: can a deaf person who cannot hear or speak clearly fulfill the obligation to recite the Shema? Could the anonymous Mishnah's interpretation of "shema" as "understand" rather than "hear" mean a deaf person could fulfill the obligation by reciting the prayer in sign language, if that is a language he or she understands?

These are questions of Jewish law best examined in a separate venue[25]; for now, it is worthwhile simply to note the importance of hearing and speech to the rabbis of the Mishnah. Similarly, the Rosh Hashanah liturgy requires Jews to "hear the sound of the shofar."[26] The Mishnaic tractate on Rosh Hashanah states, "A deaf mute, an imbecile, and a minor cannot fulfill an obligation on behalf of the many. This is the general rule: whoever is not liable to an obligation, cannot fulfill that obligation on behalf of the many" (M. Rosh Hashanah 3: 8). Kehati offers the following commentary:

> Resuming the discussion of fulfilling the obligation of blowing the shofar on behalf of others, the Mishnah teaches that a person can do so only if he himself is liable to that obligation. A deaf mute, an imbecile ... and a minor ... are not liable to the commandment of the shofar, and therefore they cannot fulfill an obligation on behalf of the many .... According to one opinion, a person who is deaf but can speak may also not fulfill this obligation on behalf of others, for the essence of the commandment is "to hear the sound of the shofar," and since he does not hear, he is exempt. (Kehati 1977)

Finally, Tannatic rulings demonstrate an impressive awareness of deafness-specific issues. For example, the existence of a separate category for an individual who had "become a deaf mute" suggests an understanding of age-of-onset (of deafness) as a critical factor in speech and language development (M. Sotah 4: 5; M. Yevamoth 14: 1). And it is clear that the Tannaim understood that deaf people communicated both manually and orally. For example, M. Gittin (5: 7) states, "A deaf mute (cheresh) may transact business by signs and be communicated with by signs" and then continues, "Ben Bathyra says, he may transact business and be communicated with by lip movements in matters concerning movable property." And M. Yevamot (14: 1) states, "Just as he marries by gesture so he may divorce by gesture."[27]

The nature of these activities (marriage, divorce, business dealings) require intelligence, reason, and knowledge *da'at*. So perhaps the rabbis (at least some of them, some of the time) understood that meaningful, abstract concepts (as well as detail) could be communicated manually, and that deaf people might have some access to *da'at*.

Conclusion

The Jewish Bible, known in Hebrew as the Torah, was the basis of the rabbinic discussion and exegesis that led to the development of the Mishnah and later Jewish law. And so it is perhaps fitting to end this chapter with a story from Torah, the story of the great leader and prophet Moses, who had a speech impairment.

According to the Book of Exodus, God commanded Moses to free the Israelites from slavery in Egypt. Moses, however, hesitated: "Please, O Lord, I have never been a man of words. I am slow of speech and slow of tongue." God responded, "Who gives man speech? Who makes him dumb or deaf or seeing or blind? Is it not I, the Lord? Now go, and I will be with you as you speak ...." Still Moses protested: "Please, O Lord, make someone else Your agent" (Exod. 4: 10–13). And then, in what I can describe only as the first reasonable accommodation in the Torah, God assured Moses that Aaron, his brother who "speaks readily," would join him and speak for him (Exod. 4: 14–16). And with that, Moses helped form a band of former slaves into a new nation, witnessed revelation, and delivered to the world the Ten Commandments.[28] Whatever one believes about the origin, truth, or veracity of the biblical text, the Torah demonstrates, through the story of Moses, the enormous potential of each human being. Moses should have been killed when he was an infant as Pharaoh had decreed the murder of all newborn Hebrew boys, and Moses was one. Imagine the implications.

Given the central role of Torah in Mishnaic and later Jewish law and tradition, it is not surprising that the Mishnah credits a person who saves a single soul with having saved a whole world (M. Sanhedrin 4: 5). It is not surprising that the Mishnah does not decree (or even contemplate) the murder of children with (or without) disabilities. It makes sense that the Mishnah is able to envision alternative means of communication for people who are deaf or who have speech impairments.

At the same time, the ancient Jews did live among the ancient Greeks and Romans. It is therefore not surprising that the rabbis, as evidenced in the Mishnaic canon, incorporated into Jewish law Greco-Roman beliefs linking hearing, speech, intelligence, and morality. It is clear, however, that the rabbis viewed all people, including deaf people, as unique individuals. The Mishnaic delineation of multiple categories of deafness resulted in not every deaf person being "categorically" disqualified or exempt from the performance of specific mitzvot.[29] The rabbis observed deaf people, paid enough attention to notice detail, and deemed deaf people worthy of life, legal rulings, and protections. From the standpoint of deaf history, these are all extremely positive developments.

AUTHOR'S NOTE: The research for this chapter began in partial fulfillment of the requirements for my master's degree in Jewish Studies, with an emphasis on Ancient Judaism, at Baltimore Hebrew University. The author gratefully acknowledges and thanks Professor Steven Fine, then of Baltimore Hebrew University, now at the University of Cincinnati, Professor Cheryl Walker of Brandeis University, the late Professor Irving Kenneth Zola (z"l) of Brandeis University, and Rabbi Jonathan Kraus of Belmont, MA, for their teaching, inspiration, and assistance. All honor is due them. All errors are mine.

Notes

1. This chapter was previously published in 2003 in *Disability Studies Quarterly* 23(2) and is reprinted here with permission.
2. As quoted in Winzer (1997: 82).
3. Lewis and Reinhold (1990: 107–108). Also note that Cicero (106 BCE–43 CE) reported that in his time, boys were required to memorize the Twelve Tables (Laws II. xxiii. 59).
4. Casson (1998: 10–11), noting that infanticide was practiced throughout ancient times, adds that the decisions of the paterfamilias were made "not

necessarily in consultation with the mother." Casson (1998: 10–11) also notes other reasons for infanticide, such as poverty (on the one hand), and the division of property among too many heirs (on the other). Carcopino (1968: 77) adds that girl babies and "bastards" were victims of exposure.

5. The Twelve Tables were instituted as a means of plebian protection against patrician magistrates, and as a means of equality before the law.

6. Individual sayings, laws, and discussions within the Mishnah are called mishnahs, and are cited according to Tractate. For example, the mishnah quoted above is located in Chapter 4 of Tractate Sanhedrin. Its citation reads "M. Sanhedrin 4: 5" because it is the fifth mishnah in Chapter 4 of Tractate Sanhedrin.

7. The Tosefta is a compilation of Tannaitic sayings not included in the Mishnaic canon. See Strack and Stemberger (1996: 149–163).

8. Translation follows Judith Abrams (1998: 118).

9. Translation follows Judith Abrams (1998: 119). On the Jerusalem Talmud, see Strack and Stemberger (1996: 164–189).

10. E.g. Euripides, Aristophanes, Sophocles, Aeschylus.

11. "Oral Torah" refers to the belief that Moses received two Torahs on Mt. Sinai, one written, one oral. The basis for this belief is in M. Avot (1: 1), and is extrapolated in part from the appearance of the plural "Torot" in Leviticus (26: 46). The phrase in Leviticus reads, "These are the decrees, the ordinances, and the teachings (*Torot*) that God gave, between Himself and the Children of Israel, at Mount Sinai, through Moses." "*Torot*" is plural of the word "Torah," suggesting that two Torahs were given to Moses. The rabbis explained that the first Torah was the written one (*Torah she bi ktav*), and the second was the oral one. For further discussion, see Elon (1994: 190–227), Safrai (1987: 35–120), and Shiffman (1991: 177–200).

12. Boman, discussing the origins of the Greek "logos" (word), notes, "Logos, word, came from... 'to speak.' The basic meaning of the root leg is, without doubt, 'to gather'... to put together in order, to arrange... The deepest level of meaning in the term 'word' is thus nothing which has to do with the function of speaking neither dynamic spokeness... nor the articulateness of utterance but the meaning, the ordered and reasonable content... Logos expresses the mental function that is highest according to Greek understanding" (Boman 1970: 67).

13. In On the Soul, Book II, 420b.5, and 420b.29 421a.1, Aristotle also said that the soul resides in the windpipe and the areas of the body that create speech, and that "voice is sound with a meaning."

14. Benderly (1980: 107) translates "dumb" as "speechless."

15. Ancient ideas of speech as an indicator of intelligence set the stage for what later became a communications debate so passionate that Benderly called it "a holy war... a conflict as fierce as any that ever sundered a party cell or shattered a religious denomination." Known initially as the "War of Methods" and later as the "oral/manual controversy," the debate

focused on whether deaf people should communicate by speaking or signing (Benderly 1980: vii–8; Brill 1984: 17; Lane 1984; Lane and Phillips 1984; Spradley and Spradley 1978; Winefield 1987).

16. Pliny (1952: Book 35, 21), however, does record a celebrated debate when the grandson of Quintus Pedius, a former consul who was appointed by Caesar as his joint heir with Augustus, was born mutus. Both Augustus and the orator Messala agreed that the grandson, also named Quintus Pedius, should have lessons in painting. Apparently the child made great progress before he died at an early age.

17. As cited in Wright (1969: 136) and Benderly (1980: 107).

18. The cochlea, inner ear, and mechanisms of hearing actually have no direct bearing on the vocal chords or the ability to speak. The reason "deaf speech" sounds different is that deaf people cannot hear how sounds are pronounced.

19. See also M. Sanhedrin (8: 4), in which hearing children of deaf adults also appear to be treated leniently.

20. *Halachah* means Jewish law.

21. The "separation" under discussion is the Heave offering (*terumah*) the portion of one's harvest that must be given to the priests in the Temple before one can eat from one's harvest. The remaining two who may not separate are "he who separates the priest's due from that which is not his own, and a non-Jew who separated from that of a Jew even by permission."

22. This prayer comes from Deuteronomy (6: 4), and articulates the Jewish belief in one God.

23. Kehati on M. Berakhot (2: 3). *Tanna* is the singular form of the Hebrew word *Tannaim*.

24. Kehati on M. Berakhot (2: 3).

25. For a more current discussion of Jewish law and deafness, for example, see Mordechai Shuchatowitz's "Halacha Concerning Jewish Deaf and Hard of Hearing" published by the Orthodox Union (undated).

26. A shofar is a ram's horn. When blown, it creates a loud sound. For a survey of the Jewish holidays, including Rosh Hashana, see Greenberg (1988).

27. Blackman (1990) alternately translates "sign" (M. Gittin 5: 7) and "gesture" (M. Yevamot 14: 1). The Hebrew in both instances stems from the root letters *reish, mem, zayin*. Alcalay (1996: 24–62) defines this, in part, as "hint, imply, sign, gesture." Blackman defines it as "sign, deaf and dumb language" (see footnote to M. Yevamot 14: 1).

28. The book of Exodus details the life of Moses.

29. *Mitzvot* is plural of *mitzvah*, a Hebrew word meaning "commandment."

References

Abrams, J. Z. (1998). *Judaism and Disability: Portrayals in Ancient Texts from the Tanach through the Bavli*. Washington, DC: Gallaudet University Press.

Alcalay, R. (1996). *The Complete Hebrew English Dictionary*. Tel Aviv, Israel: Miskal Publishing and Distribution, Ltd.

Barnes, J. (1984). *The Complete Works of Aristotle* (The Revised Oxford Translation, Vol. I, Bollinger Series LXXI.2). Princeton, NJ: Princeton University Press.

Benderly, B. L. (1980). *Dancing Without Music: Deafness in America*. Garden City, NY: Anchor Press/Doubleday.

Blackman, P. (1990). *Mishnayoth*, 2nd ed. Gateshead, England: Judaica Press.

Boman, T. (1970). *Hebrew Thought Compared with Greek*. New York, NY: Norton & Company.

Brill, R. G. (1984). *International Congresses on the Education of the Deaf: An Analytical History* (1878–1980). Washington, DC: Gallaudet University Press.

Carcopino, J. (1960). *Daily Life in Ancient Rome: The People and the City at the Height of the Empire*. New Haven, CT: Yale University Press.

Casson, L. (1998). *Everyday Life in Ancient Rome*. Baltimore, MD: Johns Hopkins University Press.

Clough, A. H. (Ed.) (2001). Lycurgus. In *Plutarch's Lives*, Vol. 1. The Dryden Translation. New York, NY: The Modern Library.

Edwards, M. L. (1995). *Physical Dsability in the Ancient Greek World*. Unpublished Doctoral Dissertation, Ann Arbor, MI: UMI Dissertation Services.

Edwards, M. L. (1996). 'Let there be a law that no deformed child shall be reared': The cultural context of deformity in the ancient Greek world. *The Ancient History Bulletin 10*(3–4), 7 –92.

Edwards, M. L. (1997). *Deaf and Dumb in Ancient Greece*. In L. J. Davis (Ed.), *The Disability Studies Reader*. New York, NY: Routledge.

Elon, M. (1994). *Jewish Law: History, Sources, Principles*. Philadelphia, PA: Jewish Publication Society.

Greenberg, I. (1988). *The Jewish Way: Living the Holidays*. New York, NY: Simon and Shuster.

Kahana, N. (Tr.) (undated). *Seder Zeraim: Berakhot. A New Translation with a Commentary by Rabbi Pinchas Kehati*. Jerusalem, Israel: Maor Wallach Press.

Kehati, P. (1966–1977). *Mishnah*. Mishnavotmevo'arot/bi yedePinhasKehati (Hebrew.) Jerusalem, Israel: HekhalShelomoh.

Lane, H. (1984). *When the Mind Hears: A History of the Deaf*. New York, NY: Random House.

Lee, D. (Tr.) (1987). *Plato: The Republic*. London, England: Penguin Classics.

Levin, E. (Tr.) (1994). *Seder Moed: Mishnah Rosh Hashana, Mishnah Megilla: A New Translation with a Commentary by Rabbi Pinchas Kehati*. Jerusalem, Israel: Maor Wallach Press.

Lewis, N., & Reinhold, M. (1990). *Roman Civilization: The Republic and the Augustan Age*, Vol. 1. New York, NY: Columbia University Press.

Lieberman, S. (1955–1988). *ToseftaKifushta: A Comprehensive Commentary on the Tosefta*, 12 vols (Hebrew.) New York, NY: Jewish Theological Seminary of America.

Pliny (1952). *Natural History*, with an English translation by H. Rackman, Vol. IX, Books 33–35, *Loeb Classical Library*. Cambridge, England: Harvard University Press.

Radutsky, E. (1993). The education of deaf people in Italy. In John Van Cleve (Ed.), *Deaf History Unveiled: Interpretations from the New Scholarship*. Washington, DC: Gallaudet University Press.

Safrai, S. (Ed.) (1987). *The Literature of the Sages: Oral Torah, Halakah, Mishna, Tosefta, Talmud, External Tractates*. Philadelphia, PA: Fortress Press.

Saunders, T. J. (Tr.) (1981). *Aristotle: The Politics*. New York, NY: Penguin books.

Shiffman, L. H. (1991). *From Text to Tradition: A History of Second Temple Rabbinic Judaism*. Hoboken, NJ: Ktav Publishing House, Inc.

Shuchatowitz, M. (undated). *Halacha Concerning Jewish Deaf and Hard of Hearing*. A publication of "Our Way" (a division of the Orthodox Union), 45 W. 36th Street, NY, NY 10018.

Strack, H. L., & Stemberger, G. (1996). *Introduction to the Talmud and Midrash* (Second Printing). M. Bockmuehl (Trans.). Minneapolis, MN: Fortress Press.

Winzer, M. A. (1997). Disability and society before the eighteenth century: Dread and despair. In L. J. Davis (Ed.), *The Disability Studies Reader*. New York, NY: Routledge.

Wright, D. (1969). *Deafness*. New York, NY: Stein and Day Publishers.

CHAPTER 3

Leprosy in Early Islam

Matthew L. Long

Notes

Books and articles written by Islamic scholars include a number of important features that may be new to nonspecialists in the field of Islam. Arabic terminology is usually translated into English and is then followed by a transliteration of the Arabic word in parentheses and italics. This is to show the reader exactly which Arabic term is being translated. Also, it is common practice to follow a Muslim author's name with two dates of death in parentheses. The first year is the date of death according to the Muslim calendar (*al-taqwīm al-hijrī*), and the second year is the date of death in the Common Era. Finally, many Arabic words are written according to standard rules of transliteration. However, more frequently occurring words, such as Qur'an, hadith, and Muhammad, are written in Standard English with no accent or diacritical marks.

Introduction and Methodology

Few studies have been undertaken in an effort to explore the subject of leprosy in the Islamic tradition. Interest in leprosy has usually been restricted to a number of specific and refined topics. For instance, many authors have been intrigued by Muhammad's statements on disease transmission in general. Michael Dols' article "The Leper in Medieval Islamic Society" (1983), along with his other work on leprosy, delved into the history of the treatment of lepers in Islamic society over many centuries, the establishment of legal proclamations on lepers, and a comparative analysis of Islamic society's treatment of lepers to that of

Christian Europe, all common topics in previous studies on Islam and leprosy. Little effort has been made to exhaustively examine the treatment of lepers in the early Muslim community or Muhammad's interaction with the leprous population.

In this chapter, I will explore the different Arabic terminology related to the English terms "leper" and "leprosy" along with the hadith and biographical literature of Muhammad and his companions (*al-Ṣaḥāba*) relating to lepers and leprosy. Unlike Dols's work, I will scrutinize the application of each term relating to leprosy, examine the characters identified as lepers, and compare and contrast the treatment of these individuals. I shall thoroughly analyze the use of each term relating to leprosy on an individual basis and then holistically to see what, if any, statements can be made about Muhammad's attitudes toward lepers and leprosy. My goal will be to reveal whether or not Muhammad and/or the early Muslim community realized a difference between certain types of skin disorders. Such a distinction would aid in explaining the divergent traditions that have plagued scholars in the past.

Obstacles in the Study of Leprosy

Investigations into the early accounts of leprosy in the Islamic tradition are problematic for two primary reasons. First, leprosy is not defined by a single term. Encountering multiple terms relating to one subject is a recurrent feature of early Islamic literature. For example, both *rasūl* and *nabī* are terms used to describe messengers/prophets and *kharaj* and *jizya* are words relating to taxation. During the early years of Islam, terminology was occasionally used arbitrarily by hadith transmitters, historians, and biographers.

Second and more importantly, incompatible traditions on the treatment of lepers exist within the hadith and biographical literature. On the one hand, Muhammad told his companions to keep their distance from leprous individuals, and permitted the practice of divorce if one marries a leper or leprosy is contracted during the marriage. Other traditions tell of Muhammad bestowing great responsibility on one his fellow Muslims who is a leper and even sharing a meal with a leper. In some instances, Muhammad stated that the disease is a curse from Allah, and such a curse is not contractible. Yet in other traditions, Muhammad suggested complete avoidance from the leper, lest the disease spread. Scalenghe (2006) best summarized the situation of the study of leprosy in the Islamic tradition: the texts are beleaguered with inconsistencies, and attitudes toward lepers are often ambiguous.

Terminology

Before examining our primary sources, it is necessary to explore the terms associated with leprosy in the Qur'an and the hadith literature. The first term is *abraṣ*. It is formed from the root *bā'- rā' - sīn* and is the only term used in the Qur'an to refer to leprosy. According to Lane (1863), *abraṣ*, literally rendered as leprous, is a person who has contracted the disease of leprosy. Leprosy (*baraṣ*) of this form is particularly "malignant" and is referred to as "leuce" (Lane 1863). Lane notes nuances of the term *baraṣ* used by Muslim lexicologists. Ibn Sīdah (d. 458/1066) in his lexicon the *Muḥkam*, al-Jawharī (d. 395/1004) in his dictionary *al-Ṣiḥāḥ*, al-Fīrūzābādī (d. 817/1415) in *al-Qāmūs*, and Murtaḍā al-Zabīdī (d. 1205/1791) in the *Tāj al-'Arūs* all characterize this type of leprosy as manifesting itself with a white color on the skin (Lane 1863).

Besides *abraṣ*, the other most frequently used term describing skin conditions is *judhām*. This second term referring to leprosy, used frequently in the hadith and sīra literature, comes from the root *jīm - dhā - mīm*. The verbal form of this root (*jadhama*) means "to cut off, or to amputate" as in a body part (Lane 1863). The cutting off of an arm, finger, or other parts of the body is how leprosy became associated with this particular Arabic root. *Judhām* and *majdhūm* are the two cognates of this root that most specifically relate to leprosy. *Majdhūm* is simply one who has been afflicted with *judhām*. Compared with the former type of leprosy, this is depicted more vividly by the philologists and lexicographers and seems to have been worse in its effects on the afflicted. In the *Tāj al-'Arūs* and *Qāmūs*, *judhām* is said to affect the appendages and can cause a "dissundering (sic)," deterioration, and decomposing of those appendages (Lane 1863). This causes the falling off of the skin and the appendages. Al-Muṭarrizī (d. 610/1213) in his dictionary *al-Mughrib* added that *judhām* causes a "craking" of the skin, and all of the scholars agree that the condition of *judhām* results in the falling of the flesh or body parts (Lane 1863).

With the wealth of information from the lexicographers at hand one may be inclined to suppose that distinguishing these two forms of leprosy would be simple. The work of the lexicographers can be a helpful guide to understanding the texts, but caution must be exercised when one attempts to strictly apply the definitions established by the lexicographers. Many of them were writing after the collection of the major hadith works and early histories of Muhammad. Their definitions may reflect knowledge of leprosy within their own milieu and not that of

Muhammad's. Moreover, many of the lexicographers tended to duplicate definitions instituted in older dictionaries; therefore, consensus on a meaning may only be a result of the continual endorsement of a previously established characterization.

One of the primary concerns when attempting to comprehend the Arabic terminology is that other skin conditions are sometimes categorized as *baraṣ* or *judhām* by the Muslim writers and English translators. For instance, *judhām* is what English translators have called elephantiasis. According to the descriptions of the grammarians, it seems *judhām* would not be elephantiasis at all if a person is losing limbs or body parts. Symptoms of elephantiasis include a great thickening of the skin, particularly in areas such as the legs. Contrarily, the Muslim dictionaries say that *judhām* is a corrosion or destruction of body parts or the skin not a thickening.

One notorious tale from the histories of Islam involves a famous Muslim hadith collector and jurist Anas ibn Mālik (d. 179/795). In *Kitāb al-Ma'ārif* written by Ibn Qutayba (d. 276/889) (1934), Anas ibn Mālik is mentioned as a notable person who contracted *baraṣ* during his lifetime. Interestingly, when this story was rendered into English, Anas ibn Mālik is not said to have leprosy but instead vitiligo or leukoderma. Both vitiligo and leukoderma are conditions in which white lesions begin appearing on the body, not dissimilar from the description of the white spots of the leprous. While the authenticity of this report regarding Ibn Mālik has been doubted by some, it nonetheless provides us pertinent information for our study on leprosy. While it appears that the Muslim lexicographers regarded *baraṣ* to be related to leprosy, other authors may have used this as a descriptor of totally different diseases and disorders of the skin (Dols 1981).

Further difficulties arise if one attempts to classify *baraṣ* and *judhām* or distinguish these diseases through the application of modern descriptions. Leprosy, also known as Hansen's disease today, has numerous subdivisions, but many physicians agree that two main forms exist: Tuberculoid and Lepromatous (Vorvick and Vyas 2009). Symptoms of both Tuberculoid leprosy and Lepromatous leprosy are skin lesions and usually a loss of pigmentation from said lesions (Vorvick and Vyas 2009). Thus, we cannot be sure if what the Muslim scholars and writers called *baraṣ* is either Tuberculoid leprosy or Lepromatous leprosy.

Some of the symptoms of Lepromatous leprosy are skin nodules, skin plaques, and thickening of the skin. Lepromatous leprosy may have been the type of leprosy that the early Muslim writers had in mind when referring to *judhām* (Dols 1981). This would make even more sense in light of the fact that English translators called *judhām* elephantiasis. Commonalities, such as the thickening of the skin, are what most likely directed English translators to label *judhām* elephantiasis instead of the more appropriate Lepromatous leprosy.

Those seeking to understand leprosy in the early history of Islam by examining only the English versions of Muhammad's biographies or the hadith will be misled by inaccurate and unspecific translations. For a better understanding of leprosy in the time of Muhammad, one must go to the Arabic sources. But even when examining the Arabic texts, one must be careful of diagnosing the exact type of leprosy plaguing individuals in early Muslim society. With this understanding of the terminology and their limitations established, I shall begin to examine the Islamic scripture and early literature to see what information these sources can provide us on leprosy and lepers.

Qur'an

The Qur'an is the primary source of knowledge and guidance for Muslims. It contains stories of the prophets who preceded Muhammad, descriptions of the Hereafter, in addition to a number of religious commands that Muslims are obliged to follow. For those seeking answers on the status of lepers in Islam or encounters that Muhammad had with leprosy, no palpable evidence can be found in the Qur'an. Only two times is leprosy mentioned in the Qur'an, and both of these instances refer to the same event.

Jesus is one of the many prophets the Qur'an mentions who came before the time of Muhammad. It is during the narratives that detail Jesus's mission and capabilities when the terms for leprosy or leprous appear in the Qur'an. The first time the term lepruous/leprosy (*abraṣ*) occurs is in the third chapter of the Qur'an, in *sūrah al-Imrān*, in verse 49.

> And [will make him (Jesus)] an apostle unto the children of Israel. (With this message) I have come unto you with a message from your Sustainer. I shall create for you out of clay, as it were, the shape of [your] destiny, and then breathe into it, so that it might become [your] destiny by God's leave; and I shall heal the blind and the leper (al-abraṣ), and bring the dead back to life by God's leave; and I shall let you know what you may eat and what you should store up in your houses. Behold, in all this there is indeed a message for you, if you are [truly] believers.

The second time the word leprosy/leprous/leper (*abraṣ*) appears is in the fifth chapter of the Qur'an, in verse 110, which is nearly identical.

On the surface, these verses reveal little about leprosy or lepers. There are no specifics on the cause of the malady and no parameters on the treatment of persons afflicted by the disease. Only through interpretive endeavors can a more refined characterization of leprosy be gleaned from the Qur'anic passages. The passages above recount that Jesus was given the power to heal those afflicted with leprosy (*abraṣ*). Leprosy is not the only malady that Jesus is able to alleviate in these two narratives. Jesus was given the power to heal those with blindness and even restore life to the deceased. Which begs the question, why are these three states grouped together in the Qur'an?

One plausible explanation of the connection between the blind, leprous, and deceased rests on the nature of these conditions. Blindness, leprosy, and death are conditions that cannot, under normal circumstances, be cured. Evidence to support this theory is evident when each individual term is thoroughly scrutinized. For instance, the type of blindness (*akmaha*) mentioned in both of the previous chapters of the Qur'an is different from other forms of blindness mentioned elsewhere. According to Hans-Wehr (1994), *akmaha* means to have been "born blind"; this is not a type of blindness that comes later in life or is due to an injury. Nor is this type of blindness to be construed as a "spiritual blindness." Some commentators attempted to argue that *akmaha* may be related to a person's unwillingness to accept the concept of one God or accept Islam; however, the linguists agree that this blindness is physiological.

The verb *'amiya* and its cognates, such as *'amū* and *'amī*, are also found in the Qur'an to describe the condition of blindness. While *'amiya* is translated as blindness, reading the word within the Qur'anic context reveals that the true definition of the word is related to a type of spiritual blindness, not a physical blindness. According to Asad (2003), *'amiya* is used in the Qur'an 20 times to refer to spiritual blindness. Three times the term is used to indicate physical blindness (24: 61; 48: 17; 80: 2). Despite these few cases, *'amiya* and its cognates are meant to relate a spiritual or religious condition of an individual rather than a physiological condition. In addition, this type of blindness is not permanent. Acceptance of Allah and Muhammad as God's messenger is the cure to most forms of *'amiya*.

It is obvious that of the two terms for blindness *akmaha* is a permanent and incurable state. Thus, blindness and death are incurable/permanent states of being, and we may reasonably conclude that the type of leprosy (*abraṣ*) is not curable either. The only means to alleviate any of these three states are through the healing abilities of a prophet. Jesus is the one prophet mentioned in the Qur'an able to heal those with leprosy, blindness, and the deceased, but this authority comes from the Divine. Thus, only through some Divine means can leprosy, or any other permanent debilitating condition, be assuaged. The concept of seeking intercession with the Divine for relief of infirmities is echoed in the hadith literature as well. My interpretation suggests that the form of leprosy identified in the Qur'an, *abraṣ*, is quite dangerous. As we begin to investigate hadith and sīra literature, we shall see that it is almost impossible to distinguish between which form of leprosy is more hazardous or infectious.

Hadith, Sīra, and Historical Literature

While the Qur'an can provide a few fragments of information on leprosy, these passages have little connection to Muhammad's experience with lepers. The hadith, sīra, and historical literature provide the best and most detailed understanding of the condition of leprosy and lepers associated with Muhammad. The hadith are oral traditions relating the words and actions of Muhammad. A hadith is composed of a chain of transmitters (*sanad* sing., *isnād* plural) and the actual text (*matn*) itself. The hadith are the second most important source of knowledge, both legal and religious, for Muslims behind the Qur'an. The sīra literature tells of the life of Muhammad, from his birth to his death, a form of biographical literature. The sīra literature does not carry the same stature, legally, as the hadith. Sīra literature is built on the Qur'an, commentaries, and hadith. It reveals the customs (*sunna*) of Muhammad; biographical literature is similar to historical accounts in that both go into vast details about events, people, places, and so on. However, sīra literature places less concern on validating sources of knowledge on Muhammad. Chains of transmissions (*isnād*) are found in numerous sīra collections, but some narratives appear in the sīra literature without these chains to validate their authenticity. Moreover, biographies of Muhammad are sometimes filled apocryphal narratives borrowed from Judeo-Christian traditions, some of which material is referred to as *Isrā'īliyyāt*. Regardless of its lesser stature, biographical literature remains an important component for those seeking knowledge on the life and actions of Muhammad.

Hadith and the Qur'an are the two major sources from which all Islamic legal rulings on leprosy and lepers originate. The topic of leprosy and lepers is discussed more often and in better detail in the hadith than in the Qur'an. Upon examination of the hadith, one can plainly see why the Muslim community acted cagily toward lepers. Perhaps the most known and quoted tradition on lepers states that Muhammad said, "One should run away from a leper (*majdhūm*) as one runs away from a lion" (Ahmad Ibn Hanbal 1993; al-Bukhārī 1997). Badr al-Dīn Aynī (d. 855/1451–1453) relates a similar version to this hadith in his *'Umdatal-qārī*. His commentary employs Ibn Nu'aym al-Iṣfahānī's (d. 430/1038) version, which exchanges "flee (*farra*)" for "fear (*taqā*)," thus generating a slightly different rendition, "one should fear a leper as one fears a lion" (1929).

In another tradition Muhammad said, "Do not fix your gaze upon the lepers (*majdhūmīn*)" (Ahmad Ibn Hanbal 1993; Ibn Māja1975). The *'Umdatal-qārī* reports that Muhammad ordered people to keep a distance of at least a spear's length from those suffering from leprosy (Aynī 1929). Finally, a tradition found in a number of hadith collections tells the story of a delegation sent to Muhammad. According to Muslim (d. 261/875) (1999), the tradition says,

> Thaqīf's delegation included a man with leprosy (majdhūm). The Prophet sent a message to him. "Go back, for we have accepted your pledge of allegiance."

While not as candid as the former traditions, it is evident that Muhammad was unwilling to directly meet an assembly of men if one among their members was a known leper.

More traditions related to lepers and leprosy, such as the tale in which God tests the leprous man, the bald man, and the blind man, can be found in hadith, but these provide little pertinent information for our study on Muhammad and his relationship with the lepers of the early Muslim community. An important observation about the hadith mentioned above is that all of these are ascribed to Muhammad and use only one of the terms when discussing leprosy, *majdhūm*. The usage of *majdhūm* instead of *abraṣ*, or one its cognates, may indicate that Muhammad recognized this form of leprosy, *majdhūm*, as a far more deadly affliction than *abraṣ*. If this is the case, then the theory that the Qur'anic term for leprosy, *abrāṣ*, was the worst of the two forms of leprosy becomes dubious.

Divorcing those infected with leprosy was a common practice in the biographical literature. Muhammad briefly married several women according to the biographical records. However, these marriages were short lived, for it was discovered, after the marriage, that these women were affected with some form of leprosy or skin disease. Some of the women suspected of contracting leprosy were Asma bint Nu'mān from the Kinda tribe and 'Amrah bint Yazīd from the Kilābiya tribe. The Islamic biographers and scholars disagree on which of the two women were impaired or if both were afflicted.

Ibn Hishām (d. 218/833) discusses marriages and wives of Muhammad. Ibn Hishām states that Asma bint Nu'mān and 'Amrah bint Yazīd were the two women Muhammad married but quickly divorced. Hishām develops the account of Muhammad's marriage to Asma further, claiming that the reasoning behind his divorce of Asma and returning her back to her tribe was that Muhammad located a white spot (*biyāḍān*) on her body. Ibn Qayyim al-Jawziyah (d. 750–751/1350) mentions in the *Zād al-ma'ād* (2006) a similar story where the Prophet saw a white spot (*biyāḍān*) on the side (*bikashahā*) of her body. The only difference between al-Jawziyah's version and Ibn Hishām's account is the location of the leprous spot on the woman's abdomen or torso. This same story including the location of the leprous mark is recorded in al-Dhahabī's (d. 748/1348) *Siyara'lām al-nubalā'* (2004) and in this version too the word used to describe the leprosy is *biyāḍān*.

Other Muslim historians writing about the companions of the Prophet asserted that Asma bint Nu'mān was not the wife marred by leprosy. Instead 'Amrah bint Yazīd was the women who Muhammad divorced because of her leprous state. Ibn Athīr's (d. 630/1233) biographical compilation the *Usd al-ghābafī al-ṣaḥāba* (1970) and Ibn 'Asākir's (d. 571/1175) immense historical work *TārīkhDimashq* (1995) indicate that it was 'Amrah who Muhammad found to be suffering from leprous spots (*biyāḍān*).

Additional women, not clearly identified in the biographies or the histories, are also said to have been divorced by Muhammad owing to leprosy. Ibn Kathīr (d. 774/1373) tells of a woman from the Ghifār tribe that Muhammad married. After the marriage, Muhammad found upon her body leprosy (*baraṣ*) in the form of a white spot (*biyāḍān*) (Ibn Kathīr 1997, 2000). A woman from al-Kilābī tribe, said to be Fāṭima bint al-Ḍaḥḥak b. Sufyān or 'Āliya bint Ẓabyān b. 'Amr b. 'Awf b. Ka'b b. 'Abd b. Abī Bakr b. Kilāb or Sanā bint Sufyān b. 'Awf b. Ka'b b. 'Abd b. Abī Bakr b. Kilāb, was divorced by Muhammad because of leprosy according to Ibn Isḥāq (d. 150–152/761, 767–769) (Ṭabarī 1998). Ibn Kathīr (2000) identifies a third woman, not named in some of the other histories, said to have contracted leprosy. Ḥamra bint al-Ḥarith b. 'Awn b. Abū al-Ḥāritha al-Murrī was also betrothed to Muhammad but was discovered to have contracted leprosy (Ibn Kathīr 2000). It is hard to determine whether only a few or all of these individuals truly contracted leprosy. Regardless, Muhammad divorced all of these women upon seeing the leprous spots upon their bodies. No record indicates the Muhammad retained a wife known to have contracted leprosy.

Biyāḍān is a new term that we are yet to explore. Coming from the root *bā' - yā' - ḍād*, it used most commonly to describe the color white. In the biographical literature, *biyāḍān* is often used synonymously with *abraṣ* or in conjunction with it. It does not literally mean leprosy, but rather acts as a description of a type of leprosy, namely *abraṣ*. Strangely, Lane (1863), whose dictionary is based on a multitude of the most famous Arabic dictionaries, makes no reference to leprosy when defining *biyāḍ*. The introduction of this new term goes further to promote the difficulty fleshing out the form of leprosy that is the more dangerous and contagious. On the one hand, the hadith seem to indicate that *judhām* is the more dangerous, yet the Qur'an along with the biographical literature indicate it is *abraṣ* and *biyāḍān* that were infectious enough to warrant divorce.

Muhammad's divorce from these women formed the legal framework for divorce and compensation in marriages with a leper. In his famous hadith collection, *al-Muwatta'*, Anas ibn Mālik enumerates a number of provisions for divorcing a husband or wife if leprosy is discovered on the spouse's body. Later Muslim legal scholars (*fuqaha*) granted divorce and determined compensation in cases of leprosy using these hadith. Rispler-Chaim (2007) spells out many of the details on divorce as it is related to leprosy, for both men and women. Interestingly, the hadith by Ibn Mālik acknowledge that there were different types of leprosy, *abraṣ* and *judhām*, yet the different types of leprosy did not change the provisions for divorce or alter compensatory amounts.

Having examined the Qur'anic and biographical accounts alongside the hadith literature, a consistent pattern begins to develop. Muhammad and the early Muslim community show disdain for the condition of leprosy and lepers. Whether it is *abraṣ* or *judhām*, all the accounts communicate a feeling of fear toward lepers, shunning and divorcing those who were afflicted by either of the two forms of leprosy. Thus, it appears as if the early Muslim community and Muhammad made no definitive distinction between *abraṣ* and *judhām*. But not all of the traditions on lepers are consistent. Further investigation into the hadith and biographical material reveals that Muhammad did not always demonstrate abhorrence toward lepers.

The first and most noteworthy contradictory tradition appears in the hadith. Inconsistencies with hadith present a greater problem than a conflicting biographical tradition due to the legal ramifications a contradictory hadith presents. The hadith in question is not located among the sound (ṣaḥīḥ) collections, that is, most legitimate hadith collections, which are the collections of al-Bukharī (d. 256/870) and Muslim. The contradictory hadith is found in the collections of Dāwūd (Dā'ūd) (d. 275/888–889) (1984, 2000) and al-Tirmidhī (d. 279/892), which are still reliable, but do not possess the same credentials as the former collections. This tradition states,

> The Prophet, peace be upon him, took a man who was suffering from leprosy (majdhūm) by the hand. He placed it [the man's hand] along with his own hand in the dish and said, "Eat with confidence and trust in Allah."

As indicated in the translation, *majdhūm* is the form of leprosy afflicting the man with whom the Prophet shared the meal. If this was a singular instance in which Muhammad acted in direct opposition to all of the previous accounts of his dealings with lepers, it would be possible to dismiss this hadith. Deviation from his customary treatment of lepers can also be located in the biographical and historical literature.

In addition to the difficulties presented by the apparent conflicting hadith, another challenging historical reference arises in the accounts of Muhammad's companions. According to Ibn Kathīr (2000), utilizing Ibn 'Asākir as his source, Mu'ayqīb b. Abu Fātima al-Dawsī was a close associate of Muhammad. So close that Mu'ayqīb was regarded as reliable transmitter of hadith and at some point in time was responsible for the care of Muhammad's signature ring (khātim). Some traditions state that Mu'ayqīb at one point contracted leprosy (al-judhām) (Ibn Kathīr 1997). Muhammad ibn Sa'd (d. 230/845) in his Ṭabaqāt Kubrá (1991) agrees that Mu'ayqīb was afflicted by the disease.

Mu'ayqīb was not only affected by leprosy but was also cured from the disease. Ibn Kathīr (2000) stated that 'Umar b. Khaṭṭāb healed Mu'ayqīb through the prescription of a "colocynth." While a number of remedies existed for certain conditions during the life of Muhammad, none of the biographical literature mentions a cure for leprosy, though in later commentaries and medical treatises, such as Ibn Qayyim al-Jawzīya's, suggest a multitude of remedies for leprosy. Many of the hadith relate that in certain circumstances leprosy may go away on its own or through divine intercession. If indeed Mu'ayqīb was already known to have been a leper while Muhammad lived, this would bolster the hadith in which Muhammad shared his meal with a leper. Furthermore, it provides a solid basis for theory that Muhammad possessed a benign attitude toward some forms of leprosy in certain situations.

Not all of the scholars agree on the validity of the story of Mu'ayqīb. Some of the historians debate whether or not Mu'ayqīb actually contracted leprosy, while others debate whether his affliction was contracted during Muhammad's lifetime or after his death (Ibn Kathīr 2000). Mu'ayqīb being radically healed may indicate, as some Islamic scholars believed, that this is a spurious account. However, Mu'ayqīb is not the only person who appears to have been cured from leprosy. 'Uways ibn Anīs al-Qarnī is a name that appears in three hadith from Muslim's Ṣaḥīḥ. In three hadith it is said the 'Umar heard Muhammad talk of a man by the name of 'Uways who was cured of leprosy (buruṣ) through supplications to God (Muslim 1999). Although some scholars consider Mu'ayqīb's revitalization as a proof of a forgery, 'Uways' story would suggest that recuperating from leprosy is a possibility. We, therefore, should not dismiss Mu'ayqīb's tale as counterfeit on these grounds. Furthermore, Ibn Sa'd's testimony, which was one of the earliest biographies on the companions of Muhammad, lends credence to the case of Mu'ayqīb's leprous state. Far more problematic is the issue of when exactly Mu'ayqīb developed this affliction.

The hadith in which Muhammad shared a meal with a man possessing leprosy is shrouded in doubt as well. No apparent evidence is presented to suggest that this is a forged (mawḍū') hadith, but commentary (sharḥ) by Islamic scholars has indicated this hadith possesses less than reputable qualities. In al-Tirmidhī's version of this hadith, he classifies this hadith as gharīb (Mubārakfūrī 2001). Gharīb is an Arabic term used to describe hadith of weaker quality due to the lack of multiple transmitters of the hadith. High-caliber hadith (mutawātir) are classified as such because of the enormous number of people who heard and transmitted the hadith. Gharīb means that the hadith in question was transmitted by one individual at some point in the chain, thereby opening the possibility of inaccuracy of the hadith. The chain (sanad) of transmission does possess a number of strong hadith transmitters, such as Jabīr ibn'Abdallāh. That the hadith is known only through Yūnus b. Muhammad on the authority of al-Mufaḍḍal b. Faḍāla is Tirmidhī's grounds for questioning this hadith's strength. It may be that this hadith is a misrepresentation of one of Muhammad's statements and actions. As the commentary continues, Tirmidhī said that Muhammad did not share the meal with the leper but rather Muhammad's close companion

'Umar (Mubārakfūrī 2001). Ibn Sa'd too believed that 'Umar did not fear leprosy and would partake in a meal with a leper (1991). If this is the case, we could conclude that more than likely the story of Mu'ayqīb may also be counterfeit and that Muhammad never recommended inter- action with lepers at such close proximity.

In the later commentaries *'Awnal-ma'būd* and *Tuhfatal-ahwadhī* exists proof of another attempt to reconcile the tradition of Muhammad eating with a leper with the antiquities of Islam. An addendum from the Islamic scholar al-Ardabīlī (d. 993/1585) states that the leper with whom Muhammad shared a meal is Mu'ayqīb b. Abu Fātima al-Dawsī, the leper mentioned as an associate of Muhammad by Ibn Sa'd and Ibn Kathīr. Al-Ardabīlī's intent was to harmonize the hadith with the his- torical records and thereby validate its authenticity. While innovative, the early histories never clearly delineate when Mu'ayqīb contracted his disease. To speculate that Mu'ayqīb was indeed the afflicted man with whom Muhammad shared a meal would do a great deal to validating this hadith, but this assumption may be anachronistic.

Dols, one of the most prolific writers on leprosy in the Islamic tradi- tion, never mentions this hadith nor does he mention any of the com- mentaries dedicated to clarifying Muhammad's relationship with those afflicted by leprosy. It may be that the given this hadith's status as *gharīb*, Islamic scholars examining leprosy have simply passed over this hadith and its commentary. However, classifying a hadith as *gharīb* does not mean that we should assume that the hadith's veracity is dimin- ished. English translators and Islamic scholars have paid little attention to the commentaries on hadith related to leprosy in the Islamic tradi- tion. I shall now turn my attention fully to the hadith commentaries in a final effort to gleam some understanding of Muhammad's opinions on leprosy.

Hadith Commentaries

Just as the Mu'ayqīb story has its subscribers, some Islamic schol- ars concede that Muhammad did share a meal with a leper. Support for this tradition is found in al-Nawawī's (d. 676/1278) *al-Adhkār*. Commentary from this work elevates the value of the hadith to good (*hasan*), greatly improving the status and reliability of this hadith (Nawawī 1988). Nawawī also produced a commentary on the hadith collection of Muslim. At one point during that commentary, it is related by Muhammad's wife, 'Ā'isha, one of the most reliable transmitters of hadith, that a leper shared both food and drink with her (Nawawī 1987).

A variation of 'Ā'isha's narration is located in early commentary of Ibn Baṭṭāl (d. 449/1057) and the later *'Umdatal-qārī*. According to the narrative, a women had come to 'Ā'isha to ask the truth in Muhammad's statement that one is to flee from a leper, and 'Ā'isha responds that she shared food and drink with a person known to have contracted leprosy (*judhām*) (Aynī 1929; Ibn Baṭṭāl 2003). It becomes difficult to believe that if the disease of leprosy, in this case *majdhūm*, were so terrible Muhammad would have permitted his wife to share a meal and drink with an infectious leper. 'Ā'isha's account provides much needed support to authenticate and validate this hadith.

While it may appear that the commentaries of Nawawī and Ibn Baṭṭāl vindicate the hadith in question, we should not rush to such a lucid conclusion. The ubiquitous theme in the hadith commentaries is the number of heterogeneous opinions on leprosy. Some of Muhammad's companions and the later Islamic scholars took softer stances on interaction with lepers, whereas other companions and scholars formulated strict policies that segregated the leprous from the rest of the Muslim community. The records will even show that companions known to support and offer compassion toward the leprous occasionally feared and restricted the afflicted in other instances. In the end, it is nearly impossible to say with any real certainty what, if any, are the "correct" or "recommended" courses of behavior when one encounters a leper, for rarely is a consensus on the matter reached by any of the scholars or even by Muhammad's own companions.

Ibn Baṭṭāl's work, *Sharḥ* of Bukhārī's *Ṣaḥīḥ* collection, is a primary example of a text teeming with multifarious opinions on permitted behavior when one encounters a leper. Unlike succeeding commentaries, Ibn Baṭṭāl's commentary addresses restrictions that may or may not have been placed upon lepers during the life of Muhammad or shortly thereafter. For instance, it is recorded that some early Muslims advocated that lepers were to be prevented from mixing with the people of the community and from entering the mosque (*masjid*) (Ibn Baṭṭāl 2003). Forbidding entrance to the mosque (*masjid*) is probably the most restrictive declaration found regarding leprosy. But no records indicate that the disease obstructed one from becoming a Muslim or suggest a leper could not remain a practicing Muslim.

More surprising are the accounts of 'Umar's interaction with lepers in Ibn Baṭṭāl's commentary. It is related that 'Umar told a leprous woman to remain in her home so as not to infect the populace (Ibn Baṭṭāl 2003). Ibn Baṭṭāl also records two nearly identical narratives that document a proclamation 'Umar made to Mu'ayqīb. 'Umar stated that when he was in company of Mu'ayqīb, he would request Mu'ayqīb to sit a distance of a spear's length from him. The figure of 'Umar, as developed by Ibn Baṭṭāl, is much different from the image of 'Umar in other commentaries and biographies; here he is a staunch proponent for the separation and isolation of lepers from the rest of the community, whereas elsewhere he is one of the only people willing to share close quarters with the leprous.

On the other hand, Ibn Baṭṭāl records a number of opinions that dissuade one from consigning harsh social restrictions upon lepers. He reports that al-Ṭabarī, the great Muslim historian and Qur'an commentator, said that many of the Salaf, the first three generations of Muslims, were ignorant of any command to keep away from those suffering from either type of leprosy, *judhām* or *baraṣ* (Aynī 1929; Ibn Baṭṭāl 2003). Furthermore, Ibn Baṭṭāl is one of, if not the, the first commentators to relate the story of 'Ā'isha and her sharing of food and drink with a individual suffering from the disease, a narration repeated in nearly every commentary attempting to elucidate Muhammad's position on leprosy. Testimony in Ibn Baṭṭāl's commentary also reveals that Muhammad and the Muslim community brought new insight of the disease and eradicated antiquated behaviors. In the days of the "people of ignorance" (*ahl al-jāhiliyya*) fear of disease transmission forced lepers into isolation, but Muhammad bucked these trends, bringing a new understanding of the disease to the Muslim community (Ibn Baṭṭāl 2003). Ibn Baṭṭāl continues citing trends of Salaf and Islamic scholars and physicians supporting the established social restrictions and those who rejected the need to separate the leprous from the remainder of the Muslim community. With the many competing opinions and attitudes on leprosy, it is difficult to discern if Ibn Baṭṭāl or, for that matter, Muhammad and his companions believed in a static set of rules governing all interactions with lepers.

Subsequent commentaries replicate the same byzantine catalog of theories and narratives as constructed in Ibn Baṭṭāl's writing. This partly due to later scholars' reliance on previous works, but I believe this was primarily caused by the lack of consensus on the subject of leprosy. Muhammad's companions and Islamic scholars encourage strict rules of quarantine for the leprous occasionally, and at other moments dismiss such notions of disease transmission as archaic. I believe that these early commentaries shaped and influenced later scholarship, which stopped arguing, through historical proofs, for the validity of one hadith over another. Instead, these later scholars sought a middle ground that would permit the variant and contradictory hadith to be reconciled. Examples of this effort to reconcile the variant hadith can be found in the writings of Nawawī and Ibn Qayyim al-Jawzīya.

Nawawī documents two statements of another Islamic scholar that further attest to the ambivalent position many held on the subject of leprosy. In his commentary on the *Saḥīḥ* collection of Muslim, Nawawī documents two opinions established by Qāḍī'Iyāḍ (d. 544/1149). 'Iyāḍ states that refraining from close contact with the leprous has its basis in Islamic law, which permits the nullification of a marriage if leprosy is discovered (Nawawī 1987). 'Iyāḍ's second statement, which was often repeated in many later commentaries, such as Ibn Ḥajar al-'Asqalānī's (d. 852/1448), permits the existence of incongruous narratives related to leprosy. He acknowledged that Muhammad did refuse to meet the delegation from Thaqīf because of the presence of a leper. He also recognized the substance of the hadith in which Muhammad shared a meal with a leper (Nawawī 1987). 'Iyāḍ agreed with the hadith that called for discretion when one encounters a leper, but, like some of his predecessors and successors, did not outright reject the hadith that seemed outwardly incompatible.

In *Healing of the Medicine of the Prophet* (1999), al-Jawzīya acknowledged that Muhammad was known to both recommend the avoidance of lepers in certain cases and allow certain interactions. Al-Jawzīya did not believe differing hadith meant that one hadith must have been inaccurate. Instead of seeing the hadith as contradictory, he affirmed the concept that Muhammad acted differently in different scenarios. Ibn Qayyim al-Jawzīya adopted a reconciliatory position that seems to have been borne out of the testimony of Qāḍī'Iyāḍ. To suggest that Muhammad's demeanor altered based upon specific situations is to suggest that Muhammad or some of his companions possessed at least a cursory understanding of leprosy.

Believing that Muhammad and the early Muslim community understood rudimentary particulars concerning the transmission of leprosy is not astonishing. Leprosy is an ancient disease; Indian and Chinese writings confirm its existence hundreds of years before the dawn of Islam. Dols (1981, 1983) cites historical records and physical proofs documenting the existence of the disease in Arabia prior to the birth of Muhammad. The first documented case of leprosy in the Middle East occurred around 500 AD, more than 100 years before Muhammad and the Muslim community (Dols 1981, 1983). Dols (1981 1983) mentions the number of figures in pre-Islamic poetry believed to have been afflicted by the disease. Based on this evidence, it stands to reason that the disease was familiar and understood by the time Islam was established in Arabia; thus, knowledge of the disease, while not formally documented, may have been known to Muhammad or at least was accessible from a companion. Given the long presence of the disease in Arabia combined with Muhammad's dissimilar treatment of lepers in the hadith and biographical literature, it is probable that Muhammad had knowledge of leprosy and its transmission.

Conclusion

This study was successful in identifying a number of the men and women Muhammad knew to have been affected by the disease. I have attempted to demonstrate that it is nearly impossible in many instances to pinpoint the form of leprosy affecting certain individuals. This predicament is due to the usage of two words by the early Muslim scholars without much prudence and to the fact that both types of leprosy share similar qualities.

Evidence from the Arabic sources clearly demonstrates that lepers were treated with a great degree of trepidation during Muhammad's lifetime. Muhammad exercised caution on permitting close contact with lepers but still thoroughly held that contagions, such as leprosy, were transmittable only through the will of God. The hadith commentaries in this study consistently display a sundry of positions held by both Muhammad's own companions and the later Muslim scholars on leprosy. I have demonstrated that though contradictory narratives pertaining to leprosy exist, later scholars adopted a much-needed position that allowed and harmonized opposing hadith. In some scenarios, I have shown that the different traditions reveal that Muhammad did not always regard leprosy as a despicable disease to be constantly feared. Rather, Muhammad's conduct was strictly driven by the context of each interaction. Unfortunately, it is not viable to distinguish exactly what form of leprosy, if indeed leprosy was the true malady, afflicted these individuals.

While I have tried to give a comprehensive overview of leprosy during Muhammad's lifetime, more can be done to advance our knowledge in the field of disability and leprosy during the early Islamic epoch. I located a number of hadith commentaries relevant to the topic of leprosy. Although I touched on many of these commentaries, further study on their contents is warranted. In addition, I attempted from the outset to limit the use of sources and traditions related to the overarching topic of disease transmission in order to concentrate strictly on leprosy. I have come to the conclusion that it is not possible or sensible to discount accounts on disease transmission. Therefore, a more exhaustive study of hadith commentaries on the general subject of disease transmission would provide greater insight to the condition of leprosy in early Islam.

References

Arabic Sources

Abū Dāwūd (Dā'ūd), Sulaymān ibn al-Ash'athal-Sijistānī. (2000). *SunanAbīDāwūd,* Vols. 1–5. Beruit, Lebanon: Dār al-Risālah al-'Ālamīyah.

al-Dhahabī, Muhammad b. Ahmad b. 'Uthmān ibn Qāmāz b. (2004) *Siyara'lām al-nubalā'*, Vols. 1–5. Beruit, Lebanon: Dār al-Kutub al-'Ilmīyah.

al-Nawawī, Muhyī al-Dīn Abī Zakarīyā Yahyá ibn Sharaf. (1987). *Sharh Sahīh Muslim* , Vols. 1–10. Beirut, Lebanon: Dār al-Qalam.

———. (1988). *Al-Adhkār al-muntakhabah min kalāmsayyidal-abrār.* Cairo, Egypt: al-Dāral-Misrīyahal-Lubnānīyah.

al-Suhaylī, Abū al-Qāsim'Abd al-Rahmān b. 'Abdallāh. (1971). *Al-Rawd al-unuf fitafsiral-Sīrahal-Nabawīyah li-IbnHishām,* Vols. 1–4. Al-Azhar: Maktabatal-Kullīyātal-Azharīyah.

———. *Rawd al-'Anf.*Retrieved from http://islamport.com/w/ser/Web/1750 /1.htm

'Aynī, Badr al-Dīn Mahmūd ibn Ahmad. (1929). *'Umdatal-qārī: sharh Sahīh al-Bukhārī* , Vols. 1–25. Egypt: Dār al-Tibā'ah al-Munīrīyah.

'Azīmābādī, Muhammad Shams al-Haqq. (1968). *'Awnal-ma'būd: sharh SunanAbīDāwūd.* al-Madīnah al-Munawwarah: al-Maktabah al-Salafīyah.

Ibn'Asākir, Abū al-Qāsim'Alī al-Hasan. (1995). *TārīkhmadīnatDimashq,* Vols. 1–80. Beirut, Lebanon: Dār al-Fikr.

Ibn Athīr,Abū al-Hasan'Alī'Izz al-Dīn. (1970). *Usd al-Ghābafi al-sahāba,* Vols. 1–7. Cairo, Egypt: Dār al-Sha'b.

Ibn Battāl, 'Alī ibn Khalaf. (2003). *Sharh IbnBattāl'alá Sahīh al-Bukhārī* , Vols. 1–10. Beirut, Lebanon: Dār al-Kutub al-'Ilmīyah.

Ibn Hajar al-'Asqalānī, Ahmad ibn 'Alī. (1978). *Fath al-Bārī: sharh Sahīh al-Bukhārī*, Vols. 1–14. Cairo, Egypt: Maktabat al-kulliyāt al-Azharīyah.

Ibn Hanbal, Ahmad ibn Muhammad. (1993). *Musnadal-ImāmAhmadibnHanbal,* Vols. 1–8. Beirut, Lebanon: al-Maktab al-Islāmī.

Ibn Kathīr, 'Amād al- Dīn al-Fidā' Ismā'īl b. 'Umar. (1997) *Al-Sīra al-Nabawiyya,* Vols. 1–4. Beirut, Lebanon: Dār al-Fikr.

Ibn Māja, Abū'Abdallāh Muhammad ibnYazīd. (1975). *Sunanal-hāfiZ Abī'AbdAllāhMuhammadibnYazīdal-QazwīniibnMājah,* Vols. 1–2. Cairo, Egypt: DārIhyā'al-Turāth al-'Arabī.

Ibn Qayyim al-Jawzīya, Muhammad b. AbīBakr. (2006). *Zād al-Ma'ad,* Vols. 1–6. Beruit, Lebanon: Al-Riyan.

Ibn Qutayba al-Dīnawarī, Abū Muhammad 'Abdallāh ibn Muslim. (1935). *Al-Ma'ārif.* Egypt: al-Matba'ah al-Islamīyah.

Ibn Sa'd, Abū'Abdallāh Muhammad. (1991). *TabaqātKubrá,* Vols. 1–9. Beruit, Lebanon: Dār al-Kutub al-'Ilmīyah.

Mubārakfūrī, Muhammad 'Abdal-Rahmān ibn 'Abdal-Rahīm. (2001). *Tuhfatalahwadhī,* Vols. 1–9. Al-Qāhirah: Dār al-Hadīth.

English Sources

Abū Dāwūd (Dā'ūd), Sulaymān ibn al-Ash'athal-Sijistānī. (1984). *Sunan Abu Dawud: English Translation with Explanatory Notes,* Vols. 1–3. Ahmad Hasan (Trans.) Lahore: Muhammad Ashraf.

Al-Ṭabarī, Abū Ja'far Muhammad b. Jarīr. (1998). *History of al-Ṭabarī: Biographies of the Prophet's Companions and their Successors* , Vol. XXXIX. EllaLandau-Tasseron (Trans.) Albany, NY: State University of New York Press.

Asad, M. (2003). *Message of the Qur'an: The Full Account of the Revealed Arabic Text Accompanied by Parallel Transliteration.* Bitton, England: Book Foundation.

Bukhārī, Muhammad ibn Ismā'īl. (1997). *Sahīh al-Bukhārī: The Translation of the Meanings of Sahīh al-Bukhārī: Arabic-English,* Vols. 1–9. Muhammad Muhsin Khan (Trans.). Riyadh: Darusalam.

Dols, M. W. (1981). Djudhām. In *Encyclopedia of Islam,* Supplement: Fascicules 5–6 (pp. 270–274). Leiden: Brill.

———. (1983). The leper in Islamic society. *Speculum: A Journal of Medieval Studies 54,* 891–916.

Ibn Ishāq, M. (1955). *Life of Muhammad: A Translation of Ishaq's Sīrat rasūl Allāh.* Alfred Guillaume (Trans.). Oxford, England: Oxford University Press.

Ibn Kathīr. (2000). *The Life of Prophet Muhammad (Al-Sīra al-Nabawiyya),* Vols. 1–4. Trevor Le Gassick (Trans.). Reading, UK: Garnet Pub.

Ibn Qayyim al-Jawzīya, Muhammad b. Abī Bakr. (1999). *Healing with the Medicine of the Prophet.* Jalal Abual Rub (Trans.) Riyadh: Darusalam.

Lane, E. W. (1863). *An Arabic-English Lexicon,* Vols. 1–8. London, England: Williams and Norgate.

Muslim ibn al-Hajjaj, Abū Husayn. (1999). *Sahīh Muslim, Arabic-English.* 'AbdulhamīdSiddīqī (Trans.) Delhi: Adam Publishers.

Scalenghe, S. (2006). Disability. In Josef W. Meri (Ed.), *Medieval Islamic Civilization: An Encyclopedia* (pp. 208–209). New York, NY: Routledge.

Vardit, Rispler-Chaim. (2007). *Disability in Islamic Law.* Netherlands: Springer.

Vorvick, L., & Vyas, J. M. (2009). *Leprosy.* Retrieved from http://www.nlm.nih.gov/medlineplus/ency/article/001347.htm.

Wehr, H. (1994). *A Dctionary of Modern Written Arabic: Arabic to English.* Ithaca, NY: Spoken Language Services.

CHAPTER 4

Vitiliginous (Sk)Inscriptions: Historical Religious Interpretations of Involuntarily Whitening Skin

Elizabeth R. Sierra

Vitiligo: Modern Medical Discourses

Vitiligo is an acquired, noncontagious hypopigmentary dermatological condition that affects approximately 1 in 200 people worldwide, mostly before age 20 and without regard to race or sex (Castanet and Ortonne 1997; Hann, Park, and Chun 1997; Gawkrodger et al. 2008; Nordlund 1997; Spritz 2008; Taïeb and Picardo 2009). In vitiligo, melanocytes in the skin and mucous membranes cease pigment production, leaving no detectable trace of themselves in established vitiliginous skin as examined in ultrastructural and histochemical studies (Castanet and Ortonne, 1997). The resulting loss of pigment gives rise to the appearance of spreading, asymmetrical patches of milky-white skin and, in some cases, poliosis or leukotrichia, terms used to refer to the complete loss of hair pigment affecting 9–45 percent of people with vitiligo (Hann, Park, and Chun 1997; Gawkrodger et al. 2008; Sehgal and Srivastava 2007).

Spritz (2008) differentiates generalized vitiligo, which is the type of vitiligo discussed throughout this work and hereafter referred to simply as "vitiligo," from other hypopigmentary disorders in the following definition:

> Generalized vitiligo is defined as an acquired pigmentary disorder characterized by depigmentation due to melanocyte loss in the regions of

involved skin, in a pattern that is nonfocal and generally bilateral across the midline, though not necessarily symmetric. This definition thus excludes various Mendelian hypopigmentary spotting disorders... which result from mutations in specific single genes and which are characterized by congenital white spotting that is relatively stable over patients' lifetimes. This definition of generalized vitiligo also excludes segmental vitiligo and some other localized forms of vitiligo... (and) many other forms of skin depigmentation, such as depigmentation resulting from contact of occupational exposure to known depigmenting agents..., depigmentation secondary to chronic inflammation, psoriasis, other forms of dermatitis, and depigmentation secondary to infection, scars, burns and various other skin insults.

Melanocyte loss in vitiligo generally follows no predictable pattern. However, at least one-third of people with vitiligo exhibit signs of Koebner's isomorphic phenomenon, in which further vitiliginous depigmentation is catalyzed by cutaneous trauma such as cuts, burns, or scrapes[1] or repeated microtraumas to bony areas of high friction, such as knees, elbows, and hands (Gawkrodger et al. 2008; Hann, Park, and Chun 1997; Huggins, Janusz, and Schwartz 2006; Sehgal and Srivastava 2007; Taïeb and Picardo 2009; Yoboue et al. 2005). Hann, Park, and Chun (1997) found that people with vitiligo who also exhibited signs of Koebnerization, poliosis, and/or depigmentation of mucous membranes were more likely to have vitiligo that is highly progressive in nature, and thus poorer prognoses in repigmentation.

Vitiligo is distinguished from other forms of depigmentation via clinical examination with a Wood's lamp,[2] which causes areas of active vitiliginous depigmentation to fluoresce with a brilliant bluish hue because of accumulation of metabolic byproduct 7-tetrahydrobiopterin (7-BH) in vitiliginous melanocytes[3] (Schallreuter et al. 1994).

Castanet and Ortonne (1997) outline three prevalent hypotheses of the etiology of melanocyte function cessation in vitiligo: The autocytotoxic hypothesis, the neural hypothesis, and the autoimmune hypothesis. These hypotheses are explained below:

> The autocytotoxic hypothesis supposes that intermediate metabolites in the melanin synthesis are melanocytotoxic. The neural hypothesis suggests that accumulation of some neurochemical mediator causes decreased melanin production. The autoimmune hypothesis is the most prevalent, and it is based mainly on the presence of melanocyte-specific antibodies that are able to induce necrosis of cultured human melanocytes. (Castanet and Ortonne 1997: 845)

Modern physicians and researchers consider vitiligo to be a disfiguring, psychologically devastating condition capable of causing severe and long-lasting disability, especially in darker-skinned people whose depigmented areas are highly contrasted with the surrounding non-depigmented skin (Gawkrodger et al. 2008; Rabenja et al. 2005; Sehgal and Srivastava 2007; Yoboue et al. 2005;). Vitiligo is considered incurable and patients are typically advised by physicians to manage symptoms through camouflage, cover, and, in advanced cases, acceleration of depigmentation by chemical means (Gawkrodger et al. 2008; Schmid-Ott et al. 2007; Taïeb and Picardo 2009; Thompson, Kent, and Smith2002). Various repigmentation treatments exist, including skin grafts and PUVA (Psoralens[4] and Ultraviolet-A) light therapy to stimulate melanin production; however, these treatments have generally poor outcomes and harmful side effects, including the risk of skin cancer and the expansion of vitiligo by Koebnerization (Gawkrodger et al. 2008; Huggins, Janusz, and Schwartz 2006; Taïeb and Picardo 2009). In a 2005 survey of 78 people with vitiligo of varying degrees of severity, Ongenae, et al. found that 97 percent of their respondents considered their vitiligo to be so disfiguring and debilitating that they would readily forfeit a year's salary for a cure. In this light, it is not surprising that many people with vitiligo are willing to subject themselves to potentially harmful treatments with low rates of patient satisfaction in hopes of recovering their previtiligo levels of pigmentation. However, they often do so at their own expense since most health insurers consider vitiligo a strictly cosmetic diagnosis and its treatment ineligible for coverage (Chernin 2004; Njoo 2000).

Ancient Interpretations/Enduring Entanglements

The moral significance attached to leprosy has blinded people to evidence. Unwarranted beliefs were long-lasting and influential...The lamentable history of social attitudes to leprosy is a lesson on the consequences of paying great attention to words, but small attention to facts. (Lewis 1987: 594)

Generalized vitiligo, often erroneously called leukoderma[5] (Panda 2005), was first referred to circa 2200 BC in the *Tarikh-e-Tib-e-Iran* (Sehgal and Srivastava 2007). It was later described circa 1500 BC in the Pharaonic medical treatise *Papyrus Ebers*,[6] in which its characteristic spreading patches of whitening skin were differentiated from the pale swelling of leprosy (Kopera 1997; Lotti, Hautmann, and Hercogová 2004; Millington and Levell 2007; Morrone 2004; Sehgal and Srivastava 2007). During the same era, the sacred Hindu texts *Atharva-vēda*, *Rig-vēda*, and *Yajur-vēda* told of a skin condition called "kilas,"[7]a word derived from the Sanskrit "kil," meaning either "that which throws away color" or "white spotted deer"(Kopera 1997; Morrone 2004; Njoo 2000; Sehgal and Srivastava 2007). In Japan, a 1200 BC collection of Shinto prayers entitled *Makatominoharai* included a description of *shira-bito* (white man), a pigmentary disorder matching vitiligo's description (Kopera 1997; Millington and Levell 2007; Morrone 2004; Njoo 2000). Four hundred years later, the *Charak Samhita*, an Indian medical compilation, coined the term *svitra*,[8,9] a word still used in India meaning "spreading whiteness" (Kopera 1997; Morrone 2004; Njoo 2000).

Hippocrates, in his Prognostic, stated that color loss complaints "are the more easily cured the more recent they are, and the younger the patients, and the more soft and fleshy the parts of the body in which they occur" (Njoo 2000: 20). In 449 BC, Herodotus wrote of the social implications of whitening skin in *Clio*, portraying vitiligo as a form of leprosy:

> If a Persian has leprosy or white sickness he is not allowed to enter into a city or to have dealings with other Persians, he must they say, have sinned against the sun. Foreigners attacked by this disorder are forced to leave the country even white pigeons are often driven away as guilty of the same offence. (Herodotus in Njoo 2000: 18; Lotti et al. 2005: 219)

The term *vitiligo* was coined around 25 BC by Greek philosopher Aulus Cornelius Celsus in *De Medicina* (Kopera 1997; Lotti, Hautmann, and Hercogová 2004; Morrone 2004; Sehgal and Srivastava 2007). There is some disagreement in the literature regarding the root of the word *vitiligo*: it is possible that it originates in the Latin *vitium*, meaning "a blemishing fault" or "defect,"[10] but many scholars hold that the root is either *vituli*, which refers to the skin of calves, or *vitelius*, the word for calf, due to vitiligo's chromatic similarity to the patchy coats of calves (Agarwal 1998; Kopera 1997; Lotti, Hautmann, and Hercogová 2004; Millington and Levell 2007; Sehgal and Srivastava 2007). The term *vitiligo vulgaris* was coined in the late 1800s and is still used today to refer to generalized vitiligo, "the acquired, progressive disorder characterized by destruction of melanocytes in the skin and other organs" (Lotti, Hautmann, and Hercogová 2004: 3).

Millington and Levell assert that the Bible did not differentiate between leprosy and vitiligo (2007), but scriptural scholarship shows otherwise.[11] The Old Testament of the Bible uses the Hebrew word *zaraath*[12] in Leviticus chapters 13 and 14 to describe an acute skin condition characterized by a "spot (or a mark) with a tendency to spread, appearing deeper than the skin, and changing the hair at the spot to white" (Lev. 13: 2–3, KJV; Vayikra 13: 2–3, Tanakh). *Zaraath* also manifested itself in a chronic form "marked by the 'swelling' character of the spot, i.e. the inflammation produces a spot in 'high-relief' as against 'bas-relief'... there is also the symptom of the hair at the spot turning white, and the appearance of raw flesh in the swelling" (Lev. 13: 10, KJV; Vayikra 13: 10, Tanakh). Acute and chronic *zaraath* have only skin and hair whitening in common, with chronic *zaraath* appearing as a swollen, inflamed eruption *on* the skin and acute *zaraath* appearing simply as spreading depigmentation *in* the skin, with color loss ultimately affecting the hair (Jastrow 1914). From a medical perspective, the symptoms given in the Old Testament for chronic *zaraath* match those of what we would now call severe psoriasis, while acute *zaraath* is the equivalent of vitiligo (Jastrow 1914; Schamberg 1899).

Scriptural and medical scholars agree that the symptoms included in the Hebrew descriptions of acute and chronic *zaraath* were not meant to be construed as a single phenomenon, but the Septuagint, the Koine Greek rendering of the Torah[13] ordered by Ptolemy and written between the third and first centuries BC, translated both acute and chronic *zaraath* into the single condition *lepra*,[14] a word used to describe the rough, scaly, and inflamed cutaneous eruption now commonly known as psoriasis (Jastrow 1914; Kopera 1997; Lewis 1987; McEwen 1911; McNiven 1985; Morrone 2004; Njoo 2000). This mistake was most likely due to the translators' unfamiliarity with lepromatous leprosy,[15] known then as *elephantiasis graecorum*[16] (Lewis 1987):

> This translation [the Septuagint], which was held in special esteem, was begun in Alexandria about 250 B.C., not many years after Manetho, a resident of that city, had made his statement as to the number of Hebrews affected with lepra at the time of the exodus from Egypt, and before the description of true leprosy as *elephantiasis graecorum*. The translators of the Septuagint, probably influenced by the words of Manetho and practically without knowledge of the condition *elephantiasis*, rendered the Hebrew word *zaraath* as *lepra*, and we are warranted in affirming that the pathological significance attaching to the word *lepra* as understood by them was that given it by Hippocrates, i.e., a condition of the skin characterized by scaliness. (McEwen 1911: 197)

Lending credence to this hypothesis, Lewis states that "(d)uring the Dark Ages leading up to the Medieval period, the word for one kind or set of skin conditions, *lepra*, came to refer to different conditions and it eventually settled in the derivative word-forms of various European languages as a word which applied to leprosy as we now know it" (Lewis 1987: 598). We see the equation of *zaraath* with *lepra* in the Vulgate, the fifth-century Latin translation of the Tanakh from Hebrew, and the eleventh-century Latin translations of the writings of several ancient Arabian physicians, including al-Hārith ibn Kaladah,[17] renderings that served to increase the confusion (Dols 1983; Jastrow 1914; McEwen 1911). The Arabian works, which combined tenets of Greek medicine[18] and scriptural instruction from the Qur'ān to form what became known as "Prophetic medicine," described both a nonleprous condition called *dal fil*, or "elephant's foot,[19]" and *judhām*,[20] or what we now call lep-romatous leprosy[21]:

> The translators into Latin, noting the similarity of idea in the words dal fil and elephantiasis, made them equivalent in their rendition. Judham or true leprosy was translated lepra. By this double error elephantiasis graecorum, the equivalent of judham, both meaning true leprosy, was made the equivalent of lepra, which term thereby came to have two meanings: scaliness of the skin [the original Hippocrates significance], and elephantiasis graecorum [leprosy]. (McEwen 1911: 198)

Thus, the Hebrew *zaraath,* a word signifying both chronic psoriasis and vitiligo, became the Greek *lepra,* meaning only chronic psoriasis. *Lepra* then subsumed the Greek *elephantiasis graecorum* and the Arabian *judhām* and *dal fil.*[22] While the comparatively sophisticated Arabic medical descriptions of leprosy provided the Western world with a foundational concept of the disease into the seventeenth century (Dols 1983), the terminological confusion upon translation proved both mys-tifying and pernicious. The aggregate translative confusion likely led to widespread misdiagnosis of a variety of nonleprous conditions such as vitiligo as leprosy, less a diagnosis than "a prediction of disfigurement and death as well as social ostracism and contempt" throughout the Western world (Dols 1983: 896; Millington and Levell 2007).[23]

Christian Europeans in the Middle Ages, following the flawed translations of the so-called Mosaic leper laws in Leviticus, engaged in centuries of persecution against people with vitiligo and other hypop-igmentary disorders (Millington and Levell 2007). Those considered leprous were forbidden to work, exiled from their communities, and sent to colonies on the margins of society with no chance of returning (Millington and Levell 2007). Accusations of leprosy were valuable political weapons, considering leprosy's implications of irrevocable sin and divine retribution; after his death, Henry IV of England was rumored to have suffered from leprosy as punishment for his execution of a rebellious archbishop[24] (McNiven 1985). In another case, exiled lepers were used as reserve soldiers in the Crusades. Jerusalem's pre-Conquest Order of St. Lazarus was converted from a hospice run by Armenian monks into a paramilitary organization in 1112 (Dols 1983; Millington and Levell 2007). "The leper knights," as they were known, were armed and sent to fight, but were defeated at the Battle of La Forbie in 1244 (Millington and Levell 2007).

Stigmatization and mistreatment of people considered leprous was not common to all ancient cultures. The Hebrews only considered Jews stricken with *zaraath* unclean, but even then this uncleanliness was considered a form of ritual impurity, not a sign of disease (Lewis 1987; Schamberg 1899). Moreover, this uncleanliness did not signify the commission of mortal sin; instead, it was akin to the Levitical taboos surrounding food consumption and the menstrual cycle:

> Other things are identified in Leviticus as unclean [e.g. a woman 'in the days of her impurity', the hare, the stork, the hoopoe, and the bat] because of their state, what they are, not because of sin in our modern sense, or disease, or because of what they have done... The commands of God are rules for holiness, to set the people apart and make them a holy people... If the high priest and perhaps the nazirite [sic] might represent the types of person who are most holy, the leper might represent something like their anti-type, the type of person who is most unclean. (Lewis 1987: 599)

The Hebrews saw *zaraath* as an issue of proper observance of religious taboo in the interest of maintaining the holiness that set them apart from gentiles, resident aliens, and pagans; thus, it was not problematic for them to live among and associate with non-Jews exhibiting signs of *zaraath* since these groups were not held to the same standards of holiness to which the Jews held themselves (Lewis 1987). In support of this assertion, McEwen points out that the Hebrew word *timme*, found in Leviticus in reference to *zaraath* and usually translated as "to pronounce unclean," may also be rendered as "to declare unfit to associate with the worshipers of Deity" (McEwen 1911). After undergoing ritual cleansing in conformity with Mosaic law, Hebrews stricken with *zaraath* were routinely readmitted to their settlement and allowed to worship (Lewis 1987).

Likewise, although medieval Islamic society considered "lepers" a moral threat to the pious due to spiritual uncleanliness, there were many who also believed that those thought to be smitten by the hand of Allah should be treated with kindness and philanthropy (Dols 1983). Caliph al-Walid I (668–715) provided his subjects with disabilities with stipends and assistants, and he is believed to have founded the first "early hospices... especially for lepers, or what were believed to be so" (Dols 1983: 896). It may be argued that these leprosariums serve as evidence of early efforts at segregation, stigmatization, and medicalization of people with various skin conditions. However, at this time most Muslims with vitiligo (*baraṣ*) were cared for in their homes and communities by family members, with those lacking family caregivers populating the leprosariums (Dols 1983). In addition, a medical compendium of physical disabilities (including vitiligo) by Arabic writer Al-Jāhiz (781–868) professes that Muslims with disabilities in the Medieval era participated fully in Islamic society, some even holding high office[25] (Dols 1983). Al-Jāhiz held that "physical ailments are not social stigmas but are what may be called signs of divine blessing or favor," praiseworthy opportunities to grow closer to an unknowable God through repentance (Dols 1983: 896). This view is similar to the ancient Hebrew belief that those with *zaraath*, having been touched by the finger of God, should be seen as an "altar of atonement" (Schamberg 1899: 165).

Sociopsychological Implications of Whitening Skin

Historically, vitiligo has been viewed as a marker of sin, a harbinger of racial harmony through the obliteration of blackness, a sign of racial transgression, cause for exile, and an occasion for capitalistic exploitation through the exhibition of people with vitiligo in freak shows (Jastrow 1914; Martin 2002; McEwen 1911; Sehgal and Srivastava 2007). Social stigma against people living in vitiliginous skins persists, with the largest burdens falling upon women of color (Porter and Beuf 1994; Rabenja et al. 2005; Sehgal and Srivastava 2007; Yoboue et al. 2005;), whose heavily-contrasted skins silently attest to modern societal biases against people with atypical appearances—attitudes and prejudices extreme enough to create disabling conditions for vitiliginous women of color (Porter and Beuf 1994; Sehgal and Srivastava 2007). Not surprisingly, researchers have determined that people with vitiligo tend to experience a markedly lower quality of life in various domains than those without (Kent and

Al'Abadie 1996; Ongenae et al. 2005; Sampogna et al. 2008; Schmid-Ott et al. 2007; Thompson, Kent, and Smith 2002), and the literature shows a need for renewed inquiry into the psychological and philosophical implications of the progressive involuntary whitening of vitiligo.

Conclusion

Vitiligo, a noncommunicable condition marked by acquired, spreading depigmentation of the skin and hair, has been addressed throughout history in both religious and secular texts. Unfortunately, translation errors paired with incomplete differentiations between similar skin conditions led to a widespread conflation of vitiligo with leprosy, a condition with dire implications of religious transgression. People with vitiligo, generally stigmatized as unclean or sinful since antiquity, continue to suffer the consequences of erroneous ancient beliefs about this condition, with the most disablement occurring among women of color. A more thorough understanding of various religious conceptions of vitiliginous skin is needed in order to interrupt both external and internalized sources of bias and stigmatization against people with vitiligo.

Notes

1. "Koebnerization" of vitiliginous skin differs from pigment loss caused primarily by skin trauma in that skin exhibiting koebnerization already manifested signs of generalized vitiligo-related pigment loss before the skin trauma that caused the depigmentation to spread.
2. A black light-emitting ultraviolet light at wavelengths of 320–400 nanometers (Schallreuter et al. 1994).
3. Areas of stabilized vitiliginous depigmentation do not exhibit this fluorescence as accumulation of 7-BH occurs only in areas of active vitiligo.
4. Psoralen is a plant-compound used in vitiligo to heighten dermal photosensitivity prior to UVA ray exposure.
5. Leukoderma is a general term meaning "white skin" that can apply to any number of depigmentation disorders. Sehgal and Srivastava (2007) differentiate leukoderma from vitiligo by stating that in leukoderma, the cause of color loss can be pinpointed as a sequelae to injury or disease, while this is not the case in vitiligo. See Note 1 in this document for more on the difference between depigmentation as a sequelae to injury or disease and koebnerization in vitiligo.
6. *Papyrus Ebers* was compiled by "itinerant priest-physicians" who collected data from Egyptian physicians and temples between 3000 and 1500 BC (Millington and Levell 2007; Todd 1921).

7. The "that which throws away color" definition of "kilas" was first identified in the 1905 translation of the *Atharva-veda* (Kopera 1997).

8. Panda (2005) gives an alternate spelling of "*Świtra*" and states that *Świtra* is also found in other ancient Indian works such as the epic poem *Mahābhārata*, the Hindu scripture *Manusmṛti*, the Buddhist scripture *VinayaPīṭaka*, and the writings of Ayurvedic physicians Caraka, Súsruta, and Vāgbhaṭṭa. Sehgal and Srivastava (2007) give the spelling as "suitra," tracing the word back to the *Manusmriti* (200 BC).

9. Other Indian terms for vitiligo include *Kilāsa, Dāruṇa, Aruṇa,* and *Śwētakuṣhta* (Kopera 1997; Panda 2005). *Śwētakuṣhta* means "white skin disease" but is commonly understood as "white leprosy" (Kopera 1997; Millington and Levell 2007; Morrone 2004).

10. Paschall argues that "vitiligo" is probably not rooted in *vitium* due to differences in meaning and vocalism (1936).

11. Although the Bible did differentiate between different forms of *zaraath*, it is important to note that all forms were addressed in the same manner (segregation and ritual cleansing).

12. Also spelled "*sāra'at*" (Jastrow 1914), *tsaraath* (Schamberg 1899), *Zoráat* (Njoo 2000), and "*zara'at*" (Lewis 1987).

13. Also known as the Pentateuch, the Torah is the highest of the sacred Jewish texts and consists of the first five books of the Hebrew Bible. In English, these are Genesis, Exodus, Leviticus, Numbers, and Deuteronomy. Leviticus chapters 13 and 14 contain the so-called leprosy laws referring to the identification and treatment of *zaraath*.

14. *Lepra* is derived from the Indo-Germanic *lap*, meaning "to scale," "to peel off" (McEwen 1911), and the Greek *lepros*, meaning "rough and scaly" and *lepis*, "a scale" (Lewis 1987).

15. One of the two principal types of leprosy, the other being Tuberculoid leprosy. Lepromatous leprosy "involves many body systems, with widespread plaques and nodules in the skin, iritis, keratitis, destruction of nasal cartilage and bone, testicular atrophy, peripheral edema, and involvement of the reticuloendothelial system. Blindness may result" (*Mosby's Medical Dictionary* 2009).

16. Lepromatous leprosy was known as *elephantiasis graecorum* in the first century BC, a term later used by second-century philosopher Celsus in his description of the disease (McEwen 1911).

17. Considered "the oldest known Arab physician and a companion of the Prophet" (Dols 1983).

18. Also called Galenic medicine after renowned Greek physician and philosopher Galen, follower of Hippocrates and foundational medical thinker (Brain 1977).

19. The Arabian physicians' clinical description of *dal fil* fits modern criteria for elephantiasis (thickening and hypertrophy of the skin and subcutaneous tissue) (*Dorland's Medical Dictionary for Health Consumers* 2007; McEwen 1911).

20. The Arabic word *judhām* means "to mutilate" or "to cut off," referring to physical disfigurement (Dols 1983). Dols goes on to describe the ancient Arab

physicians' language describing leprosy as "appropriate and more refined than that of the classical authors, and it probably influenced Byzantine nomenclature" (Dols 1983: 895).

21. To add slightly to the confusion, McEwen's "true leprosy" appears to refer to both Lepromatous and Tuberculoid leprosy (1911). Fortunately, McEwen's failure to distinguish between the two principal types of leprosy does not appreciably affect our study of vitiligo.

22. This enlarged definition of *lepra* can be seen in the 1611 AD King James Version of the Bible (McEwen 1911).

23. Incidentally, the pre-Islamic Arabic term *baraṣ*, meaning "to be white or shiny," "was definitely used to name leprosy, probably in its early stages or in its tuberculoid form, but (it) may have also been applied to other skin disorders" causing depigmentation such as vitiligo (Dols 1983: 894).

24. Henry IV may have actually died from syphilis, a disease fitting the description of the King's symptoms and that spread across Europe during his reign (Kopera 1997; McNiven 1985; Morrone 2004).

25. This attitude was also likely prevalent in Korea during the Yi Dynasty of the seventeenth century. A portrait of Chang Myeong Song, a high-ranking government official, shows vitiliginous facial and neck depigmentation, suggesting a lack of social stigma attached to vitiligo and an acknowledgment of its differentiation from leprosy, "otherwise perhaps this portrait of a ruler would have been altered to disguise the affliction" (Millington and Levell 2007: 993).

References

Agarwal, G. (1998). Vitiligo: An underestimated problem. *Family Practice 15*(Supp. 1), S19–S23.

Brain, P. (1977). Galen on the ideal of the physician. *South African Medical Journal 52*, 936–938.

Castanet, J., & Ortonne, J. P. (1997). Pathophysiology of vitiligo. *Clinics in Dermatology 15*, 845–851.

Chernin, T. (2004). Skin pigmentation disorders: More than just cosmetic? *Drug Topics 148*(22), 25.

Dols, M. (1983). The leper in medieval Islamic society. *Speculum 58*(4):891–916.

Dorland's Medical Dictionary for Health Consumers. (2007). *Elephantiasis.* Retrieved March 5, 2009, from http://medical-dictionary.thefreedictionary. com/elephantiasis

Gawkrodger, D. J., Ormerod, A. D., Shaw, L., Mauri-Sole, I., Whitton, M. E., Watts, M. J., Anstey, A. V., Ingham, J., & Young, K. (2008). Guideline for the diagnosis and management of vitiligo. *British Journal of Dermatology 159*, 1051–1076.

Hann, S., Park, Y., & Chun, W. (1997). Clinical features of vitiligo. *Clinics in Dermatology 15*, 891–897.

Huggins, R. H., Janusz, C. A., & Schwartz, R. A. (2006). Vitiligo: A sign of systemic disease. *Indian Journal of Dermatology, Venereology and Leprology 72*, 68–71.

Jastrow, M. (1914). The so-called 'leprosy' laws: An analysis of Leviticus, chapters 13 and 14. *Jewish Quarterly Review, New Series 4*(3), 357–418.

Kent, G., & Al'Abadie, M. (1996). Psychologic effects of vitiligo: A critical incident analysis. *Journal of the American Academy of Dermatology 35*(6), 895–898.

Kopera, D. (1997). Historical aspects and definition of vitiligo. *Clinics in Dermatology 15*, 841–843.

Lewis, G. (1987). A lesson from Leviticus: Leprosy. *Man, New Series 22*(4), 593–612.

Lotti, T., Hanna, D., Buggiani, G., & Urpe, M. (2005). The color of the skin: Psycho-anthropologic implications. *Journal of Cosmetic Dermatology 4*, 219–220.

Lotti, T., Hautmann, G., & Hercogová, J. (2004).Vitiligo: Disease or symptom? From the confusion of the past to current doubts. In T. Lotti & J. Hercogová (Eds.), *Vitiligo: Problems and Solutions* (pp. 1–14). New York, NY: Marcel Dekker, Inc.

Martin, C. D. (2002). *The White African-American Body*. New Brunswick, NJ: Rutgers University Press.

McEwen, E. L. (1911). The leprosy of the Bible in its medical aspect. *The Biblical World 38*(3), 194–202.

McNiven, P. (1985). The problem of Henry IV's health. *The English Historical Review 100*(397), 747–772.

Millington, G. W. M., & Levell, N. J. (2007). Vitiligo: The historical curse of depigmentation. *International Journal of Dermatology 46*, 990–995.

Morrone, A. (2004). Historical and psycho-anthropological aspects of vitiligo. In T. Lotti J. & Hercogová (Eds.), *Vitiligo: Problems and Solutions* (pp. 15–25). New York, NY: Marcel Dekker.

Mosby's Medical Dictionary, 8th edition. (2009). *Lepromatous leprosy.* Retrieved March 5, 2009, from http://medical-dictionary.thefreedictionary.com/lepromatous+leprosy

Njoo, M. D. (2000). *Vitiligo: A Review.* Doctoral dissertation, University of Amsterdam, The Netherlands.

Nordlund, J. J. (1997). The epidemiology and genetics of vitiligo. *Clinics in Dermatology 15*, 875–878.

Ongenae, K., Dierckxsens, L., Brochez, L., VanGeel, N., & Naeyaert, J. M. (2005). Quality of life and stigmatization profile in a cohort of vitiligo patients and effect of the use of camouflage. *Dermatology 210*, 279–285.

Panda, A. K. (2005). The medico historical perspective of vitiligo (Switra). *Bulletin of the Indian Institute of the History of Medicine 35*, 41–46.

Paschall, D. (1936). The origin and semantic development of Latin vitium. *Transactions and Proceedings of the American Philological Association 67*, 219–231.

Porter, J. R., & Beuf, A. H. (1994). The effect of a racially consonant medical context on adjustment of African-American patients to physical disability. *Medical Anthropology 16*, 1–16.

Rabenja, F. R., Randrianasolo, F. M. P., Ramarozatovo, L. S., Nombana, H. R., Ravelomanantena, H., & Ratrimoarivony, C. (2005). Therapeutic observation of vitiligo. *International Journal of Dermatology 44*(Suppl. 1), 46–48.

Sampogna, F., Raskovic, D., Guerra, L., Pedicelli, C., Tabolli, S., Leoni, L., Alessandroni, L., & Abeni, D. (2008). Identification of categories at risk for high quality of life impairment in patients with vitiligo. *British Journal of Dermatology 159*, 351–359.

Schallreuter, K. U., Wood, J. M., Pittelkow, M. R., Gütlich, M., Lemke, R., Rödl, W., Swanson, N. N., Hitzemann, K., & Ziegler, I. (1994). Regulation of melanin biosynthesis in the human epidermis by tetrahydrobiopterin. *Science 263*(5152), 1444–1446.

Schamberg, J. F. (1899). The nature of the leprosy of the Bible. From a medical and Biblical point of view. *The Biblical World 13*(3), 162–169.

Schmid-Ott, G., Künsebeck, H., Jecht, E., Shimshoni, R., Lazaroff, I., Schallmayer, S. Calliess, I. T., Malewski, P., Lamprecht, F., & Götz, A. (2007). Stigmatization experience, coping and sense of coherence in vitiligo patients. *Journal of the European Academy of Dermatology and Venerealogy 21*, 456–461.

Sehgal, V. N. & Srivastava, G. (2007). Vitiligo: Compendium of clinico-epidemiological features. *Indian Journal of Dermatology, Venereology, and Leprology 73*(3), 149–156.

Spritz, R. A. (2008). The genetics of generalized vitiligo. *Current Directions in Autoimmunity 10*, 244–257.

Taïeb, A., & Picardo, M. (2009). Vitiligo. *New England Journal of Medicine 360*, 160–169.

Thompson, A., Kent, G., & Smith, J. A. (2002). Living with vitiligo: Dealing with difference. *British Journal of Health Psychology 7*(2), 213–226.

Todd, T. W. (1921). Egyptian medicine: A critical study of recent claims. *American Anthropologist 23*(4), 460–470.

Yoboue, P., Sangare, A., Kaloga, M., Kouadio, A., & Djedje, M. A. (2005). Epidemiologic and etiologic features of pigmentation disorders observed during consultation at the Dermatology Center of Abidjan, Ivory Coast. *International Journal of Dermatology 44*(Suppl. 1), 33–34.

CHAPTER 5

Out of the Darkness: Examining the Rhetoric of Blindness in the Gospel of John[1]

*Jennifer L. Koosed and
Darla Schumm*

We argue that the metaphorical and literal depictions of broken bodies in the Gospel of John promote a definition of an individual's full membership in the Christian community that almost always excludes persons with disabilities. In addition, and equally troubling to us, is how such metaphors perpetuate anti-Jewish and anti-Semitic attitudes among Christians by linking the state of spiritual ignorance with being Jewish.

Focusing on the trope of blindness, as exemplified in Chapter 9, we examine how John's use of double entendre binds two meanings of blindness together—blindness as a physical state (the literal meaning) and blindness as a spiritual state (the metaphorical meaning). We have been asked: Why write a paper about the potentially damaging effects of the use of the metaphors of blindness/sight, or darkness/light, in the gospel of John with respect to both the disability community and the Jewish community? We contend that there are two primary reasons to discuss these aspects of the metaphor of blindness in tandem.

First, while scholars who work in Disability Studies have noted the dangers of metaphors such as blindness for real people who are blind, and biblical scholars who work on the Gospel of John have noted the dangers of using the blindness metaphor for real people who are Jewish, we have never seen a discussion of the ways in which the metaphor of blindness interweaves the two exclusions in the Gospel. Quite simply, we believe that this is a gap in the scholarship dealing with the Gospel of John. It is imperative that marginalized communities realize the intersections between exclusions and oppressions in an effort to combat their consequences.

To help explain our second and more complex reason for writing this chapter, we turn to the work of Adele Reinhartz (2001). In her book entitled *Befriending the Beloved Disciple*, Reinhartz draws on the literary criticism of Wayne Booth as she begins her engagement of the Gospel of John with the idea of friendship through reading. Being friends with a text can and should be just as challenging as being friends with a human being. True friendship is not just about the good times, but rather befriending engages us "with books fully, honestly, and with commitment, to address rather than to bracket the ethical considerations with which our human relationships are fraught" (Reinhartz 2001: 18). Booth's "ethical criticism" is not focused "on whether this or that book or this or that author is ethical, but rather on the complex question of who we become as we enter into relationship with one book or another" (Reinhartz 2001: 18–19). We ask the question, then, who do we become as we enter into relationship with the text of John 9?

As the constitutive metaphors for John's cosmic system, darkness and light rise to the level of macro-metaphor—in other words, they are a "powerful cluster of metaphors" that construct the "maker's world" (Booth 1988: 335). As such, the exclusions from John's textual world—if his readers adopt his world—can and do result in exclusions in the real world. World-making metaphors can be the most powerful and potentially dangerous types of metaphors. Thus, we believe it is highly important to carefully scrutinize metaphors such as those used in John 9.

Not only will we explore "reading as relationship" but also "reading in relationship," since we are responsive to each other and each other's reading. Our friendship with one another informs our "friendship" with the text. Our friendship has interdisciplinary and interreligious dimensions. Dr. Koosed is trained in biblical studies and is rooted in the Jewish tradition, while Dr. Schumm is trained in ethics and hails from the Christian tradition. We also represent degrees of physical ability and disability—Dr. Koosed is fully sighted, and Dr. Schumm is partially blind. Because of our friendship with one another we are equally committed, to paraphrase Reinhartz, to addressing and not bracketing the "real-world" effects of the use of the metaphor of blindness in John 9 on both persons with disabilities and Jews.

Blindness and Sight in the Gospel of John

In contrast to Matthew, Mark, and Luke where Jesus performs "miracles," John's Jesus performs seven "signs" (all biblical citations from the New Revised Standard Version Bible). The difference in terminology between John's Gospel and the Gospels of Matthew, Mark, and Luke points to the difference in function. In Matthew, Mark, and Luke, the miracles are often done privately, and they emerge out of faith. For example, when the woman with a hemorrhage is healed simply by reaching out and touching Jesus's tzitzit ("the fringe of his garment"), he turns and tells her: "Daughter, your faith has saved you" (Mark 5: 34, cf. Matt. 9: 24). In fact, there are times in Matthew, Mark, and Luke when faith is required in order for the miracle to work. In Mark, Jesus finds himself unable to perform miracles in his hometown because of the people's unbelief (Markk 6: 5). Jesus's signs in John, however, are public proclamations of his identity as the Christ—they move people from unbelief and ignorance to faith and knowledge. The evangelist himself declares that this is the purpose of his writings:

> Jesus did many other signs in the presence of his disciples, which are not written in this book. But these are written so that you may come to believe that Jesus is the Messiah, the Son of God, and that through believing you may have life in his name. (John 20: 30–31)

Within the seven signs, there are three signs of healing: (1) healing the Capernaum official's son (4: 46–54); (2) healing the paralytic (5: 2–9); and (3) healing the man born blind (9: 1–12). John's Gospel is highly symbolic; a healing is not just a healing. Instead, when Jesus brings broken bodies into wholeness he is foreshadowing resurrection, both the general resurrection of the dead and his own resurrection. In a sense, he is giving people a foretaste of the world to come by enacting the Kingdom of Heaven on Earth in the here and now (Lee 1994: 180).

The healing of the man born blind in Chapter 9 exemplifies John's emphasis on foreshadowing resurrection by binding the physical state of blindness with the metaphorical sense of unfaithfulness or spiritual ignorance. John plays with two meanings of blindness—literal blindness or absence of sight, and metaphorical blindness or the inability to understand or perceive—throughout the passage and also entangles them within the overarching framework of the duality of darkness and light. The employing of these two meanings of the word—physically unable to see and the inability to understand—bind the physical state of blindness to the mental or spiritual state of ignorance.

John 9 is divided into three parts. The first part recounts the physical healing, which happens in two stages: Jesus anoints the eyes with mud and spit, and then the man washes off the compact in the pool of Siloam. But before the healing even takes place, Jesus and his disciples discuss the reasons the man was born with his infirmity. When the disciples connect his blindness to sin—whether his own or his parents—Jesus replies that sin did not cause the blindness. Rather, "he was born blind so that God's works might be revealed in him" (John 9: 3).

Some commentators have hailed Jesus' response as an overturning of ideologies that link sin with disability. Jesus, however, clearly links sin and disability in other healing events (e.g., when Jesus heals the paralytic in Chapter 5, he implies that the condition was caused by sin). In addition, Church fathers such as Tertullian and Augustine understood the intricately connected symbolism of the Gospel of John to indicate that the man born blind is indeed a reference to humanity being born in sin. Jesus heals the man of his blindness using the pool of Siloam as Jesus heals all humans from their sins through the waters of baptism (Brown 1966: 381–382).

John presents several different reasons why people have disabilities, but God is behind them all. Never is the condition simply an expression of the various possibilities inherent in the human body. Never is the condition an accident. And never is the condition seen as a positive gift of God. Rather, the disability is always present for some other reason or purpose. In John 9, the implication is that God is using the man's blindness (which is characterized as an undesirable state that brings the man suffering) for God's own show of power. We question whether any link between God's will and human suffering is helpful, especially when God seems to be using the person for God's own (selfish?) purposes.

Immediately before healing the man Jesus proclaims, "As long as I am in the world, I am the light of the world" (John 9: 5), thus connecting this story with the prevalent Johannine image of light. Light is also "the basic image for life" (Lee 1994: 161), which is first introduced in the opening verses of the Gospel: "What has come into being in him was life, and the life was the light of all people" (John 1: 3–5). Jesus himself picks up on these intertwining images again in John 8:12: "I am the light of the world. Whoever follows me will never walk in darkness but will have the light of life." By giving the man born blind sight, Jesus opens his eyes to light literally and also figuratively. By opening his eyes to light, he is also giving him life, and the man becomes the embodiment of the cosmic principle of light in the world. The light is truth, and faith and knowledge and light bring eternal life.

In the second part of the passage, the man is confronted by his neighbors and then by the Pharisees, or the Jewish authorities. The purpose of these confrontations is to establish identities—first the man's and then Jesus's. As noted earlier, the physical healing of the man born blind happens in two stages—mud and washing. Likewise, his spiritual healing also occurs in two stages—the physical healing and the interrogation. The physical healing begins the turn from unbelief to belief. The interrogation then moves the man further from partial understanding of Jesus's identity to full understanding, or from partial spiritual wholeness to full spiritual wholeness. When questioned, the man first proclaims Jesus to be a prophet. But the questioning gets more intense and the Pharisees challenge the man's understanding by accusing his healer of being a sinner. The healed man proclaims that Jesus comes from God, for "Never since the world began has it been heard that anyone opened the eyes of a person born blind. If this man were not from God, he could do nothing" (John 9: 32–33). At this point, the man has moved closer to faith while the Pharisees have moved further away. Only Jesus's confirmation is required to complete the dual movement, or the second stage of the man's spiritual healing.

Jesus appears again in the third part of the narrative, thus completing the spiritual healing of the man. The Pharisees have driven the man out, and Jesus goes to find him. He asks, "'Do you believe in the Son of Man?' He answered, 'And who is he, sir? Tell me, so that I may believe in him.' Jesus said to him, 'You have seen him, and the one speaking with you is he.' 'Lord, I believe.' And he worshipped him" (John 9: 35–38). Seeing and hearing Jesus is linked to knowing and believing. It is in this moment that the literal and the symbolic meanings of seeing "perfectly" cohere (Lee 1994: 179).

The end of the story makes the links between literally and symbolically seeing even more explicit: "Jesus said, 'I came into this world for judgment so that those who do not see may see, and those who do see may become blind'" (John 9: 39). This is one of John's typical reversals using double entendres. The reversal, however, is not symmetrical. On the one hand, physical sight does not necessarily indicate spiritual wholeness. The passage continues thus: "Some of the Pharisees near him heard this and said to him, 'Surely we are not blind, are we?' Jesus said to them, 'If you were blind, you would not have sin. But now that you say "We see," your sin remains'" (John 9: 40–41). On the other hand, the man who is physically blind is also metaphorically blind, since he has no confession until after he is given his sight. It is only once his physical sight is restored that he starts to know ("to see") Jesus.

The Pharisees are blind to the truth, but they are not physically blind, nor do they become physically blind when they refuse "to see" the truth of Jesus. Through these examples, the literary images of blindness/sight, darkness/light are not only embedded in a network of exclusionary metaphors but also serve to reinforce anti-Jewish (and potentially anti-Semitic and racist) attitudes.

Competing Oppressions?

We have argued thus far that the use of the metaphor of blindness employed in John 9 can reinforce the exclusion of persons with disabilities, as well as anti-Jewish and anti-Semitic attitudes. We are not the first scholars to raise questions about biblical metaphors that may contribute to the exclusion of persons with disabilities. Nor are we the first scholars to draw attention to how interpretations of the Gospels can be detrimental to Christian-Jewish relations. We are, however, among some of the first scholars to make explicit the connections between the oppression of persons with disabilities and the Jews through the use of the metaphor of blindness in John 9, and to demonstrate why it is important to examine these oppressions simultaneously. In this section of the chapter we briefly review some of the available scholarship on John 9 and highlight how scholars critically question the exclusion and oppression of one of these groups, while at the same time maintaining, and in some instances perhaps even perpetuating, the exclusion and oppression of the other group.

In an effort to understand how the Jews are portrayed in the Gospel of John, biblical scholars place the gospel text in its historical and cultural context. Many scholars have noted that the controversy between Jesus and the Jews in John more accurately reflects the historical situation of the evangelist and his community projected back onto Jesus's own time period (Brown 1979: 40–43). John and his community may be living in a situation where they are being expelled from synagogues for professing Jesus as the Christ. The harsh rhetoric, then, of John 9 and other passages in John exemplifies intra-Jewish conflict and thus cannot necessarily be construed as anti-Jewish. This view has been recently challenged by Adele Reinhartz who suggests that it is just as likely that the impetus for the separation may have come from John's own community—a voluntary withdrawal rather than a forceful expulsion (Reinhartz 2001: 37–53).

Understanding the possible historical context, in any case, does not mitigate the damage that these passages have caused in the history of

Jewish-Christian relations. The text is no longer part of an intra-Jewish debate; rather it is part of a separate religious or Christian tradition and has been so for nearly two millennia. The possible historical context of John, the varieties of Judaism in the first century, and pressures the communities experienced during oppressive Roman rule, especially after the destruction of the second Temple, are all important considerations and can be fully explicated in scholarship and in the classroom.

But, what about the pulpit? For it is in the pulpit, or in Christian churches, where scholars have noted most directly how anti-Jewish attitudes are conveyed through interpretations of passages such as John 9. In the words of Robert W. Bullock, "The problem [of anti-Semitism] is not in the classroom. It is in church" (Bullock in Rittner and Roth 2001: 73). Bullock cites John's rhetoric in particular in his study on the effect of lectionary readings on anti-Jewish and anti-Semitic attitudes among Christians.

While it is essential to question how the language of John portrays Jews, we observe that even those scholars who critique John's depictions of the Jews often uncritically reproduce John's language of exclusion in other arenas. For example, Adele Reinhartz asks, "What, after all . . . is to distinguish those Jews whom the Johannine Jesus reviles as unbelieving descendents of the devil, blind, sinful, and incapable of understanding their own scriptures, from ourselves and the Jews around us?" (Reinhartz 2001: 15). Reinhartz clearly demonstrates the linkages between the Jews, the blind, sin, and evil. Although the images of Jews in John have been examined in commentaries on John, there still remains language that equates blindness with those who are morally and spiritually deficient.

There has also been a recent reexamination among scholars of the use of the metaphor of blindness, and John's healing narratives have been scrutinized in light of this reexamination (e.g., various articles in Eiesland and Saliers 1998; Hull 2001: 49–52). Commentators involved in Disability Studies are realizing the negative implications of John's metaphors for Christians who cannot see. Yet, the ways in which blindness is a metaphysical category of evil and, in particular, the ways in which the "Jews" in John are "blind," and therefore embody cosmic evil, is left unexamined. There are two points in the literature re-examining the use of the metaphor of blindness that we would like to address.

First, it is common for interpreters of this passage to attribute the idea that sin and disability are connected to the Jewish idea of divine punishment. The idea that the sins of the parents are visited on the children is also labeled a "Jewish idea." Whereas these ideas are certainly present in Judaism and in the Hebrew Bible, they are not exclusively so. Other peoples in the ancient world and in our world believe that God punishes sin through inflicting illness and disability.

In addition, neither the Bible nor the tradition presents a univocal perspective. The Hebrew Bible demonstrates that the idea of divine retribution was part of a lively discussion and debate. There is a general notion that God punishes those who sin throughout the Hebrew Bible, beginning with the curses on Adam, Eve, and the serpent. The question of God's justice, however, intensifies as the people undergo the tragedies of Assyrian and then Babylonian conquest. A series of competing theodicies emerge in the literature to make sense of the historical events. Some texts (the Deuteronomic History and the prophetic books) clearly attribute suffering to God's punishment. However, even the prophets hint at the opposite position: Jeremiah asks why the wicked prosper (Jer. 12: 1), and Isaiah proclaims that Israel has been punished double for its transgressions (Isa. 40: 1). The questioning reaches a fever pitch in the books of Job and Ecclesiastes. In each book, the link between suffering and evildoing is refuted.

In particular, the idea that God punishes the children for the sins of the parents was sometimes stated, other times refuted, again indicating that there was much variety in the attitudes of ancient Israel on this point. The idea that children suffer for the sins of their parents is formulated in Exodus 20:5 (see also Num. 14: 18). However, in the prophets, the proverb "The parents have eaten sour grapes, and the children's teeth are set on edge" is quoted and refuted by both Jeremiah (31: 29–30) and Ezekiel (18: 2–4). Despite unsupported claims to the contrary, there is no "traditional Jewish view of disability" (e.g., this phrase is used by Grant in Eiesland and Saliers 1998: 80).

In fact, many of the heroes and heroines of the biblical text are portrayed as having physical disabilities. Isaac becomes blind in his old age, Leah has "weak eyes," Jacob walks with a limp because of his encounter with God, and Moses stutters (Siegel 2001: 31–33). The very idea of bodily resurrection developed in Judaism as an acknowledgment that sometimes people suffered bodily torment precisely because they were righteous. The first hint of this idea appears in the book of Daniel (12: 2), a book written in response to the persecutions of Antiochus IV Epiphanes around the year 165 BCE. Resurrection then holds out the promise that as the righteous suffers in the body, the righteous will be rewarded in the body.

Second, commentators frequently reproduce John's distinctions between "the Jews" and everyone else in the gospel account as is demonstrated in the following phrase from an article by Colleen Grant (Eiesland and Saliers 1998) on John 9: "What follows Jesus' exit from the narrative are four scenes of interrogation involving at various times the man, his neighbors, the Jewish authorities, and the man's parents" (John 9:81). The problem with this statement is that all of the people in this scene are Jewish, not just the authorities. The authorities are negatively portrayed and only the authorities remain "blind" at the end of the scene. By marking the Jewishness of only the authorities, the links between Jewishness, blindness, darkness, and, therefore, evil are reinforced. Is Jewishness a disability that needs to be cured? In the Gospel of John, the blind can come to see, but "the Jews" are mired in their blindness—stubbornly clinging to it despite the obvious good news of the Christ.

Physical blindness may provide the necessary ground for faith to grow and emerge, but the person cannot remain physically blind. There are biblical scholars and disability activists alike who note that there are no blind disciples. Grant (Eiesland and Saliers 1998: 77) writes, for example, "It is true that at one level the healing stories are stories of inclusion in that Jesus heals and welcomes all sorts of people into God's reign. However, the very fact that they are physically healed by Jesus suggests that physical restoration is a necessary component of their entry into the community." Grant also cites Donald Senior, Frederick Tiffany, and Sharon Ringe, all of whom have made similar points. From her perspective working with people with disabilities and government agencies in Australia, Elizabeth Hastings writes:

> ... with all the respect due to the ten lepers, the various possessed, and the sundry blind, lame, and deaf faithful of scripture, I reckon people who have disabilities may have been better off for the last two thousand years if Our Lord had not created quite so many miraculous cures but occasionally said, "your life is perfect as it is given to you—go ye and find its purpose and meaning," and to onlookers, "this disability is an ordinary part of human being, go ye and create the miracle of a world free of discrimination." (quoted in Calder 2004: 12)

John Hull (2001) in his recent reflection on reading the Bible from his own blind perspective tries to conceive of blind men and women following Jesus through the Galilee—he cannot. Blind disciples would have been an affront to Jesus' power.

Although physical infirmity is not connected to sin in the example of the man born blind, it is, in this case, connected to ignorance of truth.

In John 9, the physical condition of blindness always also connotes metaphorical blindness as a mental or spiritual condition, or ignorance. Both the literal and metaphorical meanings of blindness are always present every time the words "blind" and "to see" are used in the story. The literal and metaphorical meanings of blindness have the potential of contaminating each other in any context. There is a danger of at least implicitly, if not explicitly, associating physically blind people with mental and spiritual incapacity, and associating Jewish people, whether blind or not, with the same shortcomings.

Metaphors Matter

Feminist and other liberationist scholars have raised awareness regarding the prevalent role that metaphors play in shaping Christian understanding and knowledge about God. According to feminist theologian Sallie McFague, people of all ages and from all walks of life rely on metaphor for learning and teaching. Metaphors teach us both the most basic and the most complex concepts. McFague writes: "For it is not geniuses who are being congratulated for their ability to use metaphor; rather, it is being asserted that metaphor is indigenous to all human learning from the simplest to the most complex" (McFague 1982: 32).

McFague highlights the primacy of the use of metaphor for the Christian community when she argues for, and subsequently articulates, a "metaphorical theology." McFague draws heavily on the work of thinkers such as Paul Ricoeur, Max Black, and I. A. Richards when defining the significance and role of metaphor for religion and religious language. Black and Richards are credited with identifying the interaction theory of metaphor. "In the simplest formulation, when we use a metaphor we have two thoughts of different things active together and supported by a single word, whose new meaning is a result of their interaction" (Richards 1965: 93; see also Black 1962). The interaction theory maintains that we must find the similarity between the two objects of comparison while preserving each object's original and indisputable distinctive quality. A tension is maintained between how the objects are alike and not alike. Therefore, the rules of metaphor are simultaneously common and arbitrary.

Ricoeur adopts Black and Richards's interaction theory of language as metaphor when, in his own view, he describes language as event. For Ricoeur, "interaction refers to the claim of rival interpretations on the subject" (Stewart 2004: 108). It is through clashing or rival interpretations that metaphors open up new ways of thinking and being in the world.

Not surprisingly, following the emergence of the interaction theory, linguistic philosophers noticed that among hearers and readers of a given metaphor there was a growing competition between the "threads of similarity" that were emphasized and chosen (Black 1954–1955). Each reader or hearer of a metaphor finds a unique thread of similarity between the objects in question. Therefore, one's context will significantly determine how one interprets and understands metaphors. There can no longer be a literal paraphrase for a metaphor because a literal paraphrase implies a universal thread of similarity and full agreement about what the metaphor means (Stewart 2004: 110).

Building on the work of Ricoeur, Black, and Richards, McFague acknowledges the primacy, complexity, and the power of metaphor when she refers to metaphor as "both our burden and our glory" (McFague 1982: 34). While McFague stresses the indigenous and empowering nature of metaphor for understanding the world (our glory), she also admits the potential danger and abuse that accompanies using metaphors (our burden). For McFague, "The greatest danger is assimilation—the shocking, powerful metaphor becomes trite and accepted" (McFague 1982: 41).

We concur with McFague that it is dangerous for metaphors to lose the significance of their initial impact. It is, however, her emphasis on how the function of metaphor has changed over time that most poignantly demonstrates for us the potentially dangerous power of metaphors. McFague notes, "in contrast to its traditional role as a mere rhetorical trope," metaphor has become "the unsubstitutable foundation of language and thought from which conceptual formulation emerges and to which it must return for its funding" (McFague 1982: 16). Melissa Stewart aptly paraphrases McFague and pinpoints the significant shift in the role of metaphors when she writes, "In other words, the grammatical or structural role that metaphor plays is not to be separated from its affective or attitudinal role" (Stewart 2004: 110). Metaphors are no longer understood as simply playing a grammatical role, but always also play an attitudinal role.

McFague's understanding of the attitudinal role of metaphor is a further expansion of Black's and Richards's interaction theory and Ricoeur's description of the interaction as clashing or rival interpretations. By suggesting that metaphor involves an interaction between two dissimilar objects, Black and Richards introduce the idea that metaphor could have functions other than just the traditional grammatical or structural role. Ricoeur pushes the concept of interaction even further and argues that not only is there an interaction between two dissimilar objects, but there is also an interaction between differing interpretations of how dissimilar objects are similar. Ricoeur's insight highlights that context will affect how metaphor is understood and interpreted. Building on Black's, Richards's, and Ricoeur's assertions, McFague adds a new dimension to the understanding of the role of metaphor. She suggests that metaphor also functions to shape or construct reality: that is, metaphor plays an attitudinal role.

It is precisely the attitudinal role of metaphor that womanist biblical scholar Renita Weems discusses when, in her book *Battered Love: Marriage, Sex, and Violence in the Hebrew Prophets*, she argues that "metaphors matter." Weems suggests that the metaphors that we employ reflect the values of the community, and often justify and reinforce the oppression of marginalized members of a community. Weems writes, "Metaphors matter because they are sometimes our first lessons in prejudice, bigotry, stereotyping, and in marginalizing others—even if only in our minds. They deserve our scrutiny because they are intrinsic to the way we live and shape reality" (Weems 1995: 107).

Like Weems, we assert that the metaphors employed by the Christian community matter, in that they help to shape both our attitudes about God and the normative standards by which membership and acceptance in the community is measured. Furthermore, metaphors require our attention and scrutiny because, as we have seen, individual and community contexts significantly shape how we understand and interpret metaphors, and these understandings and interpretations can yield damaging and exclusionary consequences.

Given the importance of metaphors, the question then becomes, "What do the metaphors we use tell us about membership in the Christian tradition?" Or, asked another way, "Who is excluded from full membership in the Christian community, and who is demonized and excluded by Christians from full membership in the human community as a result of alienating metaphors?" We endeavor to answer these questions by focusing on the metaphors used in John 9.

As we outlined earlier, the primary metaphor describing the move from ignorance to understanding, or faithlessness to faithfulness, in John 9 is that of blindness to sight, or darkness to light. Just how pervasive is this metaphor in the Christian community and in Christian worship? The gospel lectionary text from year A in the lectionary cycle and for the fourth Sunday in Lent is John 9. On that Sunday, this text is read and preached in many Christian churches throughout the country. Other examples employing the metaphors of blindness and sight, or darkness and light, include a phrase from the Nicene Creed

"God from God, light from light, true God from true God," and some popular hymns such as "Amazing Grace" ("I once was lost, but now am found, was blind, but now I see"), "I Saw the Light," and "Be Thou My Vision."

Nancy Eiesland, in her book *The Disabled God* (1994), provides some guidance for understanding the effects of metaphors such as blindness/ darkness and sight/light on persons with disabilities. Eiesland argues that for those of us whose bodies are not physically whole, but are "broken" in that they do not function as they should, language that equates physical wholeness with spiritual wholeness is not merely exclusionary, but suggests that broken bodies impede one's ability to obtain spiritual insight and understanding.

Eiesland notes some attitudes about persons with disabilities that she contends are fostered by exclusionary metaphors. She asserts that two common perceptions are that persons with disabilities are "heroic sufferers," or that a disabling condition is a result of sin. A disciple in John 9 demonstrates one of these attitudes when he asks Jesus who sinned to make the man born blind. The question may appear to be an oversimplified and extreme understanding of the cause of a disability. But, we contend that an example such as this indicates more subtle attitudes that prevail about persons with disabilities that stem in part from overt as well as covert messages we receive through metaphors employed in passages such as John 9. We would add to Eiesland's critique that the dangerous nature of exclusionary metaphors reinscribes anti-Jewish and anti-Semitic attitudes and practices.

We do not have the space to discuss all of the examples Eiesland provides demonstrating how exclusionary practices and attitudes perpetuate the idea that broken bodies impinge spiritual wholeness. We draw on her overall insistence that it is important to pay attention to language and symbols that equate spiritual wholeness with physical wholeness, and to pay attention to metaphorical language that equates darkness and blindness with spiritual ignorance in our efforts to reexamine stories such as John 9 and reevaluate their meanings and implications. In John 9, a blind man gains spiritual understanding only when he also receives physical sight. The Pharisees have physical sight but do not have spiritual understanding and are thus referred to as blind. Therefore, we cannot conclude that everyone with physical sight will also have spiritual sight. But, absent from this passage is the reverse situation of the Pharisees, the presence of a person who is physically blind but still has spiritual sight. Everyone in the story who is spiritually lost is referred to as "blind," whether they are also physically blind or not. Does this subtly suggest that although a whole body does not ensure spiritual wholeness, a broken body is not capable of spiritual wholeness, or that although physically capable of sight, a Jewish person is spiritually disabled because he or she does not "see" the "truth?" The door has certainly been opened for exclusion, if not blatantly, then at least figuratively and subtly of Jews and persons with broken and disabled bodies.

The Imperfect Perfect Body

While Eiesland identifies many examples of problematic metaphors in the Christian tradition, she also asserts that there are other examples that offer alternative and more inclusive metaphors. She argues that the broken body of the resurrected Christ is one such example. However, in order to highlight the inclusive aspect of the image of the body of the resurrected Christ, she maintains that we must shift our conception of the resurrected Christ from that of the suffering servant to that of the disabled God. This shift, Eiesland contends, is more inclusive of not only persons with disabilities but also all people. She suggests that even those persons who have able bodies will eventually age and experience the limitations of a less than whole and perfect body. For those people who are not disabled, she coins the phrase "temporarily abled." With this in mind, she asserts that the disabled God is a more representative imaging and understanding of the body of an incarnational God.

Even in John there are times when the narrative undermines metaphors that equate spiritual wholeness with physical wholeness in ways consistent with Eiesland's shift to the disabled God. Jesus' resurrection appearance to Thomas in John 20 is one such example. When Thomas questions and doubts, Jesus demonstrates to him that his resurrected body still bears the marks of the crucifixion. Thomas is invited to touch Jesus's wounds in order to experience directly the brokenness of his body so that he may believe. The brokenness of Jesus is redemptive and is not fully transformed in his resurrected body. The image of Jesus's resurrected yet still wounded body raises a question: Will people with illnesses or disabilities still bear the marks of those "imperfections" in the world to come?

In addition to the emphasis on the imperfect perfect body of the risen Christ, Jesus exclaims in this passage, "Have you believed because you have seen me? Blessed are those who have not seen and yet have come to believe" (20: 29). Here, the connection in John between literally and symbolically seeing is broken. The tensions in the narrative between these two poles—whole bodies represent whole spirits, and broken bodies can contain whole spirits—are never resolved. Rather, they serve to destabilize each other and also redeem each other.

Our reflections have led us to the following question: Should metaphors such as blindness/sight and darkness/light be used at all? Not only do they exclude Christians with disabilities but also pervade anti-Jewish attitudes within Christianity. We do not presume to be able to answer this question definitively, but we do contend that a challenge for Christians is to value all physical types by not positing a stable and perfect body as the standard for human perfection. (This, of course, needs to be done without valorizing physical illness or disability, and without minimizing the potential desire someone may have to be physically healed.) In addition, the persistence of Christian anti-Semitism requires an authentic Jewish-Christian dialogue, which cannot occur when Christian metaphors demonize Jews and position them as the blind embodiments of cosmic evil. The use of metaphors and other literary devices must be understood to have real consequences in the world, and these consequences must be recognized and interrogated. There is more than one way to be whole and holy.

Note

1. An earlier version of this chapter was published in 2005 in *Disability Studies Quarterly* 25(1) and is reprinted here with permission.

References

Black, M. (1954–1955). Metaphor. *Proceedings of the Aristotelian Society, 55,* 273–294.

Black, Max. (1962). *Models and Metaphors: Studies in Language and Philosophy.* Ithaca, NY: Cornell University Press.

Black, Max. (1979). More about metaphor. In Andrew Ortony (Ed.), *Metaphor and Thought.* Cambridge: Cambridge University Press.

Booth, Wayne C. (1988). *The Company We Keep: An Ethics of Fiction.* Berkeley: University of California Press.

Brown, Raymond E. (1966). The Gospel according to John (I–XII). In *Anchor Bible Commentary.* Garden City, NY: Doubleday & Company.

Brown, Raymond E. (1979). *The Community of the Beloved Disciple.* New York, NY: Paulist Press.

Calder, Andy. (2004). 'God has chosen this for you'—'really?' A pastoral and theological appraisal of this and some other well-known clichés used in Australia to support people with disabilities. *Journal of Religion, Disability & Health* 8(1/2), 5–19.

Eiesland, N. L. (1994). *The Disabled God: Toward a Liberatory Theology of Disability.* Nashville, TN: Abingdon Press.

Eiesland, N. L. & Saliers, D. E. (Eds.) (1998). *Human Disability and the Service of God: Reassessing Religious Practice.* Nashville, TN: Abingdon Press.

Hull, J. (2001). *In the Beginning There was Darkness: A Blind Person's Conversations with the Bible.* Harrisburg, PA: Trinity Press.

Lee, D. A. (1994). *The Symbolic Narratives of the Fourth Gospel: The Interplay of Form and Meaning.* Sheffield, England: JSOT Press.

McFague, Sallie. (1982). *Metaphorical Theology: Models of God in Religious Language.* Philadelphia, PA: Fortress Press.

Reinhartz, Adele. (2001). *Befriending the Beloved Disciple: A Jewish Reading of the Gospel of John.* New York, NY: Continuum.

Richards, I. A. [1936] (1965).*The Philosophy of Rhetoric.* Oxford: Oxford University Press.

Rittner, Carol, & John K. Roth (Eds.) (2001).*"Good News" After Auschwitz?: Christian Faith Within a Post-Holocaust World.* Macon, GA: Mercer University Press.

Siegel, Morton K. (2001). Seminal Jewish attitudes towards people with disabilities. *Journal of Religion, Health, & Disability* 5(1): 29–38.

Stewart, Melissa C. (2004). *From Plurality to Pluralism: A Study of David Tracy's Hermeneutics.* Unpublished doctoral dissertation, Vanderbilt University, Nashville, TN.

Weems, R. J. (1995). *Battered Love: Marriage, Sex, and Violence in the Hebrew Prophets.* Minneapolis, MN: Fortress Press.

CHAPTER 6

Resurrecting Deformity: Augustine on Wounded and Scarred Bodies in the Heavenly Realm

Kristi Upson-Saia

Over the past several decades, scholars of antiquity have been fixated on the body. We have pored over descriptions and representations of ancient bodies that engaged in and refrained from sexual activity, that feasted and fasted, that suffered and endured, and that were meticulously dressed, groomed, and poised in public performances and rites. Despite this far-reaching fascination with the body, we are only beginning to pay attention to disabled bodies. Within the last few years, scholars of the ancient world have begun to look afresh at representations of disability in ancient art and literature. We have begun to analyze how social, economic, medical, and religious discourses influenced notions of the "disabled," to examine how spectacles of disability were mobilized for different purposes, and to imagine how such discourses and images plausibly influenced the climate and conditions in which persons with disabilities lived (Avalos, Melcher, and Schipper 2007; Garland 1995; Rose 2003; Stiker 2006).

Scholars who study disability in the ancient world frequently note concern over the stereotypically negative ways in which disabled individuals and characters were depicted. First, disabilities were regularly cast as physical signs of an individual's weak or wayward nature.[1] For instance, it was commonly believed that soldiers who lacked an inner fighting spirit or adequate training to fight valiantly were more susceptible to sustain bodily injuries in battle. In addition, many believed that the innately weak lacked the bodily constitution to heal completely from an illness, which explained why deformities stemming from an illness lingered in some bodies and not others. Defects and disabilities were also understood to have been inflicted directly by God(s) as a punishment or portent.[2] For example, those who failed to perform sacred rites properly could be struck with an illness or impairment. Thus, disabilities were commonly understood to be the result of either an individual's deficiency or his sin. Second, healing scenes were nearly always written to praise the human or divine agents who possessed the power and virtue to "save" disabled persons from their abnormal state. In typical healing scenes, disabled persons were abstracted, emptied of their personhood, and used merely as devices to draw attention to and eulogize another, presumably more important, character.[3] Because disabled characters were frequently framed in these negative or neglectful ways, contemporary disability theorists find little worth salvaging in ancient literature. The question driving this chapter is "Is there really no discourse that redeems disfigurements and deformities in antiquity?"

With this question in mind, this essay analyzes Augustine's discussion of disabled bodies in his treatise, *City of God*. In particular, I focus on his views on deformities and disfigurements in the resurrection body. Augustine's evaluation of bodily deformities, I argue, deviates notably from his contemporaries. While he certainly agrees with the prevailing contempt for disabled bodies when he argues that *most* deformities are gross malformations that will need to be healed in the heavenly realm, Augustine surprisingly argues that other deformities will be a part of the perfect spiritual body, entirely worthy of the heavenly space. Thus, he calls into question the conventionally wholesale denigration of all bodily deformities and defects that pervaded the literature of his time.

Before we turn to Augustine's discussion of disfigured bodies, let me say a few words about terms. As disability theorists have shown, the categorizations of "normal" and "disabled" bodies are cultural constructs determined by the social values and structures of any given society at any given historical moment.[4] In other words, particular bodily features and conditions are not always—transhistorically and cross-culturally—deemed "disability." Much modern disability theory, which analyzes categories of disability in contemporary societies, therefore, does not apply seamlessly to the ancient Mediterranean context. We must analyze how ancient persons constructed their own categories to suit their sociopolitical contexts, needs, and desires.

When we turn to ancient sources, we quickly understand that the concept of disability is quite fuzzy. First and foremost, we recognize that nearly everybody in the ancient world had some sort of physical impairment. The lack of proper nutrition and hygiene, environmental and occupational hazards, coupled with a fledgling medical field that dealt insufficiently with diseases and injuries, meant that the majority of the population was affected by one or another bodily deficiency or injury.[5] It is not surprising, then, that we find no Greek or Latin terms that referenced a broad category of persons whose bodies were considered "abnormal" (in contradistinction, some might say, to the referents of the English term "disabled").[6] Although most bodies suffered some sort of impairment and although there did not seem to be an overarching concept of "disabled" persons, Greeks and Romans did indeed categorize certain bodies according to particular physical characteristics or abilities. For instance, they possessed terms to describe those whose bodies precluded them from being productive members of society (hence, disabilities defined according to economics),[7] those who were temporarily, chronically, or terminally sick (hence, disabilities related to health),[8] those who had been wounded or injured (hence disabilities related to occupational or military pursuits),[9] those with common types of physical impairment, such as the blind, lame, and deaf (hence, disabilities defined according to functional abilities),[10] and those who were "deformed," "disfigured," or "crooked" so as to be unpleasing to the eye (hence, disability related to aesthetics).[11] My analysis of resurrection bodies in this chapter will focus exclusively on the last category: bodies that were considered misshapen and deformed.

Imagining Resurrection Bodies

Augustine was not the first Christian thinker to ponder the nature of resurrection bodies. Many Christians before him crafted detailed theories, some aspects of which Augustine adopted and others from which he departed quite radically. In order to contextualize Augustine's contributions to the discussion, let me first survey the range of views about the heavenly body adduced by prior Christian writers. For the sake of brevity, I offer here only a brief synopsis of the issues raised and solutions offered by Christian thinkers prior to Augustine.[12]

Christians had long held firmly to a doctrine of bodily—or "fleshly"—resurrection despite being regularly attacked for this view. Non-Christian critics, even those who believed in the soul's continued existence after death, found nothing in the body (*corpus*) or flesh (*caro*) worth saving. Celsus, for instance, asks: "What sort of human soul is it which would still long for a body that had been subject to corruption?"

and "What kind of body is it which, after being completely corrupted, can return to its original nature, and to that self-same first condition out of which it fell into dissolution?" (as cited in Origen, *Contra Celsum* 5.14). As we see from Celsus's remarks, the major problem with a notion of bodily resurrection lies in the understanding that the body—both in life and upon death—existed in a corruptible state. In life, the body was in a continual state of flux, especially due to the natural processes of digestion: according to medical writers, the useful parts of consumed food were presumed to be absorbed into the body and transformed into blood, which, in turn, was transformed into the other bodily humors (Galen, *Nat. Fac.* I.2). The food humans consumed literally became a part of them. Upon death, moreover, the body was known to rot, decay, and decompose. Worse still, corpses became food for other creatures—fish, birds, worms, and beasts—at which time our bodies became transformed into their blood and flesh! If the body's natural state was characterized in life and death by corruptibility and change, how could such a body, opponents queried, exist alongside the incorruptible soul in an incorruptible realm in the presence of an incorruptible God?[13]

Despite these objections, many Christians felt obliged to uphold the goodness of materiality, including the material body.[14] Since the body was first formed by the Creator God and since Jesus deemed it a worthy residence while he was incarnate in the world, it must be good. Moreover, since many Christians believed that Jesus sanctified the body through his incarnation and resurrection, they sought a doctrine of bodily resurrection that was consonant with their understanding of soteriology (van Eijk 1971). They also aimed to reconcile their doctrine of resurrection with scripture. They read gospel accounts of Jesus's own resurrection in bodily form—he rose in "flesh and bones" that were handled by Thomas and that exhibited the continued ability to eat—and they supposed that their own resurrection would be similar (John 20: 24–29; Luke 24: 39–42; 1 Clement 24: 1). They also cite Ezekiel 37: 5–6 (in which God promises to raise up dry bones) and Luke 21: 18 ("not a hair on your head shall perish") as evidence that, in the resurrection, every remnant of an individual's body would be restored.[15]

The promise of bodily restoration became especially significant to the Christian psyche once opponents of Christianity began to brutally mutilate the bodies of Christian martyrs, at times, as an added insult, mincing and scattering their bodies or even consuming the beasts that earlier devoured the martyrs.[16] Persecutors hoped to demoralize Christians—who now worried about the wholeness of the martyrs' resurrection bodies—and to confound those who might volunteer to become martyrs in the future. Many Christians, however, asserted that God would retrieve every bodily bit that was scattered, consumed, or decomposed, reassuring Christians living in the age of martyrdom.[17] In fact, the doctrine of bodily resurrection enabled Christians to imagine the future, heavenly punishments their persecutors would suffer "with eternal sensibility" (Pseudo-Justin, *1 Apol.* 52).[18]

Although many Christians agreed that some sort of body would be resurrected, they did not all agree on the kind or quality of that body. According to some Christians, the great miracle of the resurrection was God's ability to identify and reassemble every part of an individual's body that had been fragmented, corrupted, scattered, and even consumed by (and thus transformed into) other creatures.[19] Simply stated, in the resurrection, God would act as the supreme reassembler and reanimator of the body; God would re-create a person's equivalent form in heaven. Other Christians scoffed at the idea that the resurrected body would be composed of bits of human flesh "vomited up" from creatures that digested them![20] While they agreed that God would indeed preserve the complete material integrity of the earthly body—gathering up all the bodily bits belonging to an individual—they also claimed that all of these bits would be thoroughly transformed into an immortal, incorruptible, and glorious new state befitting the heavenly realm (Tertullian, *De Res. Carn.* 57; Aphrahat, *Demonstration* 8; Ephraem *Serm.* 1 and *Hymns* 37.1–10; 46.16; 49.1–2, 8; Jerome, *Contra JoannemHierosolymitanum*, 23–26 and *Ep.* 84.8). They envisioned a glorified, "spiritual body" that need not be entirely equivalent to the earthly body. In this respect, they followed Paul who famously asserted:

> It is sown a physical body, it is raised a spiritual body (sw-mapneumatiko/n)...flesh and blood cannot inherit the kingdom of God, nor does the perishable inherit the imperishable...the dead will be raised incorruptible, and we will be changed. (1 Cor. 15: 44, 50, 52)

In fact, several Christians, somewhat surprisingly, embraced the flux—and even the corruption—of human bodies as part of the *process* out of which the resurrected body came to be perfectly incorruptible. For instance, Irenaeus and Gregory of Nyssa, developing the seed metaphor introduced by Paul, argued that just as some degree of rotting is necessary for seeds to sprout, so too earthly corpses decomposed as part of the process of maturation (Irenaeus, *Adv. Haer.* 5.2; 5.7; 5.10; 5.28; 5.33–34; cf. Gregory of Nyssa, *De Opificio*, 27).[21]

In addition, returning to the paradigm of digestion that so repelled their opponents, Irenaeus, Tertullian, and Cyril argued that by consuming Christ's body and blood in the Eucharistic rites Christians' corruptible bodies were being transformed by the sacraments of the church: as they digested and absorbed Christ's nature, their bodies were beginning to be changed into incorruptible beings in the here and now, a transformation that would be completed in heaven (Irenaeus, *Adv. Haer.* 5.2; Tertullian, *DeRes. Carn.* 8; Cyril of Jerusalem, *Cat.* 22.3–4; Justin *1 Apol.* 66).[22]

What did Christian writers prior to Augustine think about defects and deformities in heavenly bodies? They all—no matter what position on bodily resurrection they took—argued that deformities would not persist in heavenly bodies since deformities were signs of a body's corruptibility, which had no place in the incorruptible realm. Those who thought that bodies would be transformed and perfected had an easier time arguing that all defects would be healed. In fact, the obliteration of fleshly deformities was a *symbol* of the glorious transformation that took place as the earthly body was made incorruptible. Tertullian, for example, succinctly concludes: "If we are changed for glory, how much more for integrity!" (*De Res. Carn.* 57).[23] Those who strenuously asserted full material continuity between earthly and heavenly bodies had more trouble reconciling deformities into their position. They faced the objections of their opponents who asked:

> If "the selfsame substance is recalled to life with all its form, and lineaments, and quality, then why not with all its other characteristics? Will the blind, and the lame, and the palsied, and whoever else may have passed away with any conspicuous mark, return again with the same?" (as cited in Tertullian, *De Res. Carn.* 57)[24]

Yet even these Christian thinkers resisted the image of deformities in the resurrection. Pseudo-Justin, for instance, asserts that God would reassemble bodily bits just as an artist recasts a statue, rethrows a pot, or reassembles a mosaic: using "the same material, though fashioning it anew" (*De Res.* 6). Methodius similarly writes:

> For it is impossible for an image under the hands of the original artist to be lost, even if it be melted down again, for it may be restored; but it is possible for blemishes and injuries to be put off, for they melt away and cannot be restored; because in every work of art the best craftsman looks not for blemish or failure, but for symmetry and correctness in

his work ... [God the artist] dissolved humans again into their original materials, in order that, by remodeling, all the blemishes in them might waste away and disappear. (*Aglaophon: De Res.* I.6–7)[25]

Moreover, they liken God's correction of deformities to Jesus's healing ministry. Just as Jesus healed the blind and lame while he was incarnate, so too would God heal deformed bodies in the resurrection in order that "the flesh shall rise perfect and entire ... those dreaded difficulties of theirs will be healed" (Pseudo-Justin, *De Res.* 4). It is clear that Christian thinkers prior to Augustine found no reason to preserve deformities in the resurrection body, but rather strained to eradicate them as evidence of the heavenly body's incorruptibility and of God's mercy.

Augustine on Deformities in The Resurrection[26]

Books 21 and 22 of Augustine's *City of God* have drawn the attention of scholars for several reasons. Some wish to situate Augustine in Christian debates over the nature of the resurrected flesh: Will it be unlike or like the earthly body? And how? Others have been interested in Augustine's stance on the genitalia of resurrected bodies: Will gender—as defined by certain sexual organs of the body—continue to exist in the resurrection or not? Commentators of this section of *City of God*, however, have overlooked Augustine's rich discussion of bodily deformities and defects (*deformitas, vitium*) both in earthly and in resurrected bodies.[27] As noted above, Augustine takes inconsistent stands on whether or not there will be deformities in heavenly bodies. He does so, I argue, because he considers some bodily deformities to be incidental accidents of the body, while others are intimately linked to the individual's perfected spiritual identity that will become manifest in the resurrection. Moreover, certain bodily deformities—namely scars—serve as fruitful signs of the transformative nature of resurrection and, somewhat ironically, of the incorruptibility of the resurrection body.

Correcting and Erasing Deformities in Resurrection Bodies

Christian thinkers before Augustine were concerned that there be a material—fleshly—resurrection, though they were equally concerned that the heavenly body not be subject to corruption. They argued, therefore, that the body would be either transformed or "clothed" in incorruptibility in order to address their fear that flux and change be introduced into the realm of the changeless and incorruptible God. Thus, they could not imagine deformities and defects in the resurrection since these were key signs of the earthly body's unstable and corruptible nature. Augustine was surely aware of issues of corruptibility (as will be discussed in more detail below), but he turned the discussion of heavenly bodies onto a topic that Christian writers before him had yet to fully address: aesthetics.[28] For Augustine, deformities and defects were troublesome not only because they were inconsistent with the incorruptibility that characterized the heavenly space, but also because they were unsightly and ugly.[29]

Augustine's concern with deformities and beauty seem in part to have been driven by the objections of his opponents. Critics of Christianity found clever ways to use Christians' own texts against them, arguing that the resurrected body that Christians *must* envision—that is, if they read their scriptures faithfully—would necessarily be ugly and vile. If Christians took seriously Jesus's pledge in the gospel of Luke ("not a hair on your head shall perish"), opponents claimed, Christians must imagine a resurrected body that would be composed of all of the discarded hair—and by extension also the discarded fingernails and toenails—shed in one's lifetime. And if all of these bodily fragments were to be restored to the resurrection body, what a monstrous sight it would be! Moreover, they wondered about deformities already present in earthly bodies—the "hideousness and defects (*foeditates et vitia*)" that were present from birth or incurred accidentally in life—as well as the decay of flesh after death.[30] Would all of these unsightly aspects of the body also remain in the resurrection? And if so, they asked: "Who would not shudder at the horrid (*deformitatem*) sight? . . . and where would the beauty be?"(*De Civitate Dei* XXII.12).

We should note here that both Augustine and his opponents relied on a notion of beauty based on *symmetria*: perfect bodily proportionality and bilateral symmetry. In his treatise, *Canon*, the fifth-century BCE sculptor and art theorist Polykleitos defines bodily beauty as the perfect proportionality of fingers to palm; palm to wrist; wrist to forearm, forearm to upper arm, and so on, as well as bilateral symmetry or balance between the two halves of the body (Leftwich 1995; cf. Plotinus, *Enneades* 1.6.1).[31] While Polykleitos is credited with popularizing this definition of beauty, we find similar notions in his sixth-century BCE predecessor Pythagoras who was concerned to identify mathematical patterns of symmetry in the cosmos, as well as in the body.[32] Furthermore, physicians such as Hippocratics and Galen explicated a harmony or balance of constituents of the body (e.g., phlegm, blood, bile) and the proper proportions of bodily limbs, both of which, in their opinion, contributed to an individual's overall health (e.g., Galen, *De PlacitisHippocratis et Platonis* 5; Leftwich 1995).[33]

Moreover, we might also assume that Augustine and his contemporaries were concerned with the beauty of heavenly bodies because of the conventional link between aesthetics and virtue. Informed by physiognomy—the science of physical appearance—Greeks and Romans held that the disposition of the soul showed itself on the surface of the body through physical signs (seimei=a).[34] It was possible, therefore, to interpret an individual's character and temperament purely from his or her physical appearance. According to physiognomic taxonomies, beauty and virtue were inextricably linked, so that one man's handsome, well-proportioned looks were evidence of his praiseworthy character, while another man's ugliness and deformities were proof of his depravity and immorality.[35]

Such evaluations of bodily deformities made sense given that Greeks and Romans routinely inflicted marks (*stigmata*)—tattoos, brands, and scars—on delinquent slaves, prisoners of war, and condemned criminals, including persecuted Christians (Gustafson 2000; Jones 1987).[36] Given these contexts in which bodies were intentionally marked as a visible sign of their subjugation and ignominy, we should not be surprised that other deformed and disfigured bodies took on the connotation of disgrace through affiliation.

For these reasons, Augustine holds that heavenly bodies ought to be beautiful in keeping with the aesthetics of the heavenly space and as evidence of the perfected character and virtue of its saintly inhabitants. As Augustine himself admits, any lack of *symmetria* "offends" and is "inconsistent with the future happiness of the saints"—whether it be a lack of proportion (such as really long hair, fingernails, or toenails) or "misshapen (*pravum*)" deformities of the body. Heavenly bodies must exhibit a "harmony of parts;" "misshapen parts will be straightened, and the lack of what is seemly will be supplied" (*De Civitate Dei* XXII.19).

Augustine, however, cannot ignore his opponents' invocation of the Lukan passage that promises the retrieval of all bodily remnants. He wishes to maintain that all shed hairs, fingernails, and toenails would indeed be restored to resurrection bodies, as would also bodily defects and deformities, while he also claims that these body parts would be thoroughly transformed so as to be beautiful in keeping with the resplendence of heaven. Augustine holds both positions by ingeniously arguing that while all bodily remnants will be restored to the heavenly body, they need not return "to the places where they would cause an ugly disproportion" or remain defective. Rather they would be absorbed into "the total mass of the body." Excess hair and nail clippings, for instance, would be rejoined to the resurrection body without the "deformed enormity (*deformemenormitatem*)" (*De Civitate Dei* XXII.19). Similarly, the *substance* of bodily deformities and defects would be fully retained in the heavenly body, though the deformed *shape* of that substance would be corrected. Augustine asserts: "The restoration will be such that the deformity will disappear while the substance will be preserved intact" (*De Civitate Dei* XXII.19; cf. Augustine, *Enchiridion ad Laurentium* 87–92). Augustine succinctly concludes:

> [I]n the resurrection of the flesh, the body shall...enjoy the beauty that arises from preserving symmetry and proportion in all its members... [if] for the preservation of this beauty, any part of the body's substance, which if placed in one spot would produce a deformity, shall be distributed throughout the whole, so that neither any part, nor the symmetry of the whole, may be lost, but only the general stature of the body somewhat increased by the distribution in all the parts of that which, in one place, would have been unsightly.[37]

Borrowing the metaphor from earlier Christian writers, Augustine likens God's transformation of the body to an artist recasting a statue.

> A human artist can melt down a statue which for some reason he had cast with a deformity, and recast it in perfect beauty, so that none of its substance is lost, but only its deformity. If anything in the first figure stood out unbecomingly (*indecenterextabat*), he need not cut it off from the whole that he formed and separate it, but he can so scatter it and mix it with the whole that he neither creates an ugly thing (*foeditatemfaciat*) nor diminishes the substance. If the human artist can do this, what must we think of the almighty Artist? Will he not be able to remove and destroy all the deformities of human bodies, not only the common ones, but also the rare and monstrous? (*De Civitate Dei* XXII.19)

Even though the heavenly body is a refashioned version of the earthly body, Augustine makes plain that the integrity and continuity of an individual's identity is never compromised as he or she transitions from one realm to the next because his or her identity is based not in his or her material form but in his or her created potential for perfection. At the moment God created him or her, Augustine argues, God fashioned him or her with the potential for both spiritual and physical perfection. This potential could be realized only in part on earth, so God would restart the process in order to fully accomplish humans' created potential in the resurrection. Augustine concludes that, in the resurrection, this created identity "will come into being," or, since it has been there all along, Augustine quickly corrects himself, "rather, it will *come into view*" (*De Civitate Dei* XXII.19, emphasis added; cf. Augustine, *Enchiridion ad Laurentium* 85).[38]

Here Augustine seems to be in dialogue with Aristotle's concepts of potentiality (duna/miv) and actuality (e0nergei/a). For Aristotle, potentiality is defined by a thing's capacity to be actualized into a range of different states, whereas one's actuality is the end (telov) toward which the potential is ultimately developed. To illustrate, Aristotle uses the example of wood: while uncarved the wood has the potential to become a chair, a table, or a bowl, but once it is carved it has only one actuality. For Aristotle, a thing's actuality essentially shapes its identity (*Metaphysics* Q.6–9). Augustine takes a different stance. For him, one's true identity is found in the potential of the seed created by God and not in the actual development of that potential into one earthly form or another since God would restart and perfect the course of one's development in the resurrection.[39] It is not surprising, then, that Augustine counters Aristotle's metaphor of carved wood (which cannot be recarved once it is shaped into a particular object) with a metaphor using a different material—recast metal—to demonstrate that one's bodily development on earth is neither absolute nor irrevocable and therefore cannot be taken to be the seat of one's identity.

For Augustine, then, bodily deformities and defects are characterized as malformations in development. They are realizations of individuals' created potential and thus they will be eradicated in the resurrection body.[40] He employs the example of blindness to make this point clear. He argues that God created the eye to see and yet a defect in development undermines its created potential. In the resurrection, God will restore the sight that had been thwarted. In fact, for the sighted as well as the blind, God will further heighten the eye's spiritual sight as originally created and intended (*De Civitate Dei* XXII.1; XXII.29).

If God planned to trigger the realization of individuals' created potential in the resurrection, why did God allow malformations and deformities to develop in earthly bodies in the first place? Augustine contends that bodily deformities serve useful pedagogical purposes. They are signs that show "how this present state of mortals is one of punishment," while God's correction of such deformities is proof of God's mercy and power (*De Civitate Dei* XXII.19; XXII.21; XXI.8; XXII.20–21). Here Augustine follows the logic found in John 9:3: that the blind man was not blind due to his sins or the sins of his kin, but rather "so that God's work might be revealed through [the healing of the defect]." In fact, Augustine intriguingly notes that the terms monstrosity and monstrous (*monstrum* and *monstruosas*) share a linguistic root with the verb "to show" or "to demonstrate" (*monstrare*).[41] As Augustine sees it, monstrosities, deformities, and defects in earthly bodies are opportunities for God—through the healing of all deformities in the resurrection—to show, demonstrate, and prove that God has both the power and the mercy to heal humanity: "God will do what he has declared he will do with the bodies of humans and that no difficulty will detain God, no law of nature circumscribe God" (*De Civitate Dei* XXI.8).[42]

So far, Augustine voices the common attitude and tropes that disability studies scholars and activists find troubling. For Augustine, most bodily deformities are far too unsightly to be retained in the beautiful heavenly sphere. They can and will be eradicated because they are merely developmental malformations with no connection to Christians' true identity. Moreover, through their healing, God is able to demonstrate God's all-encompassing power over the disorders of death and sin. But this is not all Augustine has to say about heavenly deformities.

Retaining and Imparting Deformities in Resurrection Bodies

Despite Augustine's unwavering stance on the erasure of most bodily deformities in the resurrection, he simultaneously contends that certain deformities would in fact remain: namely, the bodily wounds incurred through martyrdom.[43] Although Augustine believed that martyrs' injuries would be retained, he was forced to admit that *major* injuries sustained through martyrdom would have to be rectified in the resurrection body. Severed limbs, for example, must find their way back to the resurrection body in order to satisfy the Lukan promise—surely if every hair would be restored, so too must every limb!—and to render the body bilaterally symmetrical to satisfy the requirements of heavenly beauty. In these cases, Augustine argues, since "it is fitting that the marks of their glorious wounds be seen in that immortal flesh, then in the place where the limbs were struck off or cut away . . . there will be seen scars (*cicatrices*)" (*De Civitate Dei* XXII.19). Thus, not only does Augustine insist that some deformities would be permitted to exist in the resurrection body, but also that *new* scars and marks (*cicatrices, indicia*) would be imparted in the place of wounds that were too grotesque for heaven.[44]

Augustine is quick to assert that these scars and marks should not be "considered or spoken of as defects (*vitia*)" or deformities (*deformitas*). Rather, they are "marks of virtue" (*virtutis indicia*) or "glorious marks" (*indicia gloriosorum*). They are distinct in that they will not offend in the beautiful heavenly realm: "For it will not be a deformity in them, but an honor, and in their body will shine a certain beauty, not of the body, but of virtue" (*De Civitate Dei* XXII.19). Although Augustine regularly followed the aesthetic and physiognomic conventions of his contemporaries, in this portion of his argument, he turns those conventions on their head. He dismisses absolute symmetry as the main criteria for beauty and revises the physiognomic taxonomy that interprets bodily irregularities to be indicators of vice. Against the prevailing consensus of his time, he evaluates the martyrs' deformities to be signs of virtue and holiness that are consequently to be deemed beautiful.

How can Augustine claim, on the one hand, that "all the defects that may have befallen the body will [in the resurrection] be gone," and, on the other hand, that certain wounds will remain in—and in fact that new scars will be imparted to—martyrs' resurrection bodies? I submit that the contradiction derives from two models of resurrection identity that Augustine endorses. First, as already discussed, a Christian's resurrection identity could be based in his or her created potential for perfection and, second, a Christian's resurrection identity could be based in the perfected union of body, soul, and will. Let us now examine the latter.

For Augustine, the body is fallen and corruptible not only because of its material or fleshy substance that is in a state of continual flux but more importantly because of the uncoordinated will of the body and the soul. Augustine understood the first sin to be, at its most basic level, a sin of disobedience: Adam and Eve turned from the will and commands of God toward their own will (*De Civitate Dei* XIV.11). The fitting punishment for this first disobedience was "more disobedience": from that moment on, every human's body and soul no longer obeyed his will (*De Civitate Dei* XIV.15).[45] For Augustine, then, Paul's lament—"I do not do what I will, I will not what I do" (Rom. 7: 15)—is the universal lament of all humans who exist in a fallen and corrupt state. Although after baptism Christians are released from the compulsion to disobey themselves, corruption and disobedience still linger just as listlessness persists after a serious illness; our disobedience to ourselves "still remains until our entire infirmity is healed by the advancing renewal of our inner man, day by day, when at last our outward man shall be clothed with incorruption" (*De Nuptiis et Concupiscentia* I.28).[46]

For Augustine, the corruptibility that is most problematic and incompatible with the heavenly realm is characterized not by *substance* of the body, but rather by its *disobedient state*. Augustine writes: "By the word corruptible... [is] meant that the soul is weighed down, not by just any sort of body, but by the body such as it has become as a result of sin and consequent punishment" (*De Civitate Dei* XIII.16; Alfeche 1989: 72–84). It follows that Augustine conversely defines heavenly incorruptibility as the renewed and rightly ordered body and soul, which is wholly obedient to one's will and is aligned with the will of God. The redeemed and incorruptible bodies of the resurrection will indeed be "spiritual bodies" as Paul described them: they "will be spiritual, not because they will cease to be [fleshly] bodies, but because they will have a life-giving spirit to sustain them" (*De Civitate Dei* XIII.22; Fredriksen 1991: 85–86).

Augustine intriguingly describes the sanctified state of the heavenly saints (i.e., the coordinated will and proper obedience of the body and soul) in terms of aesthetic principles of proportionality, harmony, and balance.

> The peace of the body therefore is an ordered proportionality of its components... the peace of the rational soul is the ordered agreement of knowledge and action... The peace of the heavenly city is a perfectly ordered and fully concordant fellowship in the enjoyment of God. (*De Civitate Dei* XIX.13)

By employing recognizably aesthetic terms, Augustine characterizes the beauty of the heavenly state according to not only the symmetry of body parts but also the symmetry of the body, soul, and will of each heavenly citizen.

With Augustine's unique definition of the incorruptible state in mind, we understand the acts of Christian martyrdom—and the wounds incurred in these acts—anew. By willingly submitting to and valiantly enduring martyrdom, these saints demonstrated a proper ordering of the body-soul-will, which were rightly calibrated with God's will. Martyrs' deformities, therefore, are no longer to be interpreted as evidence of the corruptible substance of material bodies (corruptibility that lacks beautiful symmetry and thus should be obliterated in the resurrection), but rather as evidence that the martyrs had overcome the corruption of the disordered body-soul-will.[47] That is, martyrs' deformities were signs of their sanctified incorruptible nature, a symmetry of body-soul-will that Augustine accordingly considered to be beautiful.

This evaluation of the martyrs' wounds and scars leads Augustine to contradict his earlier assertions that bodily deformities were malformations of individuals' created potential, that they were not to be associated with individuals' perfected identity, and therefore that they would be eradicated in the resurrection body. In this extraordinary case, martyrs' wounds and deformities were sustained when they *realized* their created potential for virtue; thus martyrs' wounds were to be linked to their true spiritual identity.[48] *These* deformities gestured not to the flawed, maldeveloped state of preresurrection bodies, but rather to martyrs' perfected virtue and identity that must be retained in the resurrection.

Augustine's insistence that wounds and scars would be prevalent signs of the martyrs' identity in heaven is perhaps most remarkable in a section in which he answers the question: how will Christians in the resurrection be able to recognize one another, given the fact that their bodies will be wholly transformed? Augustine contends that, at present, humans identify one another as embodied selves. Since we cannot recognize one another's souls, we see each others' selves only as they are cloaked in material forms. In the resurrection, on the contrary, "it will not be as it is now, when the invisible things of God are seen and understood through the things which have been made, in a mirror dimly . . . in the appearance of corporeal things which we perceive through corporeal eyes" (*De Civitate Dei* XXII.19). Christians' sight will be strengthened and perfected so that we will be able to "see" individuals' spirit and it will be that spirit by which we will identify one another. Remarkably, even while the material body is wholly transformed and, in all other ways, discontinues being a sign of Christians' identity in the resurrection (since there we will identify one another according to our spirits), wounds and scars continue to be the primary marker by which to recognize martyrs. Although Augustine readily admits that—for the sake of beauty—martyrs' wounds and scars will not actually *resemble* the marks incurred to the earthly body, their usefulness as *signs of identity* surprisingly persists from the earthly to the heavenly realm.

Augustine's use of marks and scars as signs of identity surely resonated with readers of the gospels who saw that Jesus's wounds were likewise a chief indicator of his identity. Jesus's wounds lingered in the resurrection body (John 20: 20–27), Augustine maintains, as reminders of Jesus's salvific acts of death and resurrection and ultimately they pointed to his identity as savior. It was precisely these wounds that enabled the disciples to recognize the resurrected Jesus (referencing Luke 24: 36–49, *De Civitate Dei* XXII.19), just as Odysseus and Orestes were also recognized—even though both men were in disguise—by their signature scars.[49]

Moreover, Augustine's readers were used to seeing bodies that were scarred and tattooed as an indicator of their identity and status (e.g., prisoners of war, delinquent slaves, and criminals). Such marks *focused* spectators' reading of their bodies: the scarring or the tattoo was deemed the most significant bodily sign that rendered the most salient aspects of these individuals' identity. At the same time, these marks *opened* for spectators a whole host of information—no matter how nonspecific—about the individuals' history and deeds.[50] Likewise, with the Christian martyr, the wound or scar was the bodily anchor that framed an understanding of his or her identity (*De Civitate Dei* XXII.12). Spectators who witnessed these marks were prompted to visualize the martyrs' endurance of brutal torture and death and also to recognize the virtue that undergirded and sustained them.[51] (In fact, earlier in Book 22, Augustine's discussion of martyrs' suffering may very well have been a visual guide to such imaginings. There he graphically depicts the brutal discipline of martyrs' bodies and the discipline and virtue necessary to endure such violence [*De Civitate Dei* XXII.6].)[52]

Even if the martyrs' wounds resembled those of Christ and if the wounds were incurred during noble acts, we must presume that ancient readers would have been ambivalent about Augustine's claims that deformed bodies would populate the heavenly realm, given that they also regularly witnessed the degradation of marked and scarred slaves, prisoners of war, and criminals in their midst. The sign of the wound could gesture to both honor and shame. Perhaps, though, it was precisely the fusing of offense and glory that Augustine was after. One cannot, in fact, understand the glory, beauty, and perfection into which the resurrected body is transformed without first understanding the corruption and fallenness whence it came. Augustine perhaps hoped to cull the conventional denigration of *stigmata* even while he sacralized them as signs of martyrs' virtue, holiness, and glory. As Susanna Elm has argued, "Markings, even the most horrendous, may be reversed into something positive... not despite, but *because* of their negative associations" (Elm 1996: 414).[53]

The martyrs' heavenly wounds and scars could become beautiful signs of the transformation of corruptibility into incorruptibility, degradation into glory, and suffering into reward.

The martyrs' scar in particular functioned as the perfect cipher for the paradox of the resurrection body itself. In a scar, one can see *simultaneously* the loss of the old flesh and a renewal into a new flesh.

So too, the heavenly martyrs' scars harkened back to the earthly body even while it marked the transformation of that body. It was a multivalent sign that gestured to the continuity *and* discontinuity of resurrection bodies with earthly bodies. It manifested not just the *telos*—the perfected, resurrected body—but the history of salvation in the body: from creation to fall to redemption, enabling one to apprehend the glory of resurrection and redemption, which is illuminated by the corruption and fallenness whence it has come.[54]

Reperceiving Deformities in the Terrestrial Realm

How might Augustine's discussion of heavenly wounds and scars have altered his readers' perceptions of bodily deformities in the earthly realm? By incorporating the martyrs' wounds and scars into the heavenly realm, Augustine emphasized the materiality of the resurrection body, even while he maintained that that body would be transformed into an incorruptible state. While many of his predecessors contended that the resurrection body would indeed be a body, they emptied it of its most fearful and troubling aspects: its vulnerability and fragmentation. The collective fantasy of an intact and incorruptible body in the resurrection was a salve for humans' anxiety over the precarious nature of their embodied existence. As Beth Felker Jones astutely notes: "Resurrection doctrine is indicative not only of final hopes, but also of present attitudes toward the bodies of the living" (Felker Jones 2007: 4). Earlier Christian writers attempted to alleviate their readers' anxiety by formulating a perfect heavenly body in which all deformities would be erased; they assured Christians who worried about the body's corruptibility and vulnerability that these aspects of the flesh would not persist, as signified by the healing of bodily deformities. While they upheld a doctrine of bodily resurrection, they demonstrated a devaluation of the body's corruptibility that matched their opponents and made sure to articulate a safe distance between *these* bodies here and now and *those* bodies of the heavenly sphere.

In part, Augustine follows the lead of his predecessors, arguing that most bodily deformities will be rectified in the resurrection. Yet, Augustine also accepts the vulnerability of embodied existence, which can be sanctified and, in fact, can even be evidence of an incorruptible state. By allowing wounds and scars to be present in the heavenly sphere, Augustine invites his readers to look anew at their own bodies. Instead of only despising bodily defects as signs of their fleshly corruptibility, they could now envision certain injuries, wounds, and deformities to be a product of Christian devotion. Whether they be on the extreme edges of bodily deformation (such as martyrs whose bodies were ripped apart, or ascetics who subjected themselves to rigorous bodily discipline and restraint) or merely lay Christians who endured the more normal fluctuations of the body (such as injuries, disease, and aging), the image of heavenly wounds and scars afforded all Christians the ability to consider their own deformities to be aspects of Christian identity that they might embrace.

In fact, Augustine himself encouraged such a reevalution in his sermons at the annual festival of St. Stephen, the first Christian martyr (see sermons 314–319 in Hill: 1995).[55] In these sermons, Augustine exhorted his parishioners to imitate the martyrs in "daily acts of martyrdom." Although, by that time, Christian persecution had long since ended, his Christian audience could still willingly submit themselves to God in acts of bodily devotion akin to those of the holy martyrs. By encouraging his congregation to perceive their acts of bodily discipline to be equivalent to the honorable deeds of the martyrs, Augustine closed the gap between these extraordinary saints of the Christian past and ordinary laypeople of the present; he asked: "Was Stephen not one of us? Of the same flesh and blood and the faithful servant of the same Lord?"(Sermo 317.2.3). As Augustine closed this gap, he enlarged the range of Christian pursuits that could be considered "acts of martyrdom" and he likewise enlarged the range of injuries incurred in those pursuits that could be evaluated as signs of Christian virtue and identity. When paired, Books 21 and 22 of City of God and these sermons must have affected parishioners' everyday encounters with deformed and disfigured bodies. Christians could no longer vilify all bodily defects indiscriminately since some wounds might have been sustained as part of an individual's Christian practice, and therefore might even be retained in the resurrection as a sign of his virtue and true spiritual identity.

Conclusion

As the body shifts between earthly and heavenly realms, and when all else changes in the body in order to realize an individual's true created potential and fulfill the criteria of heavenly beauty, the marks and scars of certain Christian saints remain the only constant; they straddle both earthly and heavenly bodies. They are the visible signs of the fully realized, spiritual identity of the martyrs and metonyms for the resurrection. For Augustine, scars and marks are not only to be understood as punishments from God or signs of bodily frailty and corruptibility. Rather, they could also be read as signs of incorruptibility—the renewed coordination of the body-soul-will—which is both beautiful and holy.

Augustine's views on deformities complicate the concerns of scholars that I outlined at the outset of the chapter. For sure, he depicts some bodily disfigurements as deviations from one's created potential and as a sign of earthly punishment and waywardness and he argues that such malformations will need to be corrected in the heavenly realm. But, he also argues that other bodily deformities are incurred through virtuous acts that demonstrate Christians' perfected identity, are deemed honorable and beautiful, and will be retained in the resurrection. Whereas in most ancient literature, bodily defects and deformities result from individuals' immorality or weakness, Augustine claims that in these cases they are conversely signs of Christians' virtue, nobility, and identity.

While Augustine's discussion of wounds and scars in the resurrected body did not completely overturn the contempt for bodily deformities in the ancient Mediterranean world, he certainly stands apart from his predecessors by opening the way for certain bodily marks to be reevaluated as signs of holiness. By sacralizing the heavenly wounds and scars of the martyrs and by calling for a daily imitation of the martyrs' acts, he contributed to a growing reappraisal of *stigmata*.[56] In fact, from the fifth century on, we begin to see Christians voluntarily marking their bodies as an act of religious devotion despite the explicit censure of bodily modification by biblical and ecclesial authorities (Lev. 19: 28; Elm 1996). As Susanna Elm and Maarten Hesselt van Dinter have demonstrated, some Christians tattooed or scarred their arms and foreheads with the sign of the cross or injured themselves in order to bear marks that resembled Christ's crucifixion wounds (Elm 1996: 430–437; van Dinter 2005: 36–38). Later, pilgrims and crusaders who visited the holy land also marked and tattooed their bodies as souvenirs of their holy pursuits (Lewy 2003; Purkis 2005; van Dinter 2005: 38, 40). By the time St. Francis and other holy men and women of the Middle Ages received the *stigmata* of Christ's wounds, bodily marks had become characteristically interpreted as signs of the saints' extraordinary holiness and of God's overwhelming approval (Schmucki 1991).[57]

Notes

I thank Candida Moss, Nicole Kelley, and Carly Daniel-Hughes, who provided insightful comments on an early draft of this chapter. I also received instructive feedback at the 2008 American Academy of Religion annual meeting, the

2009 American Society of Church History winter meeting (special thanks to Maureen Tilley), and the 2010 North American Patristic Society annual meeting.

1. Of course, in some cases, disabled persons were understood to possess special abilities that not only compensated for lost senses or faculties but also enhanced their social status. For a discussion of these special abilities, see Kelley (2007) and Garland (1995).
2. Holly Joan Toensing adds that disabilities and illness were also sometimes understood to be the result of demon possession (Toensing 2007).
3. Jesus's healings of disabled persons in the Gospels are culled as a prime example of this tactic. Two notable exceptions to this stereotypical use of disability are Mephibosheth, the son of Jonathan, who was beloved by his father's friend, David (2 Sam. 4: 9), and Croesus's son, who overcame his muteness and cried out to save his father from a Persian who was about to slay him (Herodotus, *Histories* I.34–35, 85). For a discussion of each, see Schipper (2006) and Rose (2003).
4. As Nicole Kelley notes, "Disability is not so much an objective reality as the product of discursive practices...that marginalize, exclude, and limit those whose bodies have certain physical traits" (Kelley 2007: 34). On the ways in which environments create "disabling" contexts, see Oliver (1996).
5. For a thorough discussion of the conditions leading to common deformities and disabilities, see Rose (2003: 15–24).
6. For a detailed discussion of terms, see Rose (2003: 11–14) and Vlahogiannis (1998: 15–21). Here I disagree with Robert Garland who construes a broader category of the disabled in antiquity (Garland 1995: 63).
7. The Greek terms a0xreio/w and pale\w mean to "render one useless" and the a)du/natoi are those who were unable to accomplish a task at hand (though this term could refer to those who are powerless for reasons other than bodily inability, such as deficiencies in education or rhetorical ability, for example).
8. The term for "weakness" incurred from illness was a)sqe/neia.
9. The Greek and Latin terms meaning "to wound or to injure" include *mulco*, katatraumati/zw, and suntitrw/skw.
10. The general terms for the physically impaired are *debilis* and phro/v, while there were also specific terms for the lame, blind, and crippled.
11. There were far more terms for deformities and disfigurement than any of the above categories, including ai)-sxov, a!morfov, kullo/v, *deformis, deformitas, distortus, extortus, foedo, pravitas,* and *turpitudo*. Of course, a taxonomy based on terms is problematic when we turn to our sources and examine individual cases. We immediately find persons whose abilities in one sense might cancel out a "disability" in another sense. For instance, although the blind poet Homer and Antigonus, the King of Macedonia, possessed physical impedi-

ments of sight, they both proved perfectly able to contribute productively to society.

12. For a thorough description and analysis of these positions, see Walker Bynum (1996: 1–114).

13. For this reason, Celsus concludes, corpses "are more worthless than dung" (Origen, *Contra Celsum* 5.14). See also Pseudo-Justin, *De Res.* 5, in which he restates his opponents' revulsion toward "vile and despicable flesh...it is not that which God should raise."

14. For a fuller discussion of these and other reasons, see Davies (1972: 448–452).

15. Clement of Rome and Jerome additionally cite Job (19: 26), which reads: "And I shall be surrounded again with my skin and in my flesh I shall see God" (1 Clement 26: 3; cf. Jerome, *Contra JoannemHierosolymitanum*, 30).

16. For a discussion of these allegations and the anxiety springing from prosecutors' alleged strategy, see Walker Bynum (1996: 49, 56, 105–106).

17. As Carolyn Walker Bynum astutely notes, the doctrine of bodily resurrection made "it possible for heroes and ordinary Christians to face...the humiliation of death and the horror of putrefaction" (Walker Bynum 1996: 47). This is certainly not to say that all Christian martyrs or spectators held to a doctrine of bodily resurrection. See, for example, a scene in the *Martyrdom of Perpetua and Felicitas* in which the catechist Saturus recounts his vision of the impending martyrdom, he states: "'We had suffered,' he said, 'and we passed out of the flesh, and we began to be carried towards the east by four angels whose hand touched us not'" (*PassiosanctarumPerpetuae et Felicitatis* 11).

18. Conversely, see Pseudo-Justin, *1 Apol.* 18–21 and Tertullian, *De Res. Carn.*56 on the embodied enjoyment of heavenly rewards.

19. See, for example, *Enoch* 60.7: "And it shall be, that those who have been destroyed in the desert, and who have been devoured by the fish of the sea, and by wild beasts, shall return, and trust in the day of the Elect One; for none shall perish in the presence of the Lord of spirits, nor shall any be capable of perishing;" and *Apocalypse of Peter* 4: "From the east to the west shall all the children of men be gathered together before my Father who lives for ever...And the wild beasts and the fowls shall he command to restore all the flesh that they have devoured, because [God] wills that people should appear; for nothing perishes before God, and nothing is impossible with him, because all things are his." By far the most detailed discussion of God's process of reassembling human bodies can be found in Athenagoras' *De Resurrectione* 2-11, 15, 25, in which Athenagoras argues that God can separate out elements of the body that either had dissolved into another element or had been absorbed into another creature during digestion.

20. See, for example, *De Res. Carn.* 32, in which Tertullian culls the example of Jonah. After three days in the bowels of the whale, Tertullian argues, Jonah's flesh would surely have been digested much like a corpse rots in its grave. He urges his readers to understand the miracle and glory of Jonah's

"resurrection"—and by extension, every other human's resurrection—as not merely the reassembly of "sinews, skin, nerves, and bones," but rather the transformation of the person. For alternate uses of the Jonah story in articulating resurrection doctrine, see the Pauline forgery, Third Corinthians, par. 6 and Justin Martyr's *Dial. Trypho* 107.

21. Compare 1 Clement 25 that upholds the immolation of the phoenix, which is necessary for the renewal of the creature, as an additional metaphor for the transformation that takes place in resurrection. Compare also Stoic views of the cyclical nature of a body's decomposition and recomposition into new material forms (e.g., Sen., *ep.* 71.16; M. Aur., *Med.* 4.21).

22. Compare Homer's description of blood enlivening the shades of the underworld in *Odyssey* 11.38f. Augustine adds baptism as one of the sacraments that transforms the body into incorruptibility, see *De Civitate Dei* 21.16; 21.25.

23. In this chapter, Tertullian collapses categories of the deformed and the dead, arguing that every corpse experiences corruption. Whether the human body "wasted away through the loss of their health, or in the long decrepitude of the grave" or both, God must repair all bodies in order to make it incorruptible. God acts not only a "restorer of the flesh, but also the repairer of its breaches." Tertullian concludes: "So that for the great future there need be no fear of blemished or defective bodies. Integrity, whether the result of preservation or restoration, will be able to lose nothing more after the time that it has been given back to it whatever it had lost."

24. Compare the similar queries cited in Pseudo-Justin, *De res.* 4: "They say that if the flesh rise, it must rise in the same manner as it falls; so that if it die with one eye, it must rise one-eyed; if lame, lame; if defective in any part of the body, in this part the man must rise deficient."

25. See also Theophilus of Antioch, who writes: "For just as a vessel, when on being fashioned it has some flaw, is remolded or remade, that it may become new and entire; so also it happens to man by death... He will rise in the resurrection whole; I mean spotless, and righteous, and immortal" (*Ad Autolycum* II.26, cf. II.38).

26. In this chapter, I address only Augustine's views later in life, as articulated in *City of God*. For a discussion of how his views evolved over time, see Rist (1994: 110–112).

27. The notable exceptions are Frank (2000a), Felker Jones (2007), Kelley (2009), and Burrus (2009).

28. The beauty associated with divine spaces has a long history. Augustine explicitly notes the promise of heavenly beauty from Romans 7:23: "Lord, I have loved the beauty of your house," but he also must have in mind the long history of Graeco-Roman literature that includes stories of divine beauty contests (e.g., between Athena, Hera, and Aphrodite, mentioned in *De Civitate Dei* IV.27). It does not seem, however, that beauty characterized the entirely of the heavenly or immortal realm. Recall, for instance, the deformity of the god

Hephaistos. Also, the *Apocalypse of Peter* depicts the bodies of the damned as deformed and grotesque (Czachesz 2003). In fact, Augustine too entertains the possibility that the damned will be resurrected with some deformities and diseases as part of their punishment (*Enchiridion* 92). (I am indebted to Nicole Kelley for this reference.)

29. To this author's knowledge, the only other reference to the issue of beauty in the heavenly realm is raised in Tertullian's treatise, *On the Resurrection*. Tertullian argues that although humans will have no need to eat or drink in the resurrection, they would still retain their teeth so as not to appear unseemly (*De Res. Carn.* 64).

30. All quotations from Augustine's *City of God* come from the Loeb Classical Library critical edition and English translation in seven volumes (Augustine 1972).

31. Unfortunately, the *Canon* is no longer extant and art historians and theorists are forced to reconstruct the contents of this influential text from citations in later works. For a list of later artist theorists who penned their own treatises on symmetry and proportionality, see Pliny's *Natural History* 35.128; 35.79–80.

32. For a discussion of Pythagoras' treatment of r9uqmo/v (compositional patterning) and summetri/a (proportional harmony), see Pollitt (1974: 12–22, 218–228, 256–258) and Hurwit (1995: 9–11).

33. J. J. Pollitt has also argued that architects such as Vitruvius may have been an additional influence (Pollitt 1995: 19–24).

34. There are several extant handbooks of physiognomy that describe how Greeks and Romans could interpret an individual's character from his physical appearance. The handbooks can be found in Foerster (1893). For detailed discussions of the science, see Evans (1935, 1969) and more recently, Barton (1994) and Frank (2000b: 145–150).

35. For this reason, the Greek term kako/v could be used interchangeably to mean both "ugly" and "evil" (Garland 1995: 88; Vlahogiannis 1998: 26–27). For examples of physiognomic depictions in Greek and Roman literature, see Garland (1995: 87–104).

36. In his seminal article, C. P. Jones demonstrates that while some ancient near eastern societies (such as Syrians, Egyptians, and Thracians) tattooed and scarred their bodies for decorative or religious purposes or to identify members of the military, Greeks and Romans persistently interpreted these customs as evidence of their "barbarian" or "uncivilized" status. Addressing the practice of marking the bodies of subordinate classes in society or of interpreting the marks of foreign cultures as proof of their profligacy, Virginia Burrus similarly remarks: "The body is marked by another and also marked as 'other'" (Burrus 2003: 405). It was not only subjugated classes, however, that were marked. Roman military expert Vegetius describes how recruits were "inscribed with permanent dots in the flesh" of their arms or hands after receiving preliminary training (Veg., *Mil.* 2.5). I thank Maria Doerfler for drawing this reference to my attention.

37. In chapters 85–92 of his *Enchiridion*, Augustine makes similar claims, such as: "They shall not rise again in their deformity, but rather with an amended and perfected body" (*Enchiridion ad Laurentium* 87).

38. In this regard, Augustine loosely follows Tertullian, who writes: "Any loss sustained by our bodies is an accident to them, but their entirety is their natural property. In this condition we are born. Even if we become injured in the womb, this is loss suffered by what is already a human being. Natural condition (*genus*) is prior to injury. As life is bestowed by God, so is it restored by Him. As we are when we receive it, so are we when we recover it. To nature, not to injury, are we restored; to our state by birth, not to our condition by accident, do we rise again" (Tertullian, *De Res. Carn.* 57).

39. Augustine seems to privilege potentiality for a few different reasons. First, he must assert the goodness of the things created by God. He writes: All things were "created by God and his unchangeable goodness who made all things good…God created it good" (*De Civitate Dei* XXII.1). So, even if a thing develops away from that goodness, away from that perfect potential, God's *original* creation is secured as good and perfect (and not to be held responsible for any malformation that subsequently develops). Second, because Augustine understands a human's potential in the seed to be equivalent to the image of God (*imago Dei*), that potential must remain the fundamental measure of individuals' identity (O'Donnell 2005).

40. Augustine must reclassify certain aspects of the body in order to maintain this claim. For instance, when he argues that female genitalia will be retained in heavenly bodies, he must contend that it "is not a defect, but a natural state," departing remarkably from Aristotle and Galen, who understood women's bodies to be underformed or malformed versions of men's bodies (Augustine, *De Civitate Dei* XXII.17; Aristotle, *De generationeanimalium* 765b–766a; Galen, *De usupartiumcorporishumani* 14.6–7).

41. Augustine here deviates from the conventional etymology that links *monstrum* with *monere*, "to warn," as related to divine admonishments and omens (for examples of this more common interpretation, see Garland 1995: 67–70).

42. Elsewhere, Augustine argues that deformities in earthly bodies ought to be viewed as part of the diversity of God's creation. In fact, the diversity of bodies is necessary to represent the fullness of creation's *beauty*: "For God, the Creator of all, knows where and when each thing ought to be, or to have been created, because he sees the similarities and diversities which can contribute to the beauty of the whole. But he who cannot see the whole is offended by the deformity of the part (*deformitatepartis*), because he is blind to that which balances it, and to which it belongs" (*De Civitate Dei* XVI.8). It is difficult to reconcile his position about the beauty of earthly deformities with his evaluation of the repulsiveness of heavenly deformities (Kelley 2009; Stiker 2006).

43. While martyrdom had ended long before Augustine's rule as bishop (over 80 years), public displays of the torture of suspected criminals, brutal public deaths of convicted criminals, and the continuation of gladiatorial contests

(despite Constantine's censure) made it very easy for Christians of Augustine's time to envision the experience of Christian martyrdom nearly a century earlier. As Gillian Clark writes: "The kind of public violence inflicted on martyrs was still familiar, and still legitimate, even if Christians were no longer at risk (except, sometimes, from other Christians) because of their faith" (Clark 1998: 105).

44. It could be that Augustine reached this conclusion after reading the *Martyrdom of Perpetua and Felicitas*. In this narrative, the heroine Perpetua receives a vision that her deceased brother, Dinocrates, was residing in a purgatory-like state. In this state, he still bore "the wound he had when he died." After fervently praying that her brother would be allowed entrance into heaven, Perpetua received a follow-up vision: now "there was Dinocrates all clean, well dressed, and refreshed. I saw a scar where the wound had been..." (*Pass. Perp.* 7–8).

45. The clearest evidence of our rebellion against our own selves is the unruly male member, which becomes aroused against our will at the most inopportune moments and yet refuses to obey our will—that is, remains limp—when the time is right (Augustine, *De Civitate Dei* XIV.16) It is also through this member that the unruliness of the body and soul—original sin—is passed from parents to children in the procreative act (*De Nuptiis et Concupiscentia* I.25, I.27).

46. I am grateful to Emma La Fleur for astutely raising the question to me of how readers with nerve injuries—those who had trouble controlling their body movements—might read Paul's promise that, with baptism, they would regain some control over their wills, as well as Augustine's claim that one's coordinated body-soul-will is an indicator of her spiritual progress. While Augustine might help to redeem certain physical deformities, he might add to the plight of others.

47. I disagree with Carolyn Walker Bynum who has argued that all of the patristic writers were anxious to incorporate elements of "corruption" to resurrected bodies because they understood such signs of flux to be antithetical to the stability that characterized the incorruptible state of resurrected Christians, and more importantly, that characterized their identity (Walker Bynum 1996: 113). While she is correct that most writers took this stance, Augustine's inclusion of martyrs' wounds are the notable exception.

48. As Carolyn Walker Bynum writes: Augustine "equated such scars with personal experience or history and thereby suggested that body is in some way a necessary conveyor of personhood or self" (Walker Bynum 1996: 98).

49. Augustine also finds precedence in the writings of fellow Christian bishop, Gregory of Nyssa who wrote the *Life of Macrina* in his tribute to his departed sister. While preparing his sister's body for burial, Gregory discovered a minute scar on her corpse that was a lingering sign (shmeion), mark (sti/gma), and reminder (mnhmo/sunon) of a breast tumor that God had healed in response to Macrina's fervent prayers, weeping, and her lifetime of ascetic service. Although Macrina did not incur the scar from an act of martyrdom, it is clear

that Gregory uses the scar of this ascetic in a similar way—as a lens through which to access her true spiritual identity. See Georgia Frank's brilliant analysis of this passage (2000a), in which she writes: "The protagonist's scar provides a postmortem point of entry into her past, thereby deepening the reader's understanding of her virtues."

50. Here my reading is inspired by Auerbach's interpretation of Odysseus' scar and especially Georgia Frank's application of Auerbach to the *Life of Macrina* (Auerbach 1953; Frank 2000a; cf. Cox Miller 2005: 24). For discussions of scars as signs that help spectators recognize identity, see also Goff (1991) and Mac Donald (1998).

51. Although she writes about the scar of an ascetic, Georgia Frank's remarks on Macrina's scar serve as a useful comparison to Augustine's use of martyrs' scars: "The protagonist's scar provides a postmortem point of entry into her past, thereby deepening the reader's understanding of her virtues" (Frank 2000a: 519). Augustine could find precedent in Graeco-Roman sources that evaluated deformities, defects, and wounds according to the honorable or dishonorable situation in which they were sustained. Christian Salazar has meticulously detailed the ways in which literary scenes that document wounding are carefully crafted as a means to measuring the hero's virtue (a)reth/) (Salazar 2000: 127–158). For instance, deformities incurred under ignoble circumstances, such as Oedipus's blindness, which followed from his own transgressions, were the subject of mockery, while other deformities that demonstrated one's courage and manliness, such as Hegesistratus's self-maiming—to escape the Spartan stocks—was celebrated and honored (Vlahogiannis, "Disabling Bodies," 24, cf. 17). Of course, we do not always find such neat and clean classifications in our sources. Robert Garland notes several instances in which military veterans were mocked for deformities that were incurred in honorable battle (Garland, *Eye of the Beholder*, 76).

52. The scars that were *imputed* by God in the heavenly realm had even greater interpretive potential. Referencing the tradition of masters marking their slaves, it constructs martyrs' identity always *in relation* to God, their master. It reminds readers of God's role in martyrs' perfected identity: it was God who originally implanted the martyrs' potential for virtue and it was God who orchestrated the opportunity of martyrdom in which the martyrs' virtue could be made manifest. The martyr, though noble, is merely the willing victim who subordinates to God's branding.

53. We need not be surprised that Christians such as Augustine would reclaim such marks that nearly always identified persons of ignominy and subjection. As Dale Martin and Judith Perkins have shown, Christians were well practiced in subverting symbols conventionally perceived as signs of degradation (such as slavery and suffering). See Dale Martin, *Slavery as Salvation: Metaphor of Slavery in Pauline Christianity* (New Haven: Yale University Press, 2000) and Judith Perkins, *Suffering Self: Pain and Narrative Representation in the Early Christian Era* (London: Routledge, 1995).

54. Georgia Frank's description of the symbolism of Macrina's scar translates well to Augustine's description of martyrs' scars: "The scar plots a stable midpoint between these two luminous moments"—the deeds of martyrdom in their wounded bodies and their true identity as made gloriously evident in their scarred posthumous bodies (Frank 2000a: 514).

55. Perhaps Augustine found inspiration for these views of heavenly deformities from the notions and devotion of relics that consumed his generation, and especially his community. The relics of the first Christian martyr, Stephen, were transferred to his town as he was completing the *City of God* (O'Donnell 2005: 174–179, 249–253). It is probable that the views of—and fervor for—the martyr's relics were refracted into Augustine's discussion of martyrs' resurrection bodies. Relics too were fragmented parts of the martyrs' body, which had been resignified as glorious and powerful despite the fact that corpses were conventionally held in disgust. The wondrous miracles produced by relics proved, for Augustine, that material bodies were transformed in the resurrection; relics were merely shadows of the transformed—though still scarred—bodies of the martyrs existing in heaven (*De Civitate Dei* XXII.9).

56. It is likely that Augustine was participating in a broader social movement that reconsidered the relationship between the material and the divine. Patricia Cox Miller has recently argued that there was a "material turn" afoot at this time, "in which the religious significance of the material world was revalued. The phrase "material turn" indicates a shift in the late ancient Christian sensibility regarding the signifying potential of the material world (including especially the human body), a shift that reconfigured the relation between materiality and meaning in a positive direction" (Cox Miller 2009: 3).

57. We might also consider how these innovations in valuing disproportionate and deformed bodies even influenced the contours of modern Western aesthetics. Tobin Siebers' work on what he terms "disability aesthetics" argues strenuously that "good" modern art is compelling only if it incorporates elements of disability that evoke "aesthetic feelings of pleasure and disgust" and "challenge ideas about how the human should be transformed and imagined" (Siebers 2006: 64, 69).

References

Alfeche, Mamerto (1989). The rising of the dead in the works of Augustine (1 Cor. 15: 35–57). *Augustiniana 39*, 54–98.

Auerbach, Erich (1953). Odysseus' scar. In Willard R. Trask (Trans.), *Mimesis: The Representation of Reality in Western Literature* (pp. 3–23). Princeton: Princeton University Press.

Augustine (1972). *The City of God Against the Pagans*, 7 vols. William M. Green (Trans.). Cambridge, MA: Harvard University Press.

Avalos, Hector, Melcher, Sarah J., & Schipper, Jeremy (Eds.). (2007). *This Abled Body: Rethinking Disabilities in Biblical Studies*. Atlanta: Society of Biblical Literature.

Barton, Tamsyn (1994). *Power and Knowledge: Astrology, Physiognomics, and Medicine under the Roman Empire*. Ann Arbor: University of Michigan Press.

Burrus, Virginia (2003). Macrina's tattoo. *Journal of Medieval and Early Modern Studies 33*(3), 403–417.

Burrus, Virginia (2009). Carnal excess: Flesh at the limits of imagination. *Journal of Early Christian Studies 17*(2), 247–265.

Clark, Gillian (1998). Bodies and blood: Late antique debate on martyrdom, virginity and resurrection. In Dominic Montserrat (Ed.), *Changing Bodies, Changing Meanings: Studies on the Human Body in Antiquity* (pp. 99–115). New York, NY: Routledge.

Cox Miller, Patricia (2005). Shifting selves in late antiquity. In David Brakke, Michael L. Satlow, & Steven Weitzman (Eds.), *Religion and the Self in Antiquity* (pp. 15–39). Bloomington: Indiana University Press.

Cox Miller, Patricia (2009). *The Corporeal Imagination: Signifying the Holy in Late Ancient Christianity*. Philadelphia: University of Pennsylvania Press.

Czachesz, István (2003). The grotesque body in the Apocalypse of Peter. In Jan N. Bremmer & IstvánCzachesz (Eds.), *The Apocalypse of Peter* (pp. 108–126). Leuven: Peeters.

Davies, J. G. (1972). Factors leading to the emergence of belief in the resurrection of the flesh. *Journal of Theological Studies 23*(2), 448–452.

Elm, Susanna (1996).'Pierced by bronze needles': Anti-Montanist charges of ritual stigmatization in their fourth-century context. *Journal of Early Christian Studies 4*(4), 409–439.

Evans, Elizabeth C. (1935). Roman descriptions of personal appearance in history and biography. *Harvard Studies in Classical Philology 46*, 43–84.

Evans, Elizabeth C. (1969). *Physiognomics in the Ancient World*. Transactions of the American Philosophical Society 59.5. Philadelphia: American Philosophical Society.

Felker Jones, Beth (2007). *Marks of His Wounds: Gender, Politics, and Bodily Resurrection*. Oxford: Oxford University Press.

Foerster, Richard (1893). *Scriptoresphysiognomonicigraecietlatini*, 2 vols. Lipsiae: B. G. Teubner.

Frank, Georgia (2000a). Macrina's scar: Homeric allusion and heroic identity in Gregory of Nyssa's life of Macrina. *Journal of Early Christian Studies 8*(4), 511–530.

Frank, Georgia (2000b). *The Memory of the Eyes: Pilgrims to Living Saints in Christian Late Antiquity*. Berkeley: University of California Press.

Fredriksen, Paula (1991). Vile bodies: Paul and Augustine on the resurrection of the flesh. In Mark S. Burrows & Paul Rorem (Eds.), *Biblical Hermeneutics in Historical Perspective: Studies in Honor of Karlfried Froehlich on His Sixtieth Birthday* (pp. 75–87). Grand Rapids: Eerdmans.

Garland, Robert (1995). *Eye of the Beholder: Deformity and Disability in the Graeco-Roman World*. Ithaca: Cornell University Press.

Goff, Barbara E. (1991). The sign of the fall: The scars of Orestes and Odysseus. *Classical Antiquity 10*, 259–267.

Gustafson, Mark (2000). The tattoo in the later Roman empire and beyond. In Jane Caplan (Ed.), *Written on the Body: The Tattoo in European and American History* (pp. 17–31). Princeton: Princeton University Press.

Hill, Edmund (1995). *Sermons 306–340. The Works of St. Augustine: A Translation for the 21st Century*, Vol. 9. New York, NY: New City Press.

Hurwit, Jeffrey M. (1995). The *Doryphoros*: Looking backward. In Barbara Hughes Fowler & Warren G. Moon (Eds.), *Polykleitos, the Doryphoros, and Tradition* (pp. 3–18). Madison: University of Wisconsin Press.

Jones, C. P. (1987). *Stigma*: Tattooing and branding in Graeco-Roman antiquity. *Journal of Roman Studies 77*, 139–155.

Kelley, Nicole (2007). Deformity and disability in Greece and Rome. In Hector Avalos, Sarah J. Melcher, & Jeremy Schipper (Eds.), *This Abled Body: Rethinking Disability in Biblical Studies* (pp. 31–45). Atlanta: Society of Biblical Literature.

Kelley, Nicole (2009). The deformed child in ancient Christianity. In Cornelia B. Horn & Robert R. Phenix (Eds.), *Children in Ancient Christianity* (pp. 199–225). Tübingen: Mohr Siebeck.

Leftwich, Gregory V. (1995). Polykleitos and Hippokratic medicine. In Barbara Hughes Fowler & Warren G. Moon (Eds.), *Polykleitos, the Doryphoros, and Tradition* (pp. 38–51). Madison: University of Wisconsin Press.

Lewy, Mordechay (2003). Jerusalem unter der Haut: Zur Geschichte der JerusalemerPilgertätowierung. *Zeitschrift für Religions- und Geistesgeschichte 55*(1), 1–39.

Mac Donald, Dennis (1998). Secrecy and recognitions in the Odyssey and Mark: Where Wrede went wrong. In Ronald F. Hock, J. Bradley Chance, & Judith Perkins (Eds.), *Ancient Fiction and Early Christian Narrative* (pp. 139–153). Atlanta: Scholars Press.

Martin, Dale (2000). *Slavery as Salvation: Metaphor of Slavery in Pauline Christianity*. New Haven: Yale University Press.

O'Donnell, James (2005). *Augustine: A New Biography*. New York, NY: Harper Collins.

Oliver, Michael (1996). *Understanding Disability: From Theory to Practice*. New York, NY: Palgrave.

Perkins, Judith (1995). *Suffering Self: Pain and Narrative Representation in the Early Christian Era*. London, UK: Routledge.

Pollitt, J. J. (1974). *The Ancient View of Greek Art*. New Haven: Yale University Press.

Pollitt, J. J. (1995). The *canon* of Polykleitos and other canons. In Barbara Hughes Fowler & Warren G. Moon (Eds.), *Polykleitos, the Doryphoros, and Tradition* (pp. 19–24). Madison: University of Wisconsin Press.

Purkis, William J. (2005). Stigmata on the first crusade. In Kate Cooper & Jeremy Gregory (Eds.), *Signs, Wonders, Miracles: Representations of Divine Power in the Life of the Church* (pp. 99–108). Woodbridge: Boydell & Brewer.

Rist, John M. (1994). *Augustine: Ancient through Baptized*. Cambridge: Cambridge University Press.

Rose, Martha L. (2003). *The Staff of Oedipus: Transforming Disability in Ancient Greece.* Ann Arbor: University of Michigan Press.

Salazar, Christine F. (2000). *The Treatment of War Wounds in Graeco-Roman Antiquity.* Leiden: Brill.

Schipper, Jeremy (2006). *Disability Studies and the Hebrew Bible: Figuring Mephibosheth in the David Story.* New York, NY: T. & T. Clark Publishers.

Schmucki, Octavian (1991). *The Stigmata of St. Francis of Assisi: A Critical Investigation in the Light of Thirteenth-Century Sources* C.F. Connors (Trans.). New York, NY: St. Bonaventure University.

Siebers, Tobin (2006). Disability aesthetics. *Journal for Cultural and Religious Theory* 7(2), 63–73.

Stiker, Henri-Jacques (2006). *A History of Disability.* William Sayers (Trans.). Ann Arbor: University of Michigan Press.

Toensing, Holly Joan (2007). 'Living among the tombs': Society, mental illness, and self-destruction in Mark 5:1-20. In Hector Avalos, Sarah J. Melcher, & Jeremy Schipper (Eds.), *This Abled Body: Rethinking Disability in Biblical Studies* (pp. 131–143). Atlanta: Society of Biblical Literature.

van Eijk, A. H. C. (1971). 'Only that can rise which has previously fallen': The history of a formula. *Journal of Theological Studies* 22(2), 517–529.

van Dinter, Maarten Hesselt (2005). *The World of Tattoo: An Illustrated History.* Amsterdam: KIT Publishers.

Vlahogiannis, Nicholas (1998). Disabling bodies. In Dominic Montserrat (Ed.), *Changing Bodies, Changing Meanings: Studies on the Human Body in Antiquity* (pp. 13–36). New York, NY: Routledge.

Walker Bynum, Carolyn (1996). *The Resurrection of the Body in Western Christianity: 200-1336.* New York, NY: Columbia University Press.

SECTION 2

Social and Philosophical Perspectives on Religion and Disability

The chapters in Section 2 probe a wide variety of social and philosophical issues such as performance of religious ritual, eugenics, constructions of Catholic sainthood, best practices for Christian missionaries working with people with disabilities, and philosophical musings on epistemology, theodicy, and death. While the topics covered and the methods employed in this section are multifarious, each essay underscores that real-life consequences are associated with religious teachings and practices. Social analysis helps to uncover how people with disabilities experience the lived realities of religious practice. Philosophical investigation delves beyond the day-to-day realities of religious practice and asks questions about how meaning is constructed among, between, and within religious traditions. This section of the book brings to light some of the best and worst ways in which we live in community with one another. The hope is that readers will see these divergent essays as provocative examples of the heterogeneity of disability and religious experience.

Arseli Dokumaci initiates Section 2 with her ethnographic research wherein she analyzes how people in Turkey with locomotive disabilities related to rheumatoid arthritis engage in daily prayers as bodily practices. The participants in this study tended to resist the alternative ways of performing daily prayers as predefined for the sick and disabled by Islam. Participants were visited at their homes and interviewed about how they adapted their movements in order to perform their daily religious duties and were asked to perform these duties for observation. Dokumaci explores how the ideological values enlivened within the Western idea of the self (such as loss of independence) undergird the boundaries between "the abled and the disabled" and how the self-challenge of the Muslim people with disabilities works with and/or against this ideologically defined boundary.

In Chapter 8, Gerald V. O'Brien and Autumn Molinari powerfully delineate the widespread use of religious metaphors by eugenics advocates in the United States and Germany, and discuss the pertinence of this issue, in both its contemporary and historical contexts, for disability studies. O'Brien and Molinari document how religious terminology, symbolism, and metaphor have always accompanied efforts to control the reproductive capacities of disabled population members, especially during the eugenics alarm period in the United States (1900–1930), as well as within the context of Nazi eugenics policies. By investigating the ongoing interplay between eugenics and American Christianity in particular, O'Brien and Molinari illuminate the contemporary cultural perception of persons with disabilities and the use of religious metaphors for social control.

In Chapter 9, Christine James offers an excellent account of the paradoxes associated with Roman Catholic traditional and contemporary teachings concerning persons with disabilities, particularly as the topic relates to sainthood and official church teachings on disability. The connection between disability and sainthood among Catholics represents a revealing dichotomy within our culture; disabled people are seen as holy and exemplary on the one hand and dependent and lesser-than on the other hand. While much of the previous literature on Catholicism and disability has emphasized the abusive elements in the church history, James addresses the theoretical construction of sainthood as it relates to disability in both positive and negative senses. James also discusses broader implications for the status of persons with disabilities and those who give care to persons with disabilities as ethical exemplars who contribute to the moral ecology of their communities.

In Chapter 10, Amy T. Wilson and Kirk Van Gilder dissect the positives and negatives associated with Christian missionary work aimed at both proselytizing a religious viewpoint and offering service to people living with a variety of disability conditions. Over the centuries, church leaders discovered that some cultures excluded their disabled population from social services normally made available to their able-bodied citizenry and responded by building mission-based schools, rehabilitation centers, churches, and health centers to address perceived marginalization. What are the negative effects of establishing mission projects in poor communities on the lives of people with disabilities? Wilson and Van Gilder suggest best practices for Christian missions when supporting people with disabilities in developing countries and offer concrete examples to support their claims.

It is important to stress that Wilson and Van Gilder neither endorse a particular religious or denominational position nor accept traditional taken-for-granted missionary perspectives. Rather, they offer a critical analysis of the strengths and weaknesses associated with historical missionary interaction with disabled communities in developing countries, while incorporating constructive suggestions for improvement.

In the final chapter of the book, Amos Yong incorporates traditional approaches to philosophy of religion with a perspective that includes key themes in disability studies, rethinking issues in epistemology, theodicy, and questions of death/afterlife as they relate and are relevant to people with disabilities. Yong demonstrates how disability perspectives have been noticeably absent in even the most recent discussions in the philosophy of religion, and how integrating disability perspectives fosters critical revision of basic questions and taken-for-granted assumptions in the field. In addition, Yong addresses how disability perspectives might play an important role in integrating philosophy and philosophy of religion into the concrete experiences of everyday life.

CHAPTER 7

Performance of Muslim Daily Prayer by Physically Disabled Practitioners

Arseli Dokumaci

Disability is the unorthodox made flesh, refusing to be normalized, neutralized, homogenized... The cripple before the stairs, the blind person before the printed page, the deaf person before the radio, the amputee before the typewriter, and the dwarf before the counter are all proof that the myriad structures and practices of material, daily life enforce the cultural standard of a universal subject with a narrow range of corporeal variation. (Thomson 1996: 24)

N̄amaz is the Muslim prayer that has to be practiced five times a day. It has a rigidly defined choreography; its time and space are strictly demarcated; there are certain rules regarding the body of its practitioner. The focus of this chapter is *namaz* and its material aspects.

Marcel Mauss (1909) launches his analysis of prayer with a critique of previous study and claims that these attempts have underestimated its single most important aspect—that is, its efficacy. Prayer's efficacy is related not only to content but also to form based on norms of time, place, and posture, which practitioners consciously or unconsciously adopt (Mauss 1909: 34). Mauss suggests that prayer is neither an event that is beyond human comprehension nor a text that one can decipher. Rather, prayer is first and foremost an institution the material practices of which can be studied through abstraction. Because of its particular qualities, *namaz* could be considered an exemplar of prayer as it is conceptualized by Mauss.

Thompson's quotation and Mauss's theoretical perspective regarding prayer highlight two important issues. First, Thompson describes disability as the materialization of divergence. Second, Mauss delineates prayer as an efficacious social phenomenon. However, once disability is seen as embodiment of the unorthodox and prayer as an institution that becomes such through embodied practices, then relevance appears between the two and spurs a simple question: How does the disabled body perform prayer? In this context, it is important to delineate what is meant by prayer or disability. Mauss's interpretation of prayer is adopted in the context of Islam with emphasis on *namaz* in the Turkish context. Turkey is a secular state and has a predominantly Muslim population that comes from different interpretive traditions with different levels of commitments. In this heterogeneous landscape, *namaz* plays a major role in maintaining a shared discursive framework and in binding the social dividing lines opened up by that landscape[1] (Henkel 2005). The primary religious references utilized are the Koran (English translations) and *İlmihal*[2] published by The Presidency of Religious Affairs of the Republic of Turkey (2004).

For purposes of this chapter, the topic of *namaz* as performed in Turkey is confined to its material performances by practitioners who have rheumatoid arthritis (RA)-related disabilities. RA is a chronic inflammatory condition of the joints that is associated with pain and swelling. Joint tissues may in time become permanently damaged, resulting in progressive disability (Newman et al. 1995; Verbrugge and Juarez 2001). Concentration on disability related to RA is salient in that the disabilities associated with RA may be at odds with the range of motion and postures required for performing *namaz*.

Performance of *Namaz* as it is Prescribed by the Rule of Conduct

According to Islamic rule, a practitioner cannot embark on *namaz* until certain rituals have been performed. These rituals pertain to the time and place of *namaz* as well as to the body of the practitioner. There are five mandatory daily prayers, and each must be performed within a specific time frame. The space for *namaz* must meet the cleanliness codes. The body must be oriented toward Mecca without any person or object blocking it. Rigorous rules about clothing and exposed body parts must be observed. Of all these prerequisites, however, *abdest* is the most intricate. *Abdest* is defined by the code as the duty reinstating the state of cleanliness, and is central to the Islamic practice of *namaz*.

The code designates three types of *abdest* that should be performed depending on the level of bodily contamination and accessibility to water. The focus of this chapter is the lesser *abdest*, the most practiced one. The formula for this *abdest* is described in the Koran as follows: "Believers, when you rise to pray wash your faces and your hands as far as the elbow, and wipe your heads and your feet to the ankle" (5: 6).[3] In addition to the four main acts ordained in this verse, in other religious resources *abdest* involves several other recommended acts. Some of these are as follows: Repeating each act three times; starting always with the right instead of the left; rinsing the mouth; cleaning the nostrils with water; wiping the earlobes with wetted forefingers (cleaning inside the ear) and wiping outside of the lobe with the thumb; and letting the water run through the fingers of the hand and toes of the feet. There are certain instances (such as calls of nature, deep sleep, light bleeding) that following *abdest* would violate it and require its repetition.

Once *abdest* is completed with completion of all rituals and requirements, *namaz* may begin. The basic unit of *namaz* is called *rekàt*. It is a series of ritual actions accompanied by recitations of verses from the Koran in Arabic. There are two *rekàts* in the morning, four at noon and late afternoon, three at sunset, and four at night prayers. Below is the formula for a single *rekàt* as in the order it is given in *Ilmihal* (The Presidency of Religious Affairs of the Republic of Turkey, 2004):

1. *Kıyam* (Stand with the feet slightly apart, raise the arms to the level of ears with palms facing forward, fingers aligned with each other while the thumb is pointing to the ear).
2. Retain the standing position but change the position of the hands either by clasping them on the chest or waist or placing them at the sides.
3. *Rükû* (The feet are kept as they are while one bows from the waist. Palms are placed on the knees. The back should be parallel to the ground.)
4. Rise up to the standing position again.
5. *Secde* (Prostration, done twice during each *rekàt* by kneeling down on the floor from the standing position. First the forehead, then the hands, and then the face should touch the ground).
6. *Celse* (Seated position while standing on legs and feet; done between the two prostrating positions. To continue to the next *rekàt*, the practitioner should rise back to *kıyam* after the second prostration by placing hands on knees. When performing the

last *rekàt* in *na:naz* (when in *celse*) the head is held loosely, then turned right and left as far as possible.

The first *rekàt* and following ones have some slight variations, but the main movements remain as described. Throughout the performance of *namaz*, communicating with the outside world, making movement that is not part of the choreography, and uttering any sound other than the recitations are strictly forbidden. Should any occur, the *rek'at* must be repeated.

The prescribed formulas for *abdest* and *namaz* require a functional body that can kneel down, stand up, lie prostrate, and raise arms. However, any of these positions and movements present problems for a person with RA disabilities. The question is raised: Does the rule of conduct presuppose a community of practitioners who are all nondisabled?

Namaz and the Alleviations for "The Disabled"

Rispler-Chaim (2007) and Bazna and Hatab (2005) examined the ways that canonical sources of Islam (primarily the Koran) address disability. Both authors concurred that disability, as a generic term (embracing all persons with disabilities), is not found in these texts. On the basis of her examination of the *fiqh* (Islamic jurisprudence), Rispler-Chaim (2007) suggests that the terms *marid* (sick person) and *marad* (disease) might actually qualify as broader terms to include both illness and disability (Rispler-Chaim 2007: 5). It is therefore reasonable to translate verses in the Koran that use variations of "the sick" as inclusive of people with disabilities. Most of these verses concern the five pillars of Islam that are demarcated as the main religious duties of a Muslim. For example, the previously quoted verse referring to *abdest* continues as follows:

> But if you are sick...take some clean sand and rub your faces and your hands with it. God does not wish to burden you; He seeks only to purify you and to perfect His favor to you, so that you may give thanks. (5: 6)

In reference to the fasting, required during the month of Ramadan, the verse states:

> But he who is ill...shall fast a similar number of days later on. God desires your well-being, not your discomfort. He desires you to fast the whole month so that you may magnify God and render thanks to Him for giving you His guidance. (2: 183)

For the practitioners having difficulty during *namaz*, it is written that

> In the creation of the heavens and the earth, and in the alternation of night and day, there are signs for men of sense; those that remember God when standing, sitting and lying down, and reflect on the creation of the heavens and the earth...(3: 191)

Two main emphases characterize these different verses: First is that no adherent is exhorted to perform the duties in the way they are described for the general population, when their physical condition prevents it. Second is that while there is almost never a total exemption[4] of "the sick" from these duties (Bazna and Hatab 2005: 25; Rispler-Chaim 2007: 26), there are different degrees of alleviation depending on one's capabilities. For instance, when unable to do the movements, the practitioner may reduce them to gestures or even to intentions of the heart (Glassé and Smith 2003: 400). Yet everyone is responsible for performing their duties whether they are healthy or not.

> ...God measures the night and the day. He knows that you cannot count the length of the vigil, and turns to you mercifully. Recite from the Koran as many verses as you are able; He knows that among you there are sick men...Recite from it, then, as many verses as you are able. (73: 20)

This and other verses are important because of the message that they give to "the sick." This message requires that "the sick" do "whatever they can within their power" (Bazna and Hatab 2005: 12), bending down, standing, moving, prostrating as deeply as possible, to the best of their ability (Rispler-Chaim 2007). The rule appears to leave the decision about modification of *namaz* to the believer. At the same time it asks for the practitioner's best effort. This reliance on interpretation is characteristic of the Koran's aim to guide rather than to ordain absolutes. The hermeneutic process regarding the Koran itself has been the subject of much study and is beyond the scope of this chapter. This chapter does, however, provide a unique interpretive approach that encourages the disabled practitioner to evaluate his or her particular embodiment. Cases such as severe stroke, or lost consciousness, or paralysis allow for an easy adherence to the alternative formulas demarcated for "the sick." Disability, however, has a myriad of complex and not always visible forms and levels of physical impediment not necessarily defined as "sickness." Disability may be congenital or acquired; may be gradual or sudden, may involve pain or not; may remit or be persistent; may affect different aspects of participation in life (for instance, participation in eating in cases of diabetes; or movement in cases of arthritis). Given this diversity, there are experiences of disability where self-evaluation of embodiment could become complicated.

Performance of *Namaz* by Physically Disabled Practitioners

Ten people who had RA-related disabilities were recruited through a Rheumatology clinic in Istanbul, Turkey. Participants were interviewed in their homes and asked how disability was affecting their everyday lives and whether they used any alternative methods to complete activities of daily living during disease exacerbation. Participation in religious duties was one of the topics covered during the interviews. Practicing Muslims were asked about how they performed the duty of *namaz* in particular. At the conclusion of the interviews, I requested them to do a set of daily tasks (which ranged from the actions included in cooking to dressing and performing *namaz*) in front of a video camera. Out of ten, three participants were practicing Muslims while the others either did not follow any religious belief or were Muslims who rarely performed ritual duties.

D.D. is a 62-year-old male who has had RA for 30 years. He is retired and living with his wife and two sons on the outskirts of İstanbul. Some of his daily adaptations include grabbing the faucet, sink, and the doorknob to bend down and stand up when using the traditional Turkish squatting toilet and taking short breaks to rest while doing strenuous activities such as gardening, walking, and shopping for groceries. When interviewed about the performance of *namaz* and *abdest*, he gave the following answers:

I: Can you perform *namaz*?
D.D.: Sure.
I: Do you prefer to do it by sitting or standing?
D.D.: No, never by sitting.
I: Are you able to prostrate, sit, and stand up with ease?
D.D.: Not at all but I force myself.
I: Why do you prefer to perform *namaz* standing?
D.D.: It's a matter of principle. Sitting, for me, means giving up on everything. What will I do then, be completely immobile? Use it or lose it! I do not want to lose it. I have to use my body. I need my body in the future. Let me show you how I perform *namaz*.

The participant stood up from the sofa with difficulty by pushing himself up and by using his arms to support his body. In order to prostrate, he first placed his right knee on the floor, while his left foot was slightly bent backwards. In the meantime, his right arm was straight as a pole fixed on the ground supporting his whole body.

> D.D.: I still try to prostrate, otherwise I might end up bedridden! Everybody is frustrated with me and they think that what I do is torture to myself! Then, I ask them: How do you expect me to quit doing these things? And when time comes for me to stand up from *secde*, I extend my right arm to the ground, make a firm fist with my hand and then I let all my weight on that arm and stand up.

While standing, he moved his left knee backwards slightly and kept the right knee bent. The right arm was positioned exactly in the way he described above. His left arm was bent backwards, and it was holding his back while he was standing up. In the end, he managed to stand up but while watching him perform *namaz*, it struck me that he was undergoing enormous pain and difficulty.

> D.D.: (Referring to the way he stood up) I always hold my knees very firmly with my hands while standing up. The knees remain in my palm. Particularly the left one, as it is more painful.
>
> I: Do you fulfill all the five prayers without exception?
>
> D.D.: Of course.
>
> I: Do you have stiffness in early morning when you are supposed to perform the first *namaz* of the day?
>
> D.D.: Yes I have pain, but I try ignoring it.
>
> I: Do you then perform *namaz* despite stiffness?
>
> D.D.: Yes sure, I perform all my duties. Missing any of them is out of the question.
>
> I: How do you perform *abdest*?
>
> D.D.: I find my ways around. For example, I couldn't move my left leg the other day. It was completely stiff. However, my bathroom is quite narrow so what I did was: I leaned back on the wall, then I grabbed the fabric of my trousers with both hands and lifted my leg up bit by bit until it reached the sink. Then, I put it there as if it were an object. Nobody knows about this incident, even my sons who share the same house with me! After that, the same leg was sizzling with pain during *namaz*. But as I told you before, I took support from my arms and forced myself up and down. I was able to fulfill my duty even that day.
>
> I: When you have difficulty, do you ask for help from your family or friends?

D.D.: Never ever, God forbid! That's precisely what I do not want to do, that's the reason why I force myself to do these things. What do you expect me to do? Ask my son to come and wash my feet?! These days, nobody should be awaiting help from others; it is not likely that somebody would come and give you a hand!

A.A. is 33-year-old male who has had RA for six years. He works full-time and lives with his mother and two sisters in the suburbs of Istanbul. He complained about having knee and ankle pain that caused him difficulty walking, standing up, and taking the bus to go to work every day. But he added that despite all these hardships, he would try to hide his disabilities, particularly in public spaces. His mother shared the same concerns about public image, as she strictly reminded me not to reveal her son's identity, believing that being referred to as disabled might not be good for her son's future prospects of marriage. I asked him about performing *namaz*, particularly at Friday services.

I: Do you have difficulties performing *namaz*?
A.A.: I do but, even so I go to Friday services every week. For example, when it is time to prostrate, I have to push myself forward as if I am falling. Because bending is almost impossible for me as my knees are pretty swollen and painful. Even when I am sitting on a sofa, as in the way I do now, I just extend my feet like this without ever fully bending them. My friends who know my situation suggest that I use a chair. But to be honest if I do that, I am worried that people might have a wrong idea about me.
I: Do you use a chair when praying alone at home then?
A.A.: (after a moment of silence) Not really...I still force myself to do it, as if it were a practice for me to get ready for the Friday services. It is also too hard for me to accept that I need a chair. I always think I am a young guy in good shape and that I should be able to do these things. I tend to see my illness like a flu or a cold that will vanish at some point. And the longer it stays, the more frustrated I become. One more activity that I cannot do as easily as I did before is a huge disappointment for me. I do not want to be there...
U.S. is 60-year-old woman with a five-year history of RA. She is an upper middle class housewife living with her husband and caretaker in a central district in Istanbul. She experiences pain and limitations of mobility in her knee joints.
U.S.: Can you see that I have pain doing this (referring to *celse*)? This is the position that is sort of a problem for me. I cannot bend my feet backwards. (While standing up she takes support by putting both of

her hands on the ground first and forces herself up. This movement indicates that it wasn't any easier for her to stand up either).

I: Do you have difficulty standing?

U.S.: No not really, I am good at it. It is only the sitting position (*celse*) that is difficult from time to time like today. But I can handle it. I even went all the way to Mecca like this and fulfilled my *Hajj* (pilgrimage) duty—without taking my weekly injections with me.

I: How did you perform *namaz* during *hajj*?

U.S.: I took a portable chair, and carried it around with me. I took it because you have to pray almost continuously during *hajj*.

I: Did you have any pain more than usual because of the physical challenges during *Hajj*?

U.S.: No, not really. Not until the last two days actually. But then I took some painkillers, and God has given me vigor to finish my duty with success.

These responses regarding *namaz* were part of a larger inquiry into other activities of daily life such as dressing, personal care, transportation, cooking, acquiring food and basic needs, and doing housework. Even though excerpts of interviews in this chapter are limited to *namaz*, the analysis will include reference to other activities of daily living in order to better communicate the material aspects of *namaz* as part of the materiality surrounding daily life.[5] Instead of receiving external help or avoiding activities altogether, most participants forced themselves to complete their basic daily tasks by way of adaptations even though forcing caused pain. The individual mechanisms for adaptation of daily activities can be considered in three categories: (a) using different composites of functional movements when the set of movements that a task required included any of their actively inflamed or previously damaged joints (such as wearing a shirt as a jumper in order to avoid using buttons), (b) manipulating the tools and space involved in tasks in order to fulfill them by minimizing the workload of limited joints (for instance, standing up from the squatting position by means of grabbing faucets and doorknobs), (c) taking longer durations to complete tasks and taking breaks throughout performances (such as shopping or gardening by pausing in between and spreading the activity over a longer period of time). In the particular case of *namaz*-performance, the participants' responses were reflective of these adaptations, and it is these that generate theoretical consideration. While performing *namaz*, the participants tended not to use the alternative methods outlined for "the sick" by the Islamic rule of conduct. Instead they employed the "standard" method for the abled by developing their own adaptations and alternatives as they did for their other daily activities. The religious commitment of the participants could have been influencing their adherence to practicing *namaz* with such tenacity. However, my perception was that the participants' persistence to perform other daily tasks was of equal intensity.

The Calculus of Disability

People are not born with RA-related disabilities but acquire them later in life in a process styled disablement (Verbrugge and Jette 1994). This body in disablement, to appropriate Susan Sontag's words (2001), "holds dual citizenship" in the kingdoms of abled and disabled and eventually becomes the resident of "that other place" (Sontag 2001: 3). However, this transitory phase does not occur haphazardly. It is accompanied by another phase that can be termed a process of re-education—or perhaps a recalibration—where the changing states of the body are continuously matched with the demands of its surroundings. While training themselves, bodies in disablement modify the "what, how, how long and how often" of their everyday lives in meticulous efforts (Verbrugge and Jette 1994: 9). In the way that a child learns to be "abled" throughout locomotor development, the person in disablement develops adapted gestures and behaviors while learning to be "less abled." Given the progressive nature of disablement process, people actually living through it may not be in a position to tell whether they are still abled or have already become disabled.[6] It is also difficult for them to determine which "Kingdom" they reside in, since they adapt to their disabilities, learning to live with and even hide them. The process of disablement, apart from being a model to understand the participants' responses here, constitutes another major concern of this study that may pose the most important questions: At what point of disablement, as R. G. A. Williams (1979) posits, does the "calculus" of disability begin? On what basis are some bodies called abled and some disabled?

When ability and disability are regarded merely in somatic terms, it might not be easy to find any formal line separating the two.[7] However, the discourse surrounding disability still forces itself no matter how resistant corporeal experiences may be. Williams (1979) writes: "[T]he non-disabled level..., tends to be a minimum level of production beyond which any activity may receive help. This is where the calculus begins" (Williams 1979: 36). The tacit line separating the abled from the disabled here is indexed to one's autonomous contribution to the socioeconomic fabric of a community. Moving beyond Williams' perspective, I posit that the very socioeconomic fabric of a community is woven by quotidian practices of bodies regardless of their physical ability.

Bruno Latour (2000) asserts that the material world around us and the daily tasks we perform do not "reflect" social relations, but they themselves "make" those relations. This approach to the materiality of everyday life experience is very close to Mauss's description of prayer as an institutionalized social force that manifests through its material practices. In fact, the perspectives of Mauss and Latour are so close that one might take their assertions a step further and postulate that quotidian activities also have a sense of choreography, even if they are not as strictly prescribed as the choreography of prayer. *Abdest*, *kıyam*, *rükû*, *secde*, or *celse* in *namaz* all have predefined gestures. Similarly, the diameter of a plastic bottle top we loosen, the number of steel stairs we walk down to reach the subway, the weight and shape of a ceramic mug we lift to have a sip of coffee, all of these daily tasks shape our material being in the world. There is a certain grip and strength needed to open a bottle, or to turn a faucet, and an exact time to cross the street during the green light phase. Hence, these everyday mathematics, calculations, textures, and degrees that surround us elicit predefined gestures that, considered on the level of physical norms, may not differ from those typical tasks performed for *namaz*. The social fabric of a community is manifest through embodied formulas, timings, textures, weights. The social world needs fingers to grip, hands to hold, elbows to carry, knees to bend, feet to walk, arms to reach, eyes to see, ears to hear, or in other words, functional bodies to perform predefined social gestures. A non-disabled body then is a body that can respond to the gestures evoked by the physicality of its surroundings.

The ability to perform appropriate gestures does not imply that disability simply arises out of bad environmental design. Even when a body is physically unable to manage elements of the physical world, a series of interventions is often introduced, whether adaptive environments or assistive devices, which aim to correct this "mismatch" between the world and the body. While accessibility is an important issue in itself, it is the very intention to fix the "mismatch" that serves to solidify the preordained social fabric. The performance of bodies could be quite distinctive, to the extent that they could include multiple physical variations. For example, even with the strict formula of *namaz*, one individual performance might not exactly coincide with the next individual performance. However, these material practices, from the moment they are ritualized or formalized, cease to be individual performances and are elevated to the status of social forces (Mauss 1909: 37). As such, routines of everyday life performed by a body in its unique ways cease being individual from the moment they give form to a certain social imposition. Routine everyday life activities enacted by individual bodies in their unique manner cease being merely individual performances but are infused by social imposition and convention. Bodies appear able to the extent that they can conform to preordained social routines and appear disabled to the extent that they cannot conform to social routine. Because of internalizing social impositions, disabled people may feel compelled to perform *namaz* in the same way that everyone else is performing *namaz*, compelled to embody the same material gestures that everyone else is embodying, even to the degree that such efforts result in physical pain and discomfort. The ability to wash one's feet during *abdest* without asking for help, the capacity to attend communal prayers without using a chair, or the performance of any taken-for-granted material gesture is where the calculus of disability begins to manifest itself.

The routine activities of daily life performed with an "ordinary sense of free and spontaneous movements" often become complicated "calculated efforts" for many people with physical limitations (Leder 1990: 36). Bodies with RA find themselves in a series of negotiations that may not even rise to the level of conscious awareness for bodies without RA. These calculated negotiations lead people with RA to question more than prejudicial social attitudes regarding disability or the level of appropriate material and social accommodations for the disabled. Disabled bodies first and foremost question the given-ness of a material order and the social assumption that they should accommodate to it even when it results in excessive pain and discomfort. The *unorthodox* practices of bodies with RA, while still contributing to a certain social fabric, at the same time become interrogators of that very fabric. Disabled bodies are in constant negotiation with their material surroundings. They face a plethora of questions (such as the number of stairs going up or down, the weight of a spoon, the height of a sink) rarely asked by the typical person climbing stairs, eating lunch, performing *abdest*, buttoning a shirt, or cutting vegetables. The physically disabled body is more than a malleable body in constant adaptation mode. It is also a body that daringly interrogates the ordinariness of materiality and the routine social arrangements and material gestures they invoke. As Tobin Siebers (2001) articulates, bodies are "capable of influencing" as well as "transforming the social languages" within which they act (Siebers 2001: 68). They are stubborn. Disabled bodies are keenly aware that their physical selves determine their perception of and negotiation with the material and social world. These negotiations, like their bodies, are often non-conforming and disclose new social categories, material expressions, and models of thinking and being, even as they strive to accommodate to the material and social worlds in which they find themselves participating.

Notes

1. Henkel (2005: 492) also draws attention to the remarkable stability of the format of *namaz* in contemporary Turkey. This is important in that the Koran, despite laying down the basic movements of *namaz*, does not by itself give precise definition of it (Mohammed 1999). It is only through the teachings of Muhammad that *namaz* is tied to a strict formula, which still may have slight variations in different denominations.
2. Henkel compares Muslim *ilmihals* to Christian catechisms and finds that they are somewhat similar with regard to basic tenets of the religious conduct. She also draws attention to their popularity in the later nineteenth century in the Ottoman/Turkish context where they served an important role in the standardization of Islamic practice (Henkel 2005: 504).
3. All quotations from the Koran are from its English translation by N. J. Dawood. The numbers following each verse in parentheses locate the verses in the Koran where the first number refers to the chapter (*sûre*) and the second one indicates its place within the chapter (*âyet*).
4. The only instance where one is totally exempted from these duties is in the cases of mental disabilities and loss of consciousness.
5. The focus of this study involves the materiality of *namaz*. The spiritual elements of *namaz* are very important but will not be addressed in this study.
6. The empirical results of this research indicate that people do not decide about their level of ability or disability solely by considering their physical status.
7. I am here referring only to experience of body, not the definition of its physicality as it is used in medical contexts.

References

Bazna, M. S., & Hatab, T. A. (2005). Disability in the Qur'an: The Islamic alternative to defining, viewing, and relating to disability. *Journal of Religion, Disability & Health 9*(1), 5–27. DOI: 10.1300/J095v09n01_02

Dawood, N. J. (2000). *The Koran,* 7th Rev. ed. London, UK: Penguin.

Glassé, C., & Smith, H. (Eds.). (2003). *The New Encyclopedia of Islam.* California: AltaMira Press.

Henkel, H. (2005). Between belief and unbelief lies the performance of salat: Meaning and efficacy of a Muslim ritual. *Journal of Royal Anthropological Institute 11*, 487–507. DOI: 10.1111/j.1467-9655.2005.00247.x

Latour, B. (2000). The Berlin key. In P. M. Graves-Brown (Ed.), *Matter, Materiality and Modern Culture* (pp. 10–21). New York, NY: Routledge.

Leder, D. (1990). *The Absent Body*. Chicago, IL: Chicago University Press.

Mauss, M. [1909] (2003). *On Prayer*. W. S. F Pickering (Ed). New York, NY: Berghahn.

Mohammed, K. (1999). The foundation of Muslim prayer. *Medieval Encounters 5*(1), 17–28. DOI:10.1163/157006799X00231

Newman, S. P., Fitzpatrick, R., Revenson, A. T., et al. (Eds.) (1995). *Understanding Rheumatoid Arthritis*. New York, NY: Routledge.

Rispler-Chaim, V. (2007). *Disability in Islamic Law*. Dordrecht: Springer.

Siebers, T. (2001). Disability in theory: From social constructionism to the new realism of the body. *American Literary History 13*(4), 737–754. DOI: 10.1093/alh/13.4.737

Sontag, S. (2001). *Illness as Metaphor and AIDS and its Metaphors*. New York, NY: Picador.

The Presidency of Religious Affairs of the Republic of Turkey. (2004). *İlmihal 1 İman ve İbadetler*. Ankara, Turkey: The Presidency of Religious Affairs. Last retrieved 2009 from www.diyanet.gov.tr/turkish/basiliyayin/webkutuplistel. asp?yid=7<http://www.diyanet.gov.tr/turkish/basiliyayin/webkutuplistel. asp?yid=7><http://www.diyanet.gov.tr/turkish/basiliyayin/webkutuplistel. asp?yid=7>

Thomson, R. G. (1996). *Extraordinary Bodies: Figuring Physical Disability in American Culture and Literature*. New York, NY: Columbia University Press.

Verbrugge, L. M., & Jette, A. M. (1994). The disablement process. *Social Science Medicine 2*(1), 1–14. DOI:10.1016/0277-9536(94)90294-1

Verbrugge, L. M., & Juarez, L. (2001). Profile of arthritis disability: II. *Arthritis Care & Research 55*(1), 102–113. DOI:10.1002/art.21694

Williams, R. G. A. (1979). Theories and measurement in disability. *Epidemiology and Community Health 33*, 32–47. DOI:10.1016/0277-9536(95)80009-9

CHAPTER 8

Religious Metaphors as a Justification for Eugenic Control: A Historical Analysis

*Gerald V. O'Brien and
Autumn Molinari*

In conjunction with efforts to complete the mapping of the Human Genome, writings that detail the prospective benefits or fears that may accompany genetic innovations have been plentiful in popular literature and other media. Advocates and opponents of such innovations, as well as more neutral observers, have employed numerous metaphoric themes in order to describe issues such as genetic engineering and testing, therapeutic human cloning, and DNA testing. While such metaphors provide an important means of describing technology that few people fully understand in nontechnical language, they also carry explicit or implied meanings related to how we think about and the value accorded to persons with disabilities as well as other "nonnormative" populations.

Religious rhetoric and concepts have been especially prevalent in both contemporary and historical discussions related to eugenics and bioethics. The perception that eugenics is a hubristic enterprise remains in contemporary discussions of new genetic technology. Decades before the initiation of the Human Genome Project, Charles Frankel (1974) wrote that

> There hovers about biomedicine the scent of ancient taboos broken, of entry into forbidden territory. It stirs to life fears that go back to the oldest myths in our civilization, and revives religious attitudes about sin,

trespass, and tinkering with the delicate harmonies of the Creation that lie just below the level of consciousness even in agnostics and atheists. (Charles Frankle 1974: 29)

As early as 1965 Philip Abelson described future genetic research as "fruit from the tree of knowledge" (Abelson 1965: 251), and more recently Jonathon Cohen contended (1999) that in engaging in genetic research "we have picked of the tempting fruit of the tree of genetic knowledge" (Cohen 1999: 8). A book on cloning is titled *Remaking Eden* (Silver 1997), the Genome Project itself has been called a "quest for the Holy Grail," and the computer program that generates the information for the Project is called "GENESIS" (Nelkin and Tancredi 1989: 13–14). A host of writers have described genetic research as a "Promethean" effort or as "Playing God" (Goodfield 1977; Howard and Rifkin 1977), and an article on genetic research published in the *Utne Reader* was titled "God in a Labcoat" (Rifkin 1998). Nelkin and Lindee noted that, in many ways, our genes have "assumed a cultural meaning similar to that of the Biblical soul" (Nelkin and Lindee 1995: 40). In their book *The DNA Mystique*, these authors provide additional examples of the application of religious metaphors and symbols within the context of contemporary genetic debates.

What is especially intriguing about these metaphors is that similar rhetoric was widely used in the past to describe or advance schemes of controlled human breeding. Some advocates of eugenics in the United States and elsewhere a century ago invoked religion as a conceptual metaphor against which eugenics could best be understood. Importantly, the cultural meaning of disability, and especially mental disability, has often been played out against the backdrop of this debate.

This chapter will describe the employment of religious rhetoric and concepts in both the United States and Nazi Germany within the context of eugenic writings as a means of framing schemes of controlled human breeding that primarily pertained to persons with disabilities. As an integral aspect of modern cultures, Western religion has often served as an important means of fostering interpersonal bonding, providing hope, direction, and meaning to people, helping to develop a communal sense of morality, and demarcating normative social behavior. At times, however, mainstream religious precepts have also served to rationalize the separation of certain subgroups from the community at large, justify social control measures, and coerce people to engage in behaviors that run contrary to their own personal sense of right and wrong.

Because of its central role in society, it is not surprising that religious and spiritual symbols and terminology have frequently been invoked metaphorically. The leaders of social movements frequently attempt to exploit such symbols, to frame their cause as a religious or spiritual one, or at least present it as compatible with mainstream religious teachings. Especially important in eugenics, in many cases religious symbolism or rhetoric will be directly incorporated within propaganda related to the movement and its goals. Efforts may also be made by movement leaders to co-opt religious leaders or networks to communicate issues or proposals, or highlight the moral or spiritual foundation of the movement (O'Brien 2009).

Similarly, supporters of social control measures often argue that they advocate such actions in part because they are in the best interests of the target group members themselves. Often, this paternalistic regard for victims easily coexists alongside concerns that the group is a threatening force that needs to be controlled for the protection of society. Altruistic arguments as a rationale for social control are included in this chapter for several reasons. First, such altruism is often described within a religious context. Control measures may be presented as a form of "Christian love," charity, or even sacrifice on the part of those who enforce measures of social control. Second, the patronizing attitude that is central to the altruistic metaphor is closely tied to the language of mainstream Christianity. The perception that God is a kindly but firm parent figure who lovingly guides and admonishes us is very similar to the way in which authoritarian institutions and groups often present themselves. Forms of social control such as imperialism, the forced acculturation of indigenous populations, and even slavery were frequently justified based on altruistic arguments. As we shall see below, so have eugenic policies such as sterilization, forced institutionalization, and even euthanasia.

A Brief Introduction to Historical Eugenics

A thorough description of the ideological, political, and scientific foundations of eugenics is beyond the scope of this chapter. However, a brief overview of the important factors that fostered the movements in the United States and Germany is important to contextualizing the issue. While eugenic proposals were present in the writings of Plato and many other early Utopian writers (Plato 1986), the seeds for the "eugenic alarm era" (1900–1930) in the United States were planted during the nineteenth century. England's Sir Francis Galton was undoubtedly the most important early influence for later eugenicists. Galton believed that most traits, both positive and negative, were hereditary in nature. He contended that humans could direct their own evolutionary course by fostering the procreation of the "most fit" members of the community (positive eugenics), while at the same time diminishing the fecundity of the "least fit" (negative eugenics) (Galton 1870, 1904, 1907, 1996). Other nineteenth-century figures whose writings influenced later eugenicists included population theorist Thomas Malthus, Herbert Spencer, the leading social Darwinism of the time, and early racial anthropologists such as Arthur de Gobineau and Houston Stewart Chamberlain (Gould 1981).

Eugenics became an important social movement in the United States shortly after 1900. Due in large part to widespread fears of the rapid growth of the "moron" and "criminalistic" elements of the population, an ideologically eclectic cadre of physicians, psychologists, zoologists, institutional administrators, and other professionals called for a national program of negative eugenics. American eugenicists embraced a hereditarian view of social problems such as poverty, feeblemindedness, crime, and sexual immorality. These problems, they argued, were primarily caused by hereditary traits that could not be changed through environmental or cultural influences. Importantly, the cause of the eugenicists was bolstered by the rediscovery of Mendel's laws of heredity in 1900 (Kevles 1985).

Leaders of the movement contended that the "unfit" segments of the population were propagating much more quickly than the "fit" groups, and would eventually take over society unless their birth rate was restricted. Eugenic proponents were successful in the initiation of compulsory sterilization programs and restrictive marriage laws in many states, as well as the large-scale development of institutions for the feebleminded, epileptic, and other "dysgenic"—or undesirable—populations (Kevles 1985; O'Brien 1999; Reilly 1991; Trent 1994). During the 1920s, they also joined forces with restrictive immigration proponents to limit the immigration of persons from countries that were seen as producing large numbers of "undesirable" immigrants (Ludmerer 1972; O'Brien 2003a).

The eugenic alarm era in the United States ended during the 1930s, although the American movement had a substantial influence on the Nazi eugenic programs (Kühl 1994). In their own efforts to purify the race of "degenerate genes," the Nazis instituted an involuntary sterilization program (modeled after those in the United States) in 1933, developed the 1935 Nuremberg Marriage Laws, and beginning in 1939 initiated a formal euthanasia program that eventually killed hundreds of thousands of persons labeled as feebleminded or insane as well as other "useless eaters" (Proctor 1988; Smith 1985). Six German mental institutions were fitted with gas chambers, and thus the primary killing apparatus of the Nazi holocaust were perfected (Aly, Chroust, and Pross 1994).

With public knowledge of the horrors of the holocaust, eugenics came to be closely connected to Nazism, and public interest in the topic therefore waned following World War II. Starting in the 1970s, however, eugenics again gradually came to be regarded as a proper subject for scholarly research and discussion. This changing view was fostered by several issues, including (a) technological innovations that allowed even severely disabled persons to survive to adulthood, and possibly to propagate, (b) the development of new reproductive technologies, such as artificial insemination, (c) the belief that there would in the future be a potential for cloning and genetic engineering to be employed as forms of positive eugenics, and (d) the growth of genetic testing as a precursor to the abortion of "impaired" fetuses. Opponents of new genetic technology often associate these developments with past efforts to advocate the creation of a Utopian society inhabited by "perfect" people. Many supporters of such technology for their part decry these comparisons as simple "fear mongering." As is normally the case in such debates, the truth lies somewhere in the middle.

Eugenicists Employment of Religion and Religious Symbols

The eugenic alarm period has been described by many of the authors of secondary works on the era as a religious endeavor, at least in the eyes of its staunchest advocates (Kevles 1985; O'Brien 1999). Ludmerer, for example, wrote that many eugenicists "came to regard the acceptance of eugenic programs as a religious duty imposed by the theory of evolution, many of them even calling the movement a secular religion" (Ludmerer 1972: 17). This relationship began early. Francis Galton himself wrote that eugenics "must be introduced into the national consciousness as a new religion" (Galton 1904: 5). Eugenics has, Galton continued, "strong claims to become an orthodox religious tenet of the future, for eugenics co-operate with the workings of nature by securing that humanity shall be represented by the fittest races" (Galton 1904: 5). In another work he added that eugenics "ought to find a welcome home in every tolerant religion," since it "extends the function of philanthropy to future generations." Eugenics, he noted, was unlike mainstream religions, however, since it "sternly forbids all forms of sentimental charity that are harmful to the race..." (Galton [1909] 1996:68–70).

American eugenicists followed Galton's lead. Albert Wiggam stated in 1923 that "eugenics means a new religion, new objects of religious endeavor, a new moral code, a new kind of education to our youth, a new conception of many of life's meanings, a new conception of the objectives of social and national life, a new social and political Bible" (Wiggam 1923: 104). Alfred Scott Warthin (1928), the President of the National Association of Physicians, told his audience at the Third Race Betterment Conference that "[o]ld faiths, old superstitions, old beliefs, old emotions" were passing away due to the light of biological research, which was "a new faith" (Warthin 1928: 89).

Most eugenicists understood that their primary goal, directing the course of human breeding, could be viewed as hubristic. They attempted to counter this assertion by contending that their proposals were consistent with divine intent and mainstream Christianity. "God," Leon Whitney wrote in 1926, "loves perfection. This great strain which God or nature developed by the kindly selective process was no doubt much greater than the race from which it sprang and must have been very dear unto God" (Whitney 1926: 4). Wiggam (1923) declared that "had Jesus been among us, he would have been president of the First Eugenics Congress" (Wiggam 1923: 110), and that "[s]cience came not to destroy the great ethical essence of the Bible but to fulfill it" (Wiggam 1923: 111). Another eugenicist added that Jesus "was born into the world without any hereditary taint," and that this physical and mental normality "is what he craved for every other child of God" (Reccord 1918: 381). "It lies within the purpose of God," wrote Samuel Batten (1908), that "every life born into the world should grow up tall and straight and should be clean and pure" (Batten 1908: 245).

In counteracting preservation measures—such as medical and sanitation innovations and poor support—not by killing the unfit, but simply by ensuring that they would not breed, eugenicists contended they were actually serving to keep the stock from becoming polluted in a humane way. According to Walter Hadden, a British physician,

> The world cannot go on deteriorating, and degenerating without ruining the designs of God that man shall aim for the highest things in life. Nowhere can it be found that the Almighty while insisting upon reproduction, insists that it shall be carried on without reason and common sense.... To reach perfection was the constant insistence of Christ. In the Sermon on the Mount, addressing the multitude he said: "Be ye

therefore perfect, even as your Father which is in heaven is perfect."
There is no justification here for perpetuating imperfection, but the contrary. (Hadden 1914: 9)

As the above quote demonstrates, biblical verses, especially the teachings of Jesus, were frequently used as examples to demonstrate that
eugenic measures were in keeping with the principles of Christianity.
Leon Whitney (1926) described the parable of the sower as analogous
to eugenics. A man who sowed good seeds in his field came to find that
weeds also had grown up, the latter being the product of an enemy who
"came and sowed tares among the wheat" while the owner slept. When
harvest came, the wheat was to be gathered and placed into barns, while
the "bad seed" was to be burned to ensure that it would no longer grow.
Whitney concluded that in carrying out this injunction, church leaders
must join forces with eugenicists and "do their part in seeing that the
seed from the human tares does not go over into the next generation"
(Whitney 1926: 16). Another eugenicist noted that Jesus had said that
"I am come that ye may have life, and that ye might have it more abun-
dantly." It was, this writer continued, "higher and more abundant life
that is the eugenic ideal" (Newman 1921: 509).

In his book *The New Decalogue of Science*, Albert Wiggam "proposed to
replace the biblical Ten Commandments with a new scientific decalogue"
that was more in line with contemporary science (Rosen 2004: 130). Wiggam
(1923) noted that eugenics was "simply the projection of the Golden Rule
down the stream of protoplasm." The "biological Golden Rule" would be to
"*[d]o unto both the born and the unborn as you would have both the born and
the unborn do unto you*" (Wiggam 1923: 110–111, italics in original). The
American Eugenics Society also co-opted religious symbolism by printing
a "Eugenics Catechism" that included the primary beliefs of the movement
("Prizes for..." 1926: 48). In her 2004 book *Preaching Eugenics*, Christine
Rosen noted that the medals given to winners of Fitter Families Contests,
which were eugenic competitions held at state and county fairs, included
an inscription from Psalm 16: "Yea, I have a goodly heritage" (Rosen 2004:
111). Rosen contended that the American Eugenics Society purposefully
included Christian symbolism in its eugenics propaganda in part to recruit
religious leaders to support its cause.

Religious rhetoric was often used in eugenic writings to describe the
breeding of "unfit" persons. Dysgenic matings, which presumably fostered the hereditary transmission of "degenerative" characteristics, were
said to be grievous sins against society or a "sacrilege" (MacMurchy
1916: 231, 234; "A New Force..." 1913: 488). Eugenicists frequently

referred to "unfit" persons, and especially the feebleminded, as evil entities or a principle source of evil in the world. Some even described feebleminded persons as an "incubus," or demon spirit (Kostir 1916: 29; Mott 1894: 175). Even prior to the turn of the century, Kate Wells wrote that "(t)he marriage of deaf-mutes is [a] 'physiological sin,' as such crimes have been well termed" (Wells 1897: 305). Warthin (1928) added that "theological terms" provided an apt means of describing eugenics. In speaking of "biological sins," he wrote that "our biologic mission is to carry on this immortal stream of germ plasm," and that any healthy person who refused to bring children into the world was committing an "unpardonable sin" (Warthin 1928: 88).

Lydia De Vilbiss (1914) argued that the belief many had previously held that feebleminded and other "defective" children were the result of divine retribution upon sinful parents was a myth. Nevertheless, she added, such children were indeed the natural result of "ignorance or sin." It was not God, however, who was responsible for the result, but rather the parents, who did not employ eugenic standards when choosing a mate and deciding to have children (De Vilbiss 1914: 554–555). In her book *Race Improvement or Eugenics*, LaReine Baker (1912) called racial degeneration "the scientists' formula for the theologian's 'fall from grace,'" and wrote that the "eugenist does not say that religion, morality, and education are ineffective, he only claims that these great forces should apply to the foundations of society instead of being spent and dissipated in a thousand less important directions" (Baker 1912: 55–56).

Some eugenicists even used religious metaphors and analogies to propose that passive euthanasia might be an acceptable form of eugenics. In discussing a famous Chicago case of infanticide of the Bollinger baby, a supposedly disabled infant, a physician wrote "(t)he human body, we are told, is the temple of the living God." A body like that "of this baby," he continued, "would be a poor receptacle for the indwelling Holy Spirit" ("Was the Doctor Right? . . . " 1916: 24). Foster Kennedy, one of the most well-known American supporters of euthanasia during the eugenic era, noted (1939) that a primary concern of legalizing the measure was that even the severely disabled or comatose had "immortal souls." Kennedy contended that even if this was true, "to release that soul from its misshapen body which only defeats in this world the soul's powers and gifts is surely to exchange, on that soul's behalf, bondage for freedom" (Kennedy 1939: 15).

According to Schwartz (1908–1909: 88), aiding "nature in her task of elimination" was in conjunction with "the best interpretation of Christian ethics" (Schwartz 1908–1909: 88). "It was not God," Huntington and Whitney (1927) added, "who made the defectives. We made them, or our forefathers did. God kills them off, for that is Nature's stern way; we make them by disregarding the laws of heredity, by preserving the weak and imbecile, and by making it easy for defectives to reproduce their kind" (Huntington and Whitney 1927: 136).

Christine Rosen (2004) describes the relationship between the eugenics movement and religious leaders in great depth. According to Rosen, a large number of clerics, especially liberals with a social reform outlook, were very interested in infusing eugenics into their religious theology. Progressivism and its focus on prevention and amelioration of disease and social problems had an important influence in many Protestant churches, and a large number of religious leaders believed that they could help usher in "the Kingdom of God on earth through reform and service."

Ministers and other clerics were especially desirable allies for those in the eugenic movement because of their roles in facilitating marriage bonds. Since an important goal of the movement was to ensure that prospective mates had considered each other's hereditary fitness prior to marriage, and many eugenicists fought for state laws that would restrict marriage among the "unfit," they also realized that the cooperation of those who administered marriages was essential. Even without such legislation, some members of the clergy, led by Walter Sumner (1914), agreed to refuse to marry couples unless they could produce health certificates providing evidence that they did not have a hereditary or communicable disease (also see "Eugenics Supported by the Church" 1912). Many eugenicists, while applauding these ministers for recognizing the importance of eugenic control, were lukewarm in their support of the certificates. This was primarily due to their belief that they would be of limited benefit, since morons would likely procreate whether married or not (Rosen 2004). Popenoe and Johnson suggested that charity given by churches to their poor members should only go to those congregants who refrained from having children (Popenoe and Johnson 1933: 227).

Eugenicists including Charles Davenport and Harry Laughlin called on mainstream churches and their leaders to not only support but also take a leading role in the movement. In 1926 the *Eugenical News* announced that the American Eugenics Society was holding a competition for those preachers who could best incorporate the issue of eugenics into their sermons. This competition, the announcement noted, was "open to any minister, priest, rabbi or student in a theological seminary of any denomination." The Society also formed a "Committee on

Cooperation with Clergymen" ("Committee on Cooperation..." 1925: 68; "Prizes for Sermons..." 1926: 48; Rosen 2004).

Taking after Galton, some eugenicists did call the Catholic Church to task for its celibacy policy. They held that those who were under the policy were presumably physically fit, well-educated, and pious individuals. To deny such prospective parents the right to have children was seen as highly dysgenic. According to Huntington and Whitney,

> We wonder that the Holy Father of the Roman Catholic Church does not go up into the mountain and view his world in the light of eugenics. We should think a farmer either crazy or hopelessly stupid if he continually killed off his best animals and let the poorer do the breeding. Yet that is what religious celibacy, as now practiced, does to the human race. (Huntington and Whitney 1927: 132).

Eugenics and Religion in Nazi Germany

German eugenicists prior to Hitler had employed Galton's conceptualization of eugenics as a religion (Lenz 1924). Writing in *Mein Kampf*, Hitler himself repeatedly used religious rhetoric to bolster his arguments for a program of state-controlled race hygiene. He contended, for example, that "if the fertility of the healthiest bearers of the nationality is...consciously and systematically promoted, the result will be a race which at least will have eliminated the germs of our present physical and hence spiritual decay" (Hitler 1971: 405). The "holiest human right" and "holiest obligation" of the people, he added, was "to see to it that the blood was preserved pure" (Hitler 1971: 402). As was the case with some of the American eugenicists, Hitler contended that a program to control the breeding of humans in order to create a more perfect race was an important way of ensuring that God was presented with the type of humans that He truly deserved, a race that reflected both the presumptive moral and aesthetic features of the deity. It was only by putting "an end to the constant and continuous original sin of racial poisoning," he wrote, that humans could "give the Almighty Creator beings such as He Himself created" (Hitler 1971:402). Likewise, he wrote that if eugenic standards for marriages were set, matrimony could become *an institution which is called upon to produce images of the Lord and not monstrosities halfway between man and ape*" (Hitler 1971:405). Reflecting these statements, a Nazi medical spokesperson argued in 1934 that "hereditary inferior" persons "remind us [more] of animal-like behavior than of the image of God ...." (Thomalia 1934: 127).

Upon coming to power in Germany, control over the breeding practices of the *Volk* became a central feature of Nazi policy. While the Nazis did not feel the need to kowtow to religious authorities in order to obtain sanction for their eugenic programs, they did attempt to show that their policies were not in opposition to the original principles of Christianity. Wilhelm Frick, Reichs minister for the Interior, wrote that it would "be considered an offense against Christian and social charity to allow hereditary defectives to continue to produce offspring [since] this would mean endless suffering to themselves in their kin in this and future generations" (Frick 1934: 36). Another advocate of German eugenics wrote in the same year that "to prevent the birth of valueless life is the true meaning of charitable love" (Thomalia 1934: 140), and Dr. Guett, the German physician who helped write the sterilization law, was quoted in the *New York Times* as saying that Nazi eugenic policies extend the concept of "neighborly love" to future generations ("Sterilization Law..." 1934: 6).

Those race hygienists who were in line with National Socialist thinking frequently noted that our love and concern for the race must supersede the personal feelings one might have for individuals, and that such sympathy was a principle hindrance to eugenic success. Responding to criticism by the Catholic Church over the sterilization policy, one Nazi official defended the Party, arguing that "They call us pagans and heretics, but this one fight in the past years has brought more religion than all theology and all priests together" ("Nazis Tighten Law..." 1935: 1).

The Nazis also appropriated religious language to support their race control policies. They developed, for example, a list of "Ten Commandments for the Choice of a Mate" (Bock 2004: 72), and Nazi leader Martin Bormann proposed a "National Socialist Catechism." Along with other Nazi doctrines, this was to provide a spiritual foundation for German youth, and "gradually supplant the Christian religions." Borman "suggested that some of the Ten Commandments could be merged with the National Socialist Catechism," and he provided examples of specific Commandments, such as "Thou shalt keep thy blood pure" (*Nazi Conspiracy and Aggression: Volume II* 1947: 61, also see Stoddard 1940: 197–200).

As with a number of American eugenicists, many of their German counterparts contended that social Darwinism was not antagonistic but rather complementary to the goals of Christianity. This was a predominant theme, for example, of Nazi propaganda films that were commissioned by the Reich to lend support for their eugenic programs.

My Victims of the Past was one of the Nazi documentary films that championed compulsory sterilization of the "hereditarily disabled." According to Leiser (1974), this film stated that it "was to misapply both Christianity and the laws of nature to nurse mentally 'inferior' criminals in an institution paid for by money 'which we could probably put to better use helping a good many strong, healthy, talented children in our population in their lives and careers.'" "If today," the narration continued, "we artificially reinstate by humane methods the great law of natural selection, then we shall also be paying respect to the law of the Creator and acknowledging His order" (Leiser 1974: 90). The film *Existence without Life* was specifically commissioned by the Nazi Government to proffer support for the euthanasia program. In this movie, "the religious language of mercy and salvation" was repeatedly employed to "call for the killing of disabled people," or, as the Nazis referred to them, "the spiritually dead" (cited in *Selling Murder* 1991).

Unlike in the United States, where eugenics was put forth as a complement to Christianity, in Nazi Germany it came to be viewed, especially during the Nazi era, as a movement beyond mainstream religion. In the totalitarian society that was Hitler's Germany, eugenic measures did not require the support of either the public or clerics, and thus Nazi propagandists did not have to expend a great deal of effort demonstrating that their goals were in keeping with existing religious precepts. While the American movement's relationship to religious authorities was characterized by its attempt to court religious leaders, the Nazis were best exemplified by their public battle with the Catholic Church to force its congregants to abide by the sterilization law and to register potential candidates for the "euthanasia" program. According to Gerhardt Wagener, the Reich Commissar for Public Health, the Hitler government believed that its eugenic legislation "shall remain the prerogative of medical and scientific experts and not of those 'entrusted with observing the processes of the soul.'" Those in the latter category, he noted, were not qualified to make judgments "upon matters affecting hygiene and medicine" (cited in Enderis 1934: 4).

Predominant Christian denominations, Hitler felt, had become corrupted by sentimentality and a belief in the sanctity of even "degenerate" human life. This philosophy was obviously influenced by Nietzsche's writings. A believer in innate caste differences, the German philosopher saw Christianity as a social equalizer, or a vehicle by which the power of the upper classes—and "higher" races—would become corroded by egalitarian doctrines (Nietzsche 1966, 1968, 1969). God's sentimental attachment to man was his undoing, Nietzsche believed, since by embracing the weak and downtrodden, He fostered the degeneration of the species. Thus, the God of contemporary Christianity had become a destroyer rather than a creator. It was therefore important for humans to take matters into their own hands and take responsibility for the creation of the Superman, in part by controlling the breeding practices of the species. In *Twilight of the Idols* (1968), Nietzsche lashed out against Christianity for its support of the "non-bred human being." He said that it represented "the *reaction* against the morality of breeding," and thus stood as the "*anti-Aryan* religion *par excellence*" (Nietzsche 1968: 57–58). Long before Hitler came on the stage, Maximilian Mügge wrote that "[o]ne of the lasting merits of the poet-philosopher Nietzsche is the fact that he has founded a Eugenic Religion, a valuable ally of the Eugenic Science" (Mügge 1909–1910: 184). "To Sir Francis Galton," Mugge continued, "belongs the honour of founding the *Science* of eugenics. To Friedrich Nietzsche belongs the honour of founding the *Religion* of eugenics" (Mügge 1909–1910 191).

In the light of Nazi race hygiene, there was no morality related to human breeding that contradicted the Hitlerian perception of racial progress. Sterilization, abortion, birth control, and euthanasia, for example, all had no moral meaning in and of themselves. Such practices were sinful if used to prevent the birth of or destroy a presumably "fit" Aryan fetus, child, or adult and virtuous if the result was to ensure that "unfit" parents would not leave behind offspring. Unmarried motherhood too was supported by the Nazis so long as both genetic parents were categorized as desirable. The National Socialists therefore supported the production of "state babies," often in government maternity homes such as the Lebensborns, as a means of compensating for high war deaths ("Germany Needs Boy Fathers" 1940; Hillel and Henry 1976).

Eugenics as an Altruistic Function

In both the United States and Nazi Germany, eugenic supporters frequently contended that their policies and proposals were beneficial not only for the nation as a whole, but indeed that they were altruistic measures that could greatly benefit those targeted by control measures. Institutionalization, sterilization, and other restrictive policies, they noted, would not only protect society from the burdensome weight of future morons but also were in keeping with the public's Christian duty to provide for and protect such "unfortunates" who could not live on their own, and who were constantly threatened by the dangers of their environment, or were incapable of making sound decisions on their own, and thus were frequently burdened by the consequences of their actions, such as raising unwanted children. Thus, discussions regarding the proper course of care given to such persons were filled with paternalistic or quasi-religious arguments that presented institutional administrators and other authorities as benevolent caregivers who were sacrificing their time to protect target group members and provide them with a higher quality of life than they otherwise could be expected to have (Smith 1985: 180). Lothrop Stoddard contended that while social control policies were "stern toward bad *stocks*," toward the individuals who comprised these stocks it was characterized by its kindness and "profound humaneness" (Stoddard 1923: 250). Those who carried out eugenic policies characterized their efforts as "spiritual" or "missionary" work (Hart 1914: 403) and described themselves as "devoted and self-sacrificing men and women" (Fernald 1904: 390).

Since eugenicists considered feebleminded persons to have the mentality of children, their rights could be controlled in the same way a child's rights might be. According to Leila Zenderland, Henry Goddard, like other eugenicists,

> drew an analogy between "defectives" and more "simple" peoples of the past. Both groups, moreover, could be compared to children.... Like children, they also ought to abrogate political, economic, and sexual independence, for these functions should be the province only of socially responsible adults. (Zenderland 1998: 200)

Many eugenicists, especially institutional administrators, argued that it was only within a properly run institution that morons would be able to live happily and safe. Such facilities, Barr wrote, served a dual purpose, benefiting both society and the individual. He wrote that "[s]ociety must be protected from pollution and tragedy on the one hand, and on the other the innocent imbecile must be saved from punishment for heedless or reckless transgression for which he is absolutely irresponsible" (Barr 1898: 487). Alexander Johnson invoked the teachings of Jesus in calling for the segregation of feebleminded children as a means of protecting them:

> the Master said that it was better for us to have a mill-stone around our necks and to be cast into the depths of the sea, than that we should cause one of these little ones to offend, or that we should offend one of these little ones. And when we as a people either by laws or by absence of

laws, expose these little ones to wrong and shame, we are incurring that condemnation.... The attitude of the state should be that of a good and loving mother to them. (Johnson 1908: 336)

Just as segregation was rationalized as being in the best interest of persons diagnosed as feebleminded as well as the society at large, so was sterilization. Even before the development of the vasectomy and salpingectomy, Martin Barr (1897) supported the castration of charges, since it would allow them to live in the community (Barr 1897: 6). Writing in the same period, Isaac Kerlin allowed one of the residents in the Pennsylvania Training School to have her "procreative organs" removed. This, he contended, "has been her salvation from vice and degradation." Kerlin added that he was "deeply thankful to the benevolent lady whose loyalty to science and comprehensive charity made this operation possible" (cited in Trent 1994: 193). In Great Britain, Winston Churchill, then the British Home Secretary, in 1910 supported calls for a national eugenic sterilization policy, contending that it "was a merciful act" since it was "cruel to shut up numbers of people in institutions for their whole lives, if by a simple operation they could be permitted to live freely in the world without causing much inconvenience to others" (cited in Cockburn 1992: 618).

The procedure itself was described by eugenicists as a painless or minor operation. Most operations were "not performed under duress and legal pressure," they noted, "but are merely instituted through persuasion of the individuals on the part of tactful physicians and prison officials" (Stoddard 1923: 249). Landman lauded the "therapeutic value" of sterilization (Landman 1934:295), a Kansas physician who performed sterilizations for the state contended that many additional persons should have "the benefit of this operation" (Hinshaw 1924: 19), and Whitney noted that the procedure was the "kindest" way of "aiding the feeble-minded" (Whitney 1929: 12).

Advocates of sterilization frequently noted that those who were subject to it were among its biggest supporters (Popenoe and Johnson 1933: 152), and that most of those "sterilized either welcome the operation or make no objection to having it performed" (Haldane 1938: 102). Gosney and Popenoe, two leaders of California's race betterment program, were especially outspoken in arguing that sterilized patients were not only helped by the measure but also highly supportive of it. Of the hundreds of patients they spoke with after being sterilized, only a handful, they said, were displeased. They noted that for many the procedure, even when involuntarily applied, gave them a sense of relief that "outweighs the feeling of loss of children." Many of the women they interviewed were "pathetic in their expression of gratitude and their wish that other women" in similar circumstances would "have the same protection" (Gosney and Popenoe 1980: 30–33). Even some eugenicists admitted, however, that a primary reason for support of sterilization among patients derived from the promise of freedom from institutionalization that it offered them (Dudziak 1986: 852).

Even the most drastic form of social control, extermination, was often supported by arguing that the action largely results from humanistic regard for the victims. Only a small number of eugenic supporters advocated infant or adult euthanasia as a form of eugenic control, but such proposals were almost always couched in paternalistic or pseudoreligious language. Martin Pernick wrote that Harry Haiselden compared the Bollinger baby, a victim of eugenic infanticide, "to the Christ child, explaining that the infant's sacrifice revealed a new rationally based testament to supercede the old religion" (Pernick 1996: 98). William Lennox spoke of the "privilege of death for the congenitally mindless" (Lennox 1938: 466) and W. Duncan McKim (1901) said that

> The surest, the simplest, the kindest, the most humane means for preventing reproduction among those whom we deem unworthy of this high privilege, is a *gentle, painless death*; and this should be administered not as a punishment, but as an expression of enlightened pity for the victims— too defective by nature to find true happiness in life—and as a duty toward the community and toward our offspring. (McKim 1901: 188)

In Germany prior to the Third Reich, a prescient 1920 book by two eminent authors supported euthanasia, referred to it as "healing intervention," and said that it was a way of "rescuing so many incurables from their suffering" (Binding and Hoche 1992: 241, 254). The language of "release," "salvation," "special treatment," and "deliverance" was frequently employed by the Nazis in discussing the program, and such terms often served as code words within official memorandum (Wertham 1966). A condolence letter sent to the family of a victim of the program noted that his death—from a fabricated cause—was a "deliverance" since it "delivered him from his suffering and spared him from institutionalization for life" (Müller-Hill 1988: 104). Advocates noted that those who did not support euthanasia were forcing thousands of "hopeless" individuals to endure unimaginable suffering (Leiser 1974: 92).

Prior to the initiation of their killing programs, the Nazis had received requests from some parents to allow their disabled children to die. The most well known of these was the Knauer case, which took place in 1938 and 1939. The parents of the "deformed child" had petitioned Hitler to allow doctors to hasten his death. Importantly, cases such as this allowed the Nazis to exploit the desire of parents such as the Knauers as a means of excusing their killing program. By so doing they attempted to frame themselves as "removing a burden" from such families (Burleigh 1994: 95; McKim 1901: 96).

Discussion

Religious rhetoric was used during the eugenic alarm period in the United States for the primary purpose of demonstrating that controlled human breeding was in keeping with the teachings of Christianity, and by the Nazis to describe their eugenic policies as a movement beyond the corrupt and overly sentimental Christianity of the day. An important barrier for the advocates of procreation control to overcome is the prevailing fear that the methods they espouse supersede or are contrary to organized religion, and therefore constitute either acts of hubris or outright heresy. Since eugenics deals with the elemental structure and composition of humans as individuals and groups, and seeks to change this composition in profound ways, it has often been viewed as an intrusion on the designs of God. Eugenic advocates have always understood that a program of controlled human breeding could be viewed as a sacrilegious effort to infringe on the Divine. Most, therefore, expended effort contending that they were acting in conjunction with rather than opposition to God's plans, as his ambassadors rather than his competitors.

Eugenic supporters explained that their goal was to improve the spiritual standing of humans by improving the race itself. In assisting the evolution of humans in a "desirable" direction, they were creating a more perfect race, which certainly must be in line with divine intent and conventional religious dogma. Samuel Batten (1908) noted that evolutionary science and organized religion were often in conflict with each other, but that eugenic programs could serve both. By allowing "unfit" persons to live but not procreate, eugenics was at the same time responding to the Christian call to aid the weak and the evolutionary uplift of the species.

For many American and German eugenicists, eugenic control fit very well with their view of the human species, which could be described as an updated version of the "Great Chain of Being." This construct, which had been in existence for hundreds of years prior to the 1900s, set each plant, animal, and "spiritual" type along a hierarchical continuum from the most basic entities to the most complex, terminating in God, the highest of all entities. Humans, because of our intermingling of animalistic (or physical) and spiritual (or mental) elements, formed the bridge that connected these two areas of the Chain together (Lovejoy 1966).

Many eugenicists tended to perceive divergent human subgroups as taking their own place on the species ladder. In this view, persons with disabilities, and most particularly those with intellectual disabilities, were often seen as forming the bridge or "missing link" between our species and the great apes. This was especially true since it was our intellectual or mental capacities that were accepted as connecting us to "higher" spiritual entities, and our base physical qualities that tied us to "lower" animals. Thus, animalistic rhetoric pervaded eugenic writings (O'Brien 2003b). "Feeble-mindedness," the leading American eugenicist wrote, for example, was a "direct inheritance" from "our animal ancestry" (Davenport 1912: 89). Such persons were, like animals, said to be relatively devoid of spiritual influence.

Hierarchical metaphors such as the Chain of Being allowed for a simplistic linear view of the human species. Moreover, while an individual or group's position on the scale was generally based on intellectual criteria, an assumption that most eugenicists held was that, with few exceptions, such a scale also served as a valid gauge of morality. "Animalistic" persons, in their view, were not only less capable than most but also less virtuous. Thus, efforts to control the propagation of such persons were righteous attempts to stamp out both immorality and uncontrollable behavior.

Importantly, as the Chain of Being demonstrates, conceptual metaphors that relate to linearity (e.g., high or rising as good or desirable, low or falling as undesirable) are extremely prevalent both in religious understanding and as a mode for describing and thus perceiving persons with disabilities. The placement of Heaven and Hell as up and down is not surprising, nor is it a shock that so many important Christian events relate to climbing a mountain or otherwise ascending. These linear metaphors also supplement paternalistic altruism, as, for example, we "go down" to "pull others up." This linear metaphor is reinforced by intelligence tests and similar scales that are often used to measure disablement.

There was also an aspect of eugenic control that related to the aesthetic aversion we have to people who have physical disabilities, especially various forms of "disfigurement." During the eugenic era, a public fascination arose related to the discussion and display of "nonnormative" bodies (Bogdan 1988; Washington 2006). In part this was because these bodies seemed to provide a possible clue to the proper demarcation of various human groups (did differing races/ethnicities constitute divergent species?) and potentially provide information about our past ancestry (did such individuals constitute an atavisitic throwback to an earlier humanity?). How could one reconcile, eugenicists wondered, the knowledge that man was created in God's image with the existence of persons who were severely disfigured or disabled?

Eugenic goals were for the most part commensurate with the objectives of the social purity movement of the late nineteenth and early twentieth century. This campaign appealed to both progressivists and moral conservatives, and counted among its goals the decrease and eventually elimination of smoking, drinking, illicit sex, venereal disease and prostitution, along with a promulgation of community and individual health and sanitation measures. Eugenicists argued that while environmental approaches could be beneficial, control of reproduction was the most important means by which the immorality that was said to be sweeping the nation could be curbed. Within the context of eugenic propaganda, males were likely to take advantage of young children or feebleminded or naïve women, and the females were sure to become prostitutes and to bear large numbers of illegitimate progeny. Members of both genders were almost certain to engage in sexual activity outside of marriage, often with multiple partners, and feebleminded persons were also apt to become sexually active with those of a different race. In their presumed hypersexuality, morons stood out as not only consummate sinners, but moreover as persons who were apt to lead others to evil.

It was especially the female moron who was considered to a principle source of societal pollution. Many eugenicists were obsessed with the reputed sexual exploits of those so labeled. They took for granted that such women were easily led astray by males in search of easy sexuality without commitment. Like a contemporary Eve or Pandora, most eugenic family studies could be traced back to the wayward female. The Kallikaks had their "nameless feeble-minded" barmaid (Goddard 1923: 29), and the Jukes were traced to the Juke sisters, including "Margaret, the mother of criminals" (Dugdale 1910: 15). Gertrude Davenport said that a man's "marriage with a woman of wandering and vicious disposition" was the reason for the "permanent downfall" of the degenerate branch of a European family that she described (Davenport 1907: 404). Family studies writers were especially likely to note when miscegenation had taken place within these families, and it was often this "racial sin" that began or exacerbated the families' decline. For example, Michael

Guyer noted that the Tribe of Ishmael, a "degenerate" Indiana family, was the result of "the progeny of a neurotic man and a half-breed woman" (Guyer 1913: 40). As Wendy Kline noted, normality—and therefore also moronity—was defined as much by "moral purity" as it was by "mental capacity" (Kline 2001: 26, 121).

As the eugenic era wore on, paternalistic rhetoric gave way increasingly to a rhetorical framing that depicted feebleminded individuals and other targeted persons with disabilities not so much as a vulnerable group in need of protection but rather as an uncontrollable quasi-human subgroup that threatened not only to cause physical and mental degeneration, but that moreover posed a real threat to the spiritual nature of the species. Because of their presumed intellectual deficits, these individuals may not have been aware of the threat they posed, but they needed to be controlled nonetheless. Eugenicists seeking to rationalize and implement this control found much to draw from and many sources of support in both the religious and scientific communities.

References

Abelson, P. H. (1965). Fruit from the tree of knowledge. *Science 149*, 251.

Aly, G., Chroust, P., & Pross, C. (1994). *Cleansing the Fatherland: Nazi Medicine and Racial Hygiene*. B. Cooper (Trans.). Baltimore, MD: The Johns Hopkins University Press.

Baker, L. H. (1912). *Race Improvement or Eugenics: A Little Book on a Great Subject*. New York, NY: Dodd, Mead and Company.

Barr, M. W. (1897). President's annual address. *Journal of Psycho-Asthenics 2*(1) 1–13.

Barr, M. W. (1898). Defective children: Their needs and their rights. *International Journal of Ethics 8*, 481–490.

Batten, S. Z. (1908). The redemption of the unfit. *The American Journal of Sociology 14*, 233–260.

Binding, K. & Hoche, A. (1992). Permitting the destruction of unworthy life: Its extent and form. W.E. Wright, (Trans.). *Issues in Law and Medicine 8*, 231–265. (Original work published 1920).

Bock, G. (2004). Nazi sterilization and reproductive policies. In *Deadly Medicine: Creating the Master Race* (pp. 61–88). Washington DC: United States Holocaust Memorial Museum.

Bogdan, R. (1988). *Freak Show*. Chicago, IL: University of Chicago Press.

Burleigh, M (1994). *Death and Deliverance: 'Euthanasia' in Germany 1900–1945*. Cambridge: Cambridge University Press.

Cockburn, A. (November 23, 1992). Beat the devil. *The Nation* 618–619.

Cohen, J. R. (1999). Creation and cloning in Jewish thought. *Hastings Center Report 29*(4), 7–12.

Committee on cooperation with Clergymen. (1925). *Eugenical News 10*(5), 68.

Davenport, C. B. (1912). The origin and control of mental defectiveness. *The PopularScience Monthly 80*, 87–90.

Davenport, G. C. (1907). Hereditary crime. *The American Journal of Sociology 13*, 402–409.

De Vilbiss, L. A. (1914). Better babies contests. *Proceedings of the First National Conference on Race Betterment* (pp. 554–555). Battle Creek, MI: Race Betterment Foundation.

Dudziak, M. L. (1986). Oliver Wendell Holmes as a eugenic reformer: Rhetoric in the writing of constitutional law. *Iowa Law Review 71*, 833–867.

Dugdale, R. L. (1910). *The Jukes: A Study in Crime, Pauperism, Disease and Heredity*, 4th ed. New York, NY: G.P. Putnam's Sons.

Enderis, G. (January 31, 1934). Reich takes over rights of states. *The New York Times*, p. 13.

Eugenics supported by the Church. (1912). *Current Literature 52*, 564–566.

Fernald, W. E. (1904). Care of the feeble-minded. *Proceedings of the National Conference on Charities and Corrections* (pp. 380–390). Press of Fred J. Heer.

Frankel, C. (March, 1974). The specter of eugenics. *Commentary 57*, 25–33.

Frick, W. (1934). German population and race politics. A. Hellmer (Trans.). *Eugenical News, 19* 33–38.

Galton, F. (1870). *Hereditary Genius*. New York, NY: D. Appleton and Co.

Galton, F. (1904). Eugenics: Its definition, scope, and aims, *The American Journal of Sociology 11*, 1–25.

Galton, F. (1907). *Inquiries into Human Faculty and Its Development*. Reprint. New York, NY: E.P. Dutton & Co. (Original work published 1883).

Galton, F. (1996). *Essays in Eugenics*. Reprint. Washington, DC: Scott Townsend Publishers. (Original work published 1909).

Germany needs boy fathers. (1940). *The Living Age 358*, 136–139.

Goddard, H. H. (1923). *The Kallikak Family: A Study in the Heredity of Feeble-Mindedness*, Rev. ed. New York, NY: The MacMillan Company. (Original work published 1912).

Goodfield, J. (1977). *Playing God: Genetic Engineering and the Manipulation of Life*. New York, NY: Harper Colophon Books.

Gosney, E. S., & Popenoe, P. (1980). *Sterilization for Human Betterment*. Reprint, New York, NY: The MacMillan Company. (Original work published 1929).

Gould, S. J. (1981). *The Mismeasure of Man*. New York, NY: W.W. Norton and Co.

Guyer, M. F. (1913). Sterilization. *Proceedings of the Wisconsin Conference on Charities and Corrections* (pp. 33–60). Madison, WI: Bobbs-Merrill Company.

Hadden, W. J. (1914). *The Science of Eugenics and Sex Life: The Regeneration of the Human Race*, 2nd ed. Chicago, IL: W. R. Vansant.

Haldane, J. B. S. (1938). *Heredity and Politics.* New York, NY: W.W. Norton & Company.

Hart, H. H. (1914). Segregation. *Proceedings of the First National Conference on Race Betterment* (pp. 403–408.) Battle Creek, MI: Race Betterment Foundation.

Hillel, M., & Henry C. (1976). *Of Pure Blood.* E. Mossbacher (Trans.). New York, NY: McGraw–Hill Book Co.

Hinshaw, T. E. (1924). Physician's report. In *Twenty-Second Biennial Report of the State Training School, Winfield Kansas.* Topeka, KS: Kansas State Printing Plant.

Hitler, A. (1971). *Mein kampf.* R. Manheim (Trans.). Reprint. Boston, MA: Houghton Mifflin Co. (Original work published 1925).

Howard, T., & Rifkin, J. (1977). *Who Should Play God?* New York, NY: Dell Publishing Co., Inc.

Huntington, E., & Whitney, L. F. (1927). *The Builders of America.* New York, NY: William Morrow and Co.

Johnson, A. (1908). Custodial care. In *Proceedings of the National Conference of Charities and Correction* (pp. 333–336). Fort Wayne, IN: Press of Fort Wayne Printing Co.

Kennedy, F. (May 20, 1939). Euthanasia: To be or not to be. *Colliers 103*, 15–16.

Kevles, D. J. (1985). *In the Name of Eugenics.* New York, NY: Alfred A. Knopf.

Kline, W. (2001). *Building a Better Race: Gender, Sexuality and Eugenics from the Turn of the Century to the Baby Boom.* Berkeley: University of California Press.

Kostir, M. S. (1916). *The Family of Sam Sixty.* Mansfield, OH: Press of Ohio State Reformatory.

Kühl, S. (1994). *The Nazi Connection: Eugenics, American Racism, and German National Socialism.* New York, NY: Oxford University Press.

Landman, J. H. (1934). Race betterment by human sterilization. *Scientific American 150*, 292–295.

Leiser, E. (1974). *Nazi cinema.* G. Mander & D. Wilson (Trans.). New York, NY: McMillan Publishing Co., Inc.

Lennox, W. G. (1938). Should they live? *The American Scholar 7*, 454–466.

Lenz, F. (1924). Eugenics in Germany. P. Popenoe (Trans.). *The Journal of Heredity 15*, 223–231.

Lovejoy, A. (1966). *The Great Chain of Being.* Cambridge, MA: Harvard University Press.

Ludmerer, K. M. (1972). *Genetics and American Society.* Baltimore, MD: Johns Hopkins University Press.

MacMurchy, H. (1916). The relation of feeble-mindedness to other social problems. *Proceedings of the National Conference on Charities and Correction* (pp. 229–235). Chicago, IL: The Hildmann Printing Co.

McKim, W. D. (1901). *Heredity and Human Progress.* New York, NY: G.P. Putnam's Sons.

Mott, A. J. (1894). The education and custody of the imbecile. In *Proceedings of the National Conference on Charities and Corrections* (pp. 168–179). Boston, MA: Press of Geo. H. Ellis.

Mügge, M. A. (1909–1910). Eugenics and the superman: A racial science, and a racial religion. *The Eugenics Review 1*, 184–193.

Müller-Hill, B. (1988). *Murderous Science: Elimination by Scientific Selection of Jews, Gypsies and Others: Germany 1933–1945*. G.R. Fraser (Trans.). New York, NY: Oxford University Press.

Nazi Conspiracy and Aggression: Volume II. (1947). Office of United States Chief of Counsel for Prosecution of Axis Criminality. Washington, DC: United States Government Printing Office.

Nazis tighten law on sterilization: Answer Catholics. (July 18, 1935). *The New York Times*, p. 1.

Nelkin, D., & Lindee, M. S. (1995). *The DNA Mystique: The Gene as a Cultural Icon*. New York, NY: W.H. Freeman and Co.

Nelkin, D., & Tancredi, L. (1989). *Dangerous Diagnostics: The Social Power of Biological Information*. Basic Books.

A new force in the war on feeble-mindedness. (1913). *The Survey 19*, 487–489.

Newman, H. H. (1921). *Readings in Evolution, Genetics, and Eugenics*. Chicago, IL: University of Chicago Press.

Nietzsche, F. (1966). *Beyond Good and Evil*. W. Kaufman (Trans.). New York, NY: Vintage Books. (Original work published 1886).

Nietzsche, F. (1968). *Twilight of the Idols/The Antichrist*. R. J. Hollingdale (Trans.). Reprint. New York, NY: Penguin Books. (Original work published 1889).

Nietzsche, F. (1969). *Thus Spoke Zarathustra*. R. J. Hollingdale (Trans.). Reprint. New York, NY: Penguin Books. (Original work published 1885).

O'Brien, G. V. (1999). Protecting the social body: Use of the organism metaphor in fighting the 'menace of the feeble-minded.' *Mental Retardation 37*, 188–200.

O'Brien, G. V. (2003a). Indigestible food, conquering hordes, and waste materials: Metaphors of immigrants and the early immigration restriction debate in the United States. *Metaphor and Symbol 18*, 33–47.

O'Brien, G. V. (2003b). Persons with cognitive disabilities, the argument from marginal cases and social work ethics. *Social Work 48*, 331–337.

O'Brien, G. V. (2009). Metaphors and the pejorative framing of marginalized groups: Implications for social work education. *Journal of Social Work Education*, 45, 29–46.

Pernick, M. S. (1996). *The Black Stork: Eugenics and the Death of "Defective" Babies in American Medicine and Motion Pictures Since 1915*. New York, NY: Oxford University Press.

Plato. (1986). *The Republic* (Reprint). Desmond Lee Harmondsworth (Trans.) Middlesex, England: Penguin Books, Ltd.

Popenoe, P., & Johnson, R. H. (1933). *Applied Eugenics*. New York, NY: The MacMillan Co.

Prizes for sermons on eugenics. (1926). *Eugenical News 11*(3), 48.

Proctor, R. (1988). *Racial Hygiene: Medicine under the Nazis.* Cambridge, MA: Harvard University Press.

Reccord, A. P. (1918). A perfectly normal child. *The Survey 41,* 381.

Reilly, P. R. (1991). *The Surgical Solution: A History of Involuntary Sterilization in the United States.* Baltimore, MD: Johns Hopkins University Press.

Rifkin, J. (May 1, 1998). God in a labcoat: Can we control the biotech revolution before it controls us? *Utne Reader 87,* 66.

Rosen, C. (2004). *Preaching Eugenics: Religious Leaders and the American Eugenics Movement.* Oxford, England: Oxford University Press.

Schwartz, K. (1908–1909). Nature's corrective principle in social evolution. *Journal of Psycho-Asthenics 13,* 74–90.

Selling Murder: The Killing Films of the Third Reich. (1991). London: Domino Films.

Silver, L. M. (1997). *Remaking Eden: Cloning and Beyond in a Brave New World.* New York, NY: Avon Books.

Smith, J. D. (1985). *Minds Made Feeble: The Myth and Legacy of the Kallikaks.* Austin, TX: Pro-ed.

Sterilization law is termed humane. (January 22, 1934). *The New York Times,* p. 6.

Stoddard, L. (1923). *The Revolt Against Civilization.* New York, NY: Charles Scribner's Sons.

Stoddard, L. (1940). *Into the Darkness: Nazi Germany Today.* New York, NY: Duell, Sloan & Pearce, Inc.

Sumner, W. T. (1914). The health certificate – A safeguard against vicious selection in marriage. In *Proceedings of the First National Conference on Race Betterment* (pp. 443–446). Battle Creek, MI: Race Betterment Foundation.

Thomalia, C. (1934). The sterilization law in Germany. *Scientific American 151,* 126–127.

Trent, J. W. (1994). *Inventing the Feeble Mind: A History of Mental Retardation in the United States.* Berkeley, CA: University of California Press.

Warthin, A. S. (1928). A biologic philosophy or religion a necessary foundation for race betterment. In *Proceedings of the Third Race Betterment Conference* (pp. 86–90). Battle Creek, MI: Race Betterment Foundation.

Was the doctor right? Some independent opinions. (January 3, 1916). *The Independent 85,* 23–27.

Washington, H. A. (2006). *Medical Apartheid: The Dark History of Medical Experimentation on Black Americans from Colonial Times to the Present.* NewYork, NY: Harlem Moon Broadway Books.

Wells, K. G. (1897). State regulation of marriage. In *Proceedings of the National Conference of Charities and Correction* (pp. 302–308). Boston, MA: Geo. H. Ellis.

Wertham, F. (1966). *A Sign for Cain – An Exploration of Human Violence.* New York, NY: The MacMillan Co.

Whitney, E. A. (1929). A plea for the control of the feeble-mindedness. *Eugenics 2*(5), 12–13.

Whitney, L. F. (1926). *The Source of Crime.* Reprinted from Christian Work Magazine by the American Eugenics Society, Inc.

Wiggam, A. E. (1923). *The New Decalogue of Science.* Indianapolis, IN: Bobbs–Merrill Company.

Zenderland, L. (1998). *Measuring Minds: Henry Herbert Goddard and the Origins of American Intelligence Testing.* Cambridge, England: Cambridge University Press.

CHAPTER 9

Catholicism and Disability: Sacred and Profane

Christine James

Recent publications on disability and social justice list the advantages of the "natural law" approach, rather than liberal or contractarian ethics (Tollefsen 2009). The natural law theory can be combined with what Robert George calls "moral ecology," an understanding that the ethical context of a community often influences the ethical behavior of individuals and that institutions have a moral imperative to create the proper moral ecology for their members.

This concept of moral ecology gives a context for how Catholicism understands disability. Part of providing a good moral ecology is emphasizing exemplary individuals who make upright choices. For Catholics, these individuals are the saints, who are both exemplars and intercessory figures. Biographies of saints often involve descriptions (either in the neutral sense of describing accurately, or in a somewhat more negative sense of "marketing" or "packaging") of overcoming disability or of having a special relationship with God because of their disability. Historically, we might not be able to verify that certain saints had what we would now call a disability, but there are saints who appeared to experience certain kinds of suffering that might be called disabilities. These include two types of disability, physical and cognitive. Physical disabilities would include epilepsy; cognitive disabilities include examples of "simple-mindedness," such as St. Theresa of Lisieux. Her message of the "Little Way" holds that being more "simple," childlike, and dependent on others is to be closer to God. Modern-day examples (such as Audrey Santo, a child with physical and cognitive disabilities) explicitly relate having a disability to the working of miracles. The Santo case involved both neutral descriptions of her disability and a certain marketing strategy involving Web sites and commemorative items for sale. However, the family's home diocese is supporting the process of beatification and has begun that process as of September 2008.

Some Catholics hold an unorthodox belief that saints are "victim souls" who suffer for all of us, as Christ suffered. Most Catholics do not hold this particular belief, but there is a strong connection between sainthood and disability among Catholics that deserves more attention. In the past few years, with the growing field of Disability Studies, books referring to saints' disabilities have been published, and a recent conference on sainthood and disability was held at a university in the United Kingdom. (The conference was Historicizing Disability: The Middle Ages and After and took place at York University in December 2006, and one such book was Andri Vauchez/Jean Birrell's *Sainthood in the Later Middle Ages*, which came out in the late 1990s and makes some reference to disability.)

This focus on the metaphysics of disability as a holy, or sacred, state can be compared with the official church statements on disability. In November 1978, there was a Pastoral Statement of U.S. Catholic Bishops on People with Disabilities. This statement emphasizes inclusion, interaction, and wholeness of the church and openly acknowledges that people with disabilities do not want pity but participation. The document recommends that on the national level, bishops should designate "ministry to people with disabilities" as a "special focus" for the future. In December 2000, the Vatican's Committee for the Jubilee Day produced a special statement on persons with disabilities, emphasizing the duties of the civil and ecclesiastical community. Their stated goal was to reconcile church leadership with the disabled in recognition of past wrongs. However, a few years later, the Vatican decided not to sign on with the UN Convention on the Rights of Persons with Disabilities, because it included a clause requiring member nations to provide "sexual and reproductive health and population-based public health programs" to people with disabilities (there was concern that this might be misused to promote abortions.)

The connection between disability and sainthood among Catholics represents a revealing dichotomy within our society—disabled persons are seen as both dependent and lesser-than, and constructed as holy and greater-than. There is a combination of somewhat condescending, patriarchal treatment on the one hand, and "putting on a pedestal" on the other. But in light of natural law and moral ecology, there seems to be a connection between saints as exemplars and the construction of the right moral ecology. These positive and negative conceptualizations of persons with disabilities, as well as the treatment of persons with disability by society and by church leaders, are indeed an indicator of how well society lives up to natural law (all disabled persons capable of citizenship). Some of the Catholic documentation succeeds and makes the right recommendations according to the natural law approach, yet it does not reconcile or transcend the dichotomy of patriarchal condescending treatment versus putting on pedestals. Much of the previous literature on Catholicism and disability has emphasized the negative, abusive situations in church history; this chapter will address the theoretical construction of sainthood as it relates to disability in extremely positive and negative senses.

The Roman Catholic Church has a dual view of the status of persons with disabilities in the church community. On the one hand, persons with disabilities have often been upheld as saints, as moral exemplars, or as figures who can intercede on behalf of others. In contrast, the recent statements of the Roman Catholic Church policy show an acknowledgment of abuse and neglect of persons with disabilities and gives a clear message to governmental organizations that the rights and goals of such persons must be respected. In a profound sense, the church is just now living up to the promise of its natural law perspective on personhood and full church community life for persons with disabilities. I will contrast natural law theories that have recently discussed disability, such as those by Tollefsen and George, with Rawlsian and contractarian views on disability, such as Nussbaum's capabilities approach. Next, the connection between sainthood and disability will be addressed with specific attention to a particular set of saints whose disabilities and suffering gave them a special moral status in the (unorthodox) concept of "victim souls" in the twentieth century. This possibility that persons with disabilities could have a holy or sacred state is contrasted with pastoral statements and the Vatican's response to the recent United Nations Convention on the Rights of Persons with Disabilities (2006). The final section will discuss broader implications for the status of persons with disabilities and those who give care to persons with disabilities as ethical exemplars.

The Ethical Context of Communities

The status of persons with disabilities in the Roman Catholic community can be understood through a variety of theoretical approaches. In past centuries, the Catholic Church has often failed to provide persons with disabilities with accommodation and access to full membership in community.[1] The last 40 years have seen a change, with a series of pastoral statements enjoining members of the clergy to alter how they treat members of their parishes with disabilities.

The treatment of members of a community arises from the community's key assumptions about the value of its members as moral agents. One such foundational approach to catholic community can be called the "natural law approach." Catholic views on sexuality and reproduction come from natural law theory: the notion that human life follows a natural order, that the biological functions of having children should occur in a proper order after marriage, and that the church community should set the proper supportive context for such life activities. Human flourishing, on this model, is directly related to human needs being met through active engagement with the community. The community membership and role of persons with disabilities, and the importance of the role played by their caregivers in their communities, has been a source of debate in recent years.

In her 2006 book, *Frontiers of Justice: Disability, Nationality, and Species Membership*, Martha Nussbaum describes community in terms of contractarian ethics, taking inspiration from the work of John Rawls. Nussbaum argues that given the Rawlsian determination of justice, persons with disabilities still have other specific capabilities that justify their moral status, rights, and privileges in community. For Rawls, membership in the social contract and justice within the contract is governed by maximum liberty (until one's liberty infringes on that of another), social inequality accepted only as long as it is necessary for the good of the whole, and social mobility for those who contribute to society using their own work, abilities, talents, and capabilities. While Nussbaum (2006) argued that persons with disabilities clearly have capabilities, and that these capabilities render them able to participate in the just social contract, she received some criticism in response to the book. One reviewer in *Philosophical Books* argued that Nussbaum never successfully balanced the "tension between impartiality and mutual advantage" present in much of the Rawls-inspired literature; that the need to derive justice in the impartial context of the original position leaves us without a way to balance out advantage and disadvantage (Lamey 2007: 379). Another reviewer in the *Scandinavian Journal of Disability Research* noted that even if Nussbaum's recommendation of moral rights for persons with disabilities were morally acceptable and enacted, "they remain compensatory, rather than based on genuine and equal worth" (Hanisch 2007: 135). The issue of inequality remains a lingering problem for Rawls-inspired contractarian views on disability.

While Nussbaum is criticized for not openly addressing the problem of inequality, natural law theorists, such as Christopher Tollefsen and Robert George, hold that natural law theory upholds a view of community that celebrates diverse abilities and disabilities as a natural part of the community. Rather than asking how to model politics around the concepts of justice, freedom, and equality, Tollefsen argues that the state has a teleological purpose: to serve a set of human needs, needs understood by way of a particular account of human flourishing (Tollefsen 2009: 5). In this account of human flourishing, there is room for multiple types of naturally ordered lives, there is no assumption that everyone is self-sufficient, and the roles of the dependent, person with disability, and the dependency worker all hold moral value as members of the state and community. What is significant in the natural law approach is that the state is not merely a limiting force that sets boundaries within which just behavior is defined and enforced. Instead, according to Robert George, the state and community exist to actively cultivate a proper moral ecology. "Ecology" here refers to a place in which the right moral beings and the right moral attitudes can grow and flourish. For George, "moral ecology" arises from an understanding that the ethical context of a community often influences the ethical behavior of individuals who make up that community. Furthermore, institutions have a moral imperative to create the proper moral ecology for their members (George 1993; George and Tollefsen 2008).

How Catholicism Connects Saints and Disability

A central means by which communities cultivate the proper moral ecology discussed by George is by upholding exemplary individuals, those who make morally upright choices who can be followed as exemplars. In Roman Catholic communities, there are many exemplary figures, including godparents and confirmation sponsors. But saints are arguably the most unique exemplary role models because they serve a dual purpose. First, saints lead exemplary lives, described in vivid detail through their good works during their lifetime, and often by their willingness to be martyred for their faith. Second, saints can be called upon through prayer to act as intercessory figures, men and women who act to aid those who have engaged in bad behavior to help them secure forgiveness for their sins. This intercession can be done through specific actions or healings on earth, or through the saint communicating special requests to God in heaven, as Father, Son, or Holy Spirit. One prays to saints as well as directly to God, since saints are upheld as having special roles (either as the patron saint for a specific illness, profession, or need; or as one's own patron saint via confirmation names or the feast day of one's birth.) To understand the role of the saint and the proper way to make requests of the saints, one must have a grasp of the saints' biography, the story of their life and how they came to be blessed. The biographies of saints can be understood in a number of ways: as a description of the historical events of their lives, and as a marketing or packaging tool illustrating a particular vision of what it is to be a good Catholic. Thus, the saints stand as a model for how each Catholic should live and how each Catholic life contributes to the proper moral ecology (a Kingdom of God on earth, in which each member is able to flourish to the best of his or her own abilities, whatever they may be.)

Many Catholic saints have been disabled, and in the saint's biography, the disability is often celebrated as a reason why that saint was especially close to God. Even in cases where a saint is not described as having been disabled, the saint can be described as having a special healing power over a particular type of disability. For example, St. Dymphna was the daughter of an Irish chieftain named Damon. In grief over his wife's death, Damon attempted to rape Dymphna, who resisted her father's sexual advances and fled to Belgium. Damon followed her to Belgium, found her, and beheaded her. Although St. Dymphna did not have a disability in her lifetime, she is known as the patron saint of persons with dementia, Alzheimer's, and emotional disabilities (O'Malley 1999: 86). One can contrast the St. Dymphna example with that of St. Germaine Cousin, the patron saint of persons with physical disabilities. St. Germaine Cousin was born in sixteenth-century France with a disability, a deformed hand and a debilitating skin infection called scrofula (Mulcahy 1909). In the Catholic concept of sainthood, it is often the case that either the saints are involved in miraculous events for others, helping others to overcome disabilities through their intercession, or the saints are said to have a special relationship with God specifically because of their disability.

Another distinction can be drawn between two types of disability and their treatment in Catholic saint biographies. Physical disabilities are often treated slightly differently than cognitive disabilities. One such example of cognitive disabilities in sainthood is the story of St. Thérèse of Lisieux, also known as "The Little Flower." The cornerstone of the story of St. Thérèse is that being as "simple" as possible, and being dependent on others, is the cornerstone of the "Little Way" to becoming closer to God.

But for St. Thérèse of Lisieux, the key to becoming close to God involved not merely being simple, but also suffering. Thérèse is often cited as one of the first "victim souls," a controversial belief among some Catholics that gained a great following at the turn of the last century. The victim soul is a person who believes that he or she suffers as Christ suffered for others, and as such, he or she gains closeness to Christ as the supreme victim, and his or her suffering renews the redemption that Christ's suffering secured for the faithful. Paulin Giloteaux, the author of *Victim Souls* (1927) was inspired to maintain great personal piety from the life of St. Thérèse of Lisieux, who he said set the pattern for the modern victim way with her "insatiable thirst for suffering . . . this victim life is nothing but the Christian life lived with immense attention to suffering" (Kane 2002: 100).

The influence of the victim soul concept extended throughout the twentieth century, in some cases featuring a continuing line from one victim soul to another. For example, St. Thérèse of Lisieux figures prominently in the visions of Marthe Robin, an invalid since age 16, who saw her own vocation as suffering as a victim soul. In 1918, Marthe began to believe that her own body was the site of the cosmic battle against evil that Jesus Christ had fought and won. A victim of delicate health in childhood, in her teens she suffered severe headaches, a coma, and ultimately paralysis of her legs, leaving her permanently bedridden. While comatose, Marthe had three visions of St. Thérèse of Lisieux, who told her that she would survive to extend St. Thérèse's work throughout the entire world. By 1925, Marthe had formally dedicated herself as a victim soul (Kane 2002: 111). Marthe Robin ceased sleeping, and became blind in 1939; but she remained "joyful" and inspired the founding of more than 70 *foyers de charité* (retreat centers) around the world—her biographers describe her remarkable and paradoxical *immobile voyage* (unmoving journey) (Kane 2002: 112). In her article "Victim Spirituality in Catholicism," Paula M. Kane (2002) argues that Catholic religious communities, such as the Catholic Worker houses, were also inspired by the concept of victim souls and that some who believe in the unorthodox idea of victim souls believe that St. Thérèse of Lisieux foretold the coming of a network legion of victim souls throughout the world.

Although she has not usually been represented as such, a lay embodiment of the victim mentality that Poulain criticized was Dorothy Day, the most famous American convert to Catholicism in the 1920s. Day's favorite image for the Catholic Worker Movement that she founded was that of "suffering victim." While Day externalized her identification with victims—the poor, homeless and abandoned of America's cities— and promoted solidarity with the immigrant poor by rejecting American materialism, she remained powerfully attracted to the victim mentality. Its exercises in self-abasement and "cultivation of worldly failure" were instilled through the movement's retreat theology (associated with Father John Hugo of Pittsburgh) and found kindred lay spirits in the Catholic Worker Houses. (Fisher 1989: 50; Kane 2002: 101–102)

The connection between the idea of victim souls as redemptive figures and saints as intercessory figures is still very much a part of Catholic thought, orthodox or not. Consider the recent example of Audrey Santos, a girl who was born in Worcester, MA, in 1984. She nearly drowned at the age of three and suffered severe physical and cognitive disabilities as a result of the accident. Kept alive at home with a variety of life support machines, caregivers, and visiting pilgrims, Audrey died in 2007 at the age of 23. The possibility that Audrey was working miracles, even in her disabled state of suffering, was documented through a series of events monitored by the church in the family home (Levenson 2008). In 1993, a painting of the Virgin Mary in the home appeared to weep. Eucharists produced blood, oil formed on the home's walls and inside a priest's cup, and sick persons who came to the home were healed (Ailworth 2008; Barry 1998). A variety of souvenir items, including a film, books, and keychains, were sold online (and are still being sold via the Little Audrey Santo Foundation Price List Web site.) In 1998, 10,000 people celebrated mass in a stadium with Audrey, who was brought in by ambulance (Tench 2007).

Members of the Little Audrey Santo Foundation launched a campaign in 2008 to begin the process of her beatification and canonization (necessary steps to becoming a saint recognized by the Roman Catholic Church.) Bishop Robert J. McManus of the Diocese of Worcester gave the group canonical recognition, supporting their bid to persuade the Vatican to begin the process (Ailworth 2008; Pham 2009). Robert Keane, clerk of the Santo foundation, has said he believes one posthumous miracle has occurred because of Audrey's intercession. In order for one to be declared a saint, at least two posthumous miracles must be performed. The former Bishop of Worcester, the Most. Rev. Daniel P. Reilly, noted in 1999 that the "most striking evidence of the presence of God in the Santo home is seen in the dedication of the family to Audrey.

Their constant respect for her dignity as a child of God is a poignant reminder that God touches our lives through the love and devotion of others" (Reilly 1999: 2). However, the Bishop notes that the possibility that Audrey has suffered severe cognitive impairment is detrimental to her ability to intercede with God and become a saint:

> In the case of Audrey herself, more study is needed from medical and other professionals regarding her level of awareness and her ability to communicate with the people around her. This is critical to the basis of the claim of her ability to intercede with God. In the meantime, I urge continued prayers *for* Audrey and her family. But praying *to* Audrey is not acceptable in Catholic teaching. (Reilly 1999: 2, original emphasis)

The Bishop's statement is ironic considering the historical connection between disabilities, including cognitive disabilities, and sainthood. Scholarship on this connection has increased in the last few years, including a conference on disability in history that took place at the University of York in December 2006, and that included sessions on disability and sainthood in time periods from the Middle Ages, Jacobean England, and the Renaissance. The University's Deputy Vice-Chancellor Professor Felicity Riddy said, "We are working hard at York to raise disability awareness, and the Historicising Disability Conference could not be more timely" (Garner 2006). In 1997, Cambridge University Press published the book *Sainthood in the Later Middle Ages* by Andri Vauchez, which also draws connections between sainthood and disabilities.

The connection between sainthood and victim souls, and an earlier mysticism of the suffering of Christ's Passion, brings a specific metaphysical status of sacred, holy nature to the saints involved in suffering and disabilities. As they take on suffering for others, they take on a Christ-like purity:

> Victim souls are not culpable for their personal suffering, which God is using in order to redeem someone else. The phenomenon of vicarious suffering is hardly unique to Roman Catholicism. Indeed, the identification of a scapegoat—someone who wards off threats to the group by bearing the afflictions and wrongdoing of the community—has been a feature in many world religions and social formations. Hasidic Jews speak of *zaddik*, for example, as a righteous man who embodies the Torah but who also partially bears the sins of his generation. (Kane 2002: 85)

As such, the saints with disabilities (and arguably, the concept of victim souls) are part of a long tradition of persons who suffer for others and as such attain a significant moral status in their community.

Metaphysics of Disability: Holy States versus Official Church Statements on Disability

Given the high value placed on the mystic suffering for others model, one might expect that official Roman Catholic and Vatican statements on disability would reflect that holy status. But the Reilly statement on Audrey Santo from 1999 is more closely aligned with the Catholic Church's stated policies on disability. In November 1978, a Pastoral Statement of U.S. Catholic Bishops on People with Disabilities was produced. It emphasized inclusion of persons with disabilities in church rituals, the value of interaction with persons with disabilities, and the notion that the wholeness of the church warrants such interaction and inclusion. The statement also upholds that "people with disabilities do not want pity, but participation" (1978).

The statement begins with an invocation of the New Testament Jesus, "Who heard the cry for recognition from the people with disabilities of Judea and Samaria 2,000 years ago" (1978). The intended audience of the statement is clergy members, and a variety of specific pastoral missions are described and encouraged. Bishops are enjoined to designate "ministry to people with disabilities" as a "special focus" of the church for the future:

> As pastors of the Church in America, we are committed to working for a deeper understanding of both the pain and the potential of our neighbors who are blind, deaf, mentally retarded, emotionally impaired, who have special learning problems, or who suffer from single or multiple physical handicaps—all those whom disability may set apart. We call upon people of good will to reexamine their attitudes toward their brothers and sisters with disabilities and promote their well-being, acting with the sense of justice and the compassion that the Lord so clearly desires. Further, realizing the unique gifts individuals with disabilities have to offer the Church, we wish to address the need for their integration into the Christian community and their fuller participation in its life. (U.S. Conference of Catholic Bishops 1978: Section 1)

The statement makes no reference to the notion of saints as persons with disabilities who play any special role in the church, as victim souls, or as any other type of intercessory figures. The statement features language that assumes a distinct hierarchy in which the person with disabilities is described as less than those who are without disabilities, or as "marginal": "The Church finds its true identity when it fully integrates itself with these marginal people, including those who suffer from physical and psychological disabilities" (1978: Section 12). The statement does acknowledge that persons with disabilities have a special place in the "shadow of the cross":

> They bring with them a special insight into the meaning of life; for they live, more than the rest of us perhaps, in the shadow of the cross. And out of their experience they forge virtues like courage, patience, perseverance, compassion and sensitivity that should serve as an inspiration to all Christians. (1978: Section 13)

Following sections include specific injunctions to use innovative means to include persons with disabilities in services and in parish life. Similar points are made by the Catholic Bishops' Conference of England and Wales in their 1981 pastoral statement on persons with disabilities, entitled "All People Together." This pastoral statement has served as the basis for many Catholic statements on persons with disabilities since it was written.

A more theologically based statement, "The International Year of Disabled Persons," was written by Pope John Paul II in 1981. Since the 1970s the Vatican has released many statements on the place of persons with disabilities in the Church. This statement is selected because it offers a brief theological basis for the integration of persons with disabilities. In 1985, Chicago Cardinal Joseph Bernadin produced his statement, "Access to the Sacraments of Initiation and Reconciliation for Developmentally Disabled Persons." The statement for the Archdiocese of Chicago became accepted as the theological rationale for the access to the Sacraments of Initiation and Reconciliation for people with cognitive disabilities in many archdioceses in the United States. The influence of Bernadin's statement can be seen in the United States Conference of Catholic Bishops' Pastoral Statements dealing with disability. These included "Guidelines for Celebration of the Sacraments with Persons with Disabilities" from 1995, the "Pastoral Statement of U.S. Catholic Bishops on People with Disabilities" in 1999, and "The Bishops Pastoral Statement on People with Disabilities at 30: Bright Past, Bold Future" from 2008. (United States Conference of Catholic Bishops 1995, 1999, 2008). Based strongly on "Relationship Theology," it upholds the idea that relationships between people and the creation of the right moral community is paramount (Bernardin 1985). Especially in regard to persons with cognitive disabilities, the relationship between members of the church community and with God is more important than whether or not the person understands or comprehends the sacraments. Bernadin's statement is commensurate with natural law theory and the cultivation of the proper moral ecology in the Roman Catholic community.[2]

Perhaps this notion of the community and inclusion of those with disabilities was an influence on the December 2000 Vatican's Committee for the Jubilee Day Special Statement on Persons with Disabilities. A central tenet of Relationship Theology is that bonds between people that have been broken should be healed and mended, the Vatican statement has as its goal the reconciliation of church leadership with the disabled persons, in recognition of past wrongs (Vatican Committee for the Jubilie Day 2000). Citing a number of international, secular documents on human rights, the Vatican argues that certain duties are to be enacted by civil community members in the church, as well as those who are members of the ecclesiastical community:

> The General Assembly of the United Nations took the initiative of establishing December 3 as World Day for Persons with Disabilities. (resolution 47/3 taken on December 14, 1992)
>
> In 1998 the United Nations' Human Rights Commission declared, with resolution 1998/31 taken in April, that:
>> Every person with disabilities has the right to protection from discrimination and to equal and full enjoyment of his or her individual human rights, as it is also laid down in instructions given in:
>>> The Universal Declaration on Human Rights,
>>>
>>> The International Agreement on Civil and Political Rights,
>>>
>>> The International Agreement on Economic, Social and Cultural Rights,
>>>
>>> By the International Convention on the elimination of all forms of discrimination against women
>> By the International Convention on the rights of the child
>>> By the Convention on "professional rehabilitation and work (persons with disabilities)" number 159 of the International Labour Organisation.

It is unusual for a Vatican document to take its cue from secular organizations such as the United Nations, but the Roman Catholic Church at this time sought to regain its ethical voice after years of scandals involving abuse of children. The document's goal of correcting past wrongs and healing bonds within the church community was in direct reference to specific wrongs, such as those outlined in Nancy Scheper-Hughes and Sargent's 1999 article, "Institutionalized Sex Abuse and the Catholic Church." Scheper-Hughes and Sargent (1999) highlight specific instances of abuse (from neglect to extreme sexual abuse) in Catholic contexts internationally, including Brazil, the United States, and Ireland. Perhaps in alignment with the 1900s belief in "victim souls," Roman Catholics in many countries had been taught to believe that child death was not a tragedy, but a "special grace." Scheper-Hughes and Sargent and many other scholars give a sociohistorical critique of examples of children mistreated in the church, clarifying the way that the church fostered a connection between poverty, unplanned pregnancies, celibacy, and ignorance about sexual practices. This atmosphere of poverty, ignorance, and unquestioning submission to authority led to increasing numbers of child abuse cases. Such cases were covered up, sometimes involving collusion between archdiocese officials, priests, nuns, and parents.

In an effort to heal its past and acknowledge (in some small way) its ill-treatment of children and the disabled, the Vatican's introductory statement (2000) notes that

> Disability is not a punishment, it is a place where normality and stereotypes are challenged and the Church and society are moved to search for that crucial point at which the human person is fully himself. This paper aims to help discover that the person with disability is a privileged interlocutor of society and the Church.

While the Vatican's statement does not uphold any notion that persons with disabilities can have a special status with intercession or "victim soul" roles, it does give the status of disabled persons as privileged interlocutor, one who is in dialogue with the church and potentially an interrogating example with which church policies and activities can be pressed and tested.

Another reason that the church entered into dialogue with statements on human rights from secular bodies such as the United Nations was so that it could make statements and use its voice in international politics to influence governmental policies on persons with disabilities. In section II of the document, the church describes its role as

> ...connecting policies of government bodies and their acceptance on the part of citizens, must stimulate direct assumption of responsibility

> by individuals in all forms, from the protection of rights, to fiscal contribution to support assistance services, to adhering to programmes of prevention, to the promotion of legislative measures which indicate in every field of social life the collective will to respect parity of rights for persons with disabilities. If this is a criterion, which cannot be avoided for the Christian, it can in any case be a criterion of choice for every type of society. (2000)

In this section, the Vatican is giving a clear charge that the active church community member should be in dialogue with government, have a voice in public life, and actively promote and support specific legislation and policies that will give parity and equality to persons with disabilities. In the final section of the statement, the issue of shaping the social order more broadly, and monitoring the quality of life of those who may have limited access to information, is addressed:

> It is a sad fact that persons with disabilities are vulnerable to the change in social, political and economic movements. For example, it is foreseen that the present social transformation will result in an economic order in the 21st century, in which knowledge will be the main resource, rather than manpower, natural resources or capital; a social order in which inequality based on knowledge will be the greatest challenge; in public policies in which the government is unable to solve social and economic problems. (2000)

So while the Catholic Church is still assuming a hierarchy, in which persons with disabilities must be protected and watched over, the issue of their quality of life is addressed in new ways (especially with added attention to governmental policy and statements of human rights from organizations outside the church, such as the United Nations.)

In contrast, a few years later in 2006, the Vatican decided not to sign on with the United Nations General Assembly's "Convention on the Rights of Persons with Disabilities," because it included a clause requiring member nations to provide "Sexual and reproductive health" and population-based public health programs" to people with disabilities. The Vatican's concern here was that the latest UN Convention would be used to promote abortion, particularly abortion of fetuses that were found to have disabilities. It is also significant to note that the United States did not sign on to the Convention either (Westen 2006).

From Disability and Sainthood to Broader Society

The status of persons with disabilities, and especially saints with disabilities, in the Catholic Church is complex. Persons with disabilities are seen as both dependent on others and "lesser-than." In some historical cases, persons with cognitive disabilities were assumed to be unable to partake in basic Catholic rituals and sacraments because they could not fully comprehend them. The possibility of Audrey Santo as an interceding saint is called into question, depending on the level of neural activity still occurring in her brain. Yet, at the same time, persons with disabilities and saints with disabilities have been constructed as holy, sacred, and as taking part in the suffering of Christ—clearly a relationship in which they are "greater-than" the average church community member, since they can intercede or be prayed to, or are closer to Christ because of their suffering. In these cases, the disabled person holds a binary status as both "the least of my brothers" and as redemptive locus of pain and power that can aid others to achieve salvation.

Is this merely a romanticization of the situation of persons with disabilities? Is it a tenuous connection between the Passion of Christ and its mystical modern-day cognate in the lived experiences of people such as St. Thérèse of Lisieux, Marthe Robin, Audrey Santo, St. Germaine Cousin, and St. Dymphna? The fact that so many of the "victim souls" have been female is a serious point of concern for many scholars—the victim soul concept is fraught with a variety of sexist mores, including a condescending patriarchal treatment (in which men of the church watch women suffer, or cause their suffering though abuse and flagellation, or by neglect) while at the same time deigning to put the women victim souls on pedestals and celebrate their suffering for the church and for others.

One area where the church has indeed been consistent is in celebrating the special miraculous nature of families and parents that rise to the occasion and take care of children with disabilities. An article in the *Niedziela Sunday Catholic Magazine* by Lilla Danilecka, "Every Child Is A Holy History" from 2006, upholds the holy status of families that care for disabled children:

> Christine and Pol-Marie are Belgian and they are founders of the Belgian branch of the adoptive work called Emmanuel-SOS-Adoption. They got married 33 years ago and dreamt of having five children. Then God entered their lives and gave them nineteen kids, including nine disabled or chronically ill ones. They often smile, they are humble and their eyes are full of God's peace... (Danilecka 2006: 1)

Christiane Boldo notes that her children remind her that every human life is precious and sacred, and that one must do whatever they can to help make a disabled person's life worthy (Danilecka 2006). This is a clear connection to the teleological focus of natural law theory, in which the community exists to help every individual live up to their full potentiality. The article ends with instructions for Catholics between the ages of 18 and 28 on how to volunteer to help a family with disabled children.

The church's acknowledgment that caregivers of persons with disabilities deserve gratitude and that their work is valued as a part of the church community is certainly admirable. In light of the current dialogue between natural law theory (Tollefsen and George) and Rawlsian contractarian capabilities approach (Nussbaum), it does point to the church's recent shift in disability issues as an indicator of society as a whole and its current struggle with rights for disabled persons. Perhaps if we uphold persons with disabilities as exemplars, we can see their moral fortitude as a model and the moral fortitude of those who care for persons with disabilities as having a central place in construction of the right moral ecology for society as a whole. This is a special type of moral model, one in which the person with disabilities and those who give that person care are models to inspire the right moral community and actions on the parts of individuals in that community. It is not about trying to be a disabled saint or caregiver, it is about how the community *treats* persons with disabilities and those who give care as members of *our* community:

> On the part of the disabled, hostility, discrimination, and indifference result in an environment which is more antagonistic to their flourishing than it need be, or than is reasonable. On the part of the dependency worker (the caregiver), indifference and lack of respect result in a sense that their work is unappreciated, and that they would be better off doing something more socially valued and financially remunerative. How can we see these concerns... such that they are proper concerns of the state? (Tollefsen 2009: 16)

Clearly the Roman Catholic Church has tried to find a voice in secular international politics by entering into dialogue on the international stage with the United Nations and its recent statements on disability. In fact, the international community and its attention to scandals in the Catholic Church may have inspired some of the better shifts in policy and may have proven the need for an international agreement such as the 2006 Convention on the Rights of Persons with Disabilities. The treatment of persons with disabilities by church leaders has served as an indicator, or interlocutor, of how well society lives up to natural law theory—even when the Catholic Church itself has previously fallen short of natural law.

Notes

1. Additional discussion of the church history on access, and current instructions for increasing accessibility, can be found in McNulty, Dennis C. (2009). *Church Access for Persons with Disabilities: Catholic Teachings, Practical Suggestions and Resources*. Retrieved January 2010 http://www.catholicdisabilityteachings.com/Need%20to%20be%20written/Misc%20Resources.htm

2. For further discussion of the church approach to disability in the 1980s, see John Paul II, Pope, *The International Year of Disabled Persons* (Washington: National Catholic Office for Persons with Disabilities, 1981).

References

Ailworth, E. (2008). Sainthood is sought for 'Little Audrey'. *The Boston Globe*. Retrieved November 2009 from http://www.boston.com/news/local/articles/2008/09/14/sainthood_is_sought_for_little_audrey/?page=full

Barry, E. (1998). The strange case of Audrey Santo. *The Boston Phoenix*. Retrieved November 2009 from http://bostonphoenix.com/archive/features/97/12/25/AUDREY_SANTO.html

Bernardin, J. C. (1985). *Access to the Sacraments of Initiation and Reconciliation for Developmentally Disabled Persons*. Chicago, IL: Liturgy Training Publications.

Catholic Bishops' Conference of England and Wales. (1981). *All People Together*. CTS: London.

Danilecka, L. (2006). Every child is a holy history. *Niedziela Sunday Catholic Magazine*. Retrieved November 2009 from http://sunday.niedziela.pl/artykul.php? dz=swiat&id_art=00043

Fisher, J. (1989). *The Catholic Counterculture in America, 1933–1962*. Chapel Hill, NC: University of North Carolina Press.

Garner, D. (2006). *Disability in History – York Provides a Unique Perspective*. University of York Press Release. Retrieved June 2009 from http://www.york.ac.uk/admin/presspr/pressreleases/disabilityhistory.htm

George, R. P. (1993). *Making Men Moral*. Oxford, UK: Oxford University Press.

George, R. P., & Tollefsen, C. (2008). *Embryo: A Defense of Human Life*. New York, NY: Doubleday.

Giloteaux, P. (1927). *Victim Souls*. Switzerland: Benziger Brothers, out of print.

Hanisch, H. (2007). (Review of Martha Nussbaum's *Frontiers of justice: Disability, nationality, and species membership*). *Scandinavian Journal of Disability Research* 9(2), 133–136.

John Paul II, Pope. (1981). *The International Year of Disabled Persons*. Washington, DC: National Catholic Office for Persons with Disabilities.

Kane, P. M. (2002). 'She offered herself up': The victim soul and victim spirituality in Catholicism. *Church History* 71(1), 80–119.

Lamey, A. (2007). (Review of Martha Nussbaum's *Frontiers of justice: Disability, nationality, and species membership*). *Philosophical Books* 48(4), 376–382.

Levenson, M. (2008). Bid to canonize girl draws mixed reaction: Skeptics question claims of miracles. *The Boston Globe*. Retrieved November 2009 from http://www.boston.com/news/local/articles/2008/10/13/bid_to_canonize_girl_draws_mixed_reaction/?s_campaign=8315

Little Audrey Santo Foundation Price List. Retrieved November 2009 from http://www.littleaudreysanto.org/Item_List.htm

McNulty, D. C. (2009). *Church Access for Persons with Disabilities: Catholic Teachings, Practical Suggestions and Resources*. Retrieved January 2010 from http://www.catholicdisabilityteachings.com/Need%20to%20be%20written/Misc%20Resources.htm

Mulcahy, C. (1909). St. Germaine Cousin. In *The Catholic Encyclopedia*. New York, NY: Robert Appleton Company. Retrieved November 2009 from http://www.newadvent.org/cathen/06474a.htm

Nussbaum, M. (2006). *Frontiers of Justice: Disability, Nationality, and Species Membership*, Cambridge, MA: Harvard University Press.

O'Malley, V. J. (1999). *Ordinary Suffering of Extraordinary Saints*. Huntington, IN: Our Sunday Visitor Press.

Pham, C. (2009). Little Audrey Santo's mother to appear on Catholic TV talk show to discuss beatification? *Catholic Exchange* June 22. Retrieved November 2009 from http://catholicexchange.com/2009/06/22/119680/

Reilly, D. P. (1999). *Diocese Issues Interim Findings on Miraculous Claims: Statement by Most Reverend Daniel P. Reilly, Bishop of Worcester*. Turin, Italy: CESNUR, Center for Studies on New Religions. Retrieved November 2009 from http://www.cesnur.org/testi/Worcester.htm

Scheper-Hughes, N., & Sargent, C. (Eds.). (1999). Institutionalized sex abuse and the Catholic Church. In *Small Wars: The Cultural Politics of Childhood*. Berkeley, CA: University of California Press.

Tench, M. (2007). A tearful farewell to Little Audrey. *The Boston Globe*. Retrieved from http://www.boston.com/news/local/articles/2007/04/19/a_tearful_farewell_to_little_audrey/

Tollefsen, C. (2009). Disability and social justice. Unpublished manuscript.

United Nations General Assembly. (2006). *Convention on the Rights of Persons with Disabilities*. Retrieved from http://www.un.org/esa/socdev/enable/rights/ahcfinalrepe.htm

United States Conference of Catholic Bishops. (1995). *Guidelines for Celebration of the Sacraments with Persons with Disabilities*. Washington, DC: National Catholic Office for Persons with Disabilities.

United States Conference of Catholic Bishops. (1999). *Pastoral Statement of U.S. Catholic Bishops on People with Disabilities*. Washington, DC: National Catholic

Office for Persons with Disabilities, 1978 version edited by Father George Kuryvial, O.M.I., updated 1989 and 1999. Retrieved November 2009 from http://www.ncpd.org/pastoral_statement_1978.htm and Feb. 2010 from http://www.ncpd.org/views-news-policy/policy/church/bishops/pastoral

United States Conference of Catholic Bishops. (2008). The bishops pastoral statement on people with disabilities at 30: Bright past, bold future. Webinar and toolkit. Retrieved January 2010 from http://www.ncpd.org/webinars/2008-08-13

Vatican Committee for the Jubilee Day of the Community with Persons with Disabilities. (2000). *The Person with Disabilities: The Duties of the Civil and Ecclesial Community.* Retrieved November 2009 from http://www.vatican.va/jubilee_2000/jubilevents/jub_disabled_20001203_scheda5_en.htm

Westen, J. (2006). *Vatican Refuses to Sign UN Disabilities Rights Treaty over Pro-abortion Language: First Time 'Sexual and Reproductive Health' Rights Included within an International Treaty.* Retrieved January 2010 from http://www.lifesite-news.com/ldn/2006/dec/06121406.html

CHAPTER 10

Best Practices for Faith-Based Organizations Working with Deaf Communities in Developing Countries

Amy T. Wilson and Kirk Van Gilder

For centuries, missionaries from the North have journeyed to far-away lands to propagate and practice their religious beliefs. During their travels many discovered that some cultures and societies marginalized their disabled population and excluded them from those social services normally made available to their able-bodied citizenry. In response to this marginalization, and guided by their charitable philanthropic and religious beliefs, missionaries built schools, rehabilitation centers, churches, and health centers for those who would not ordinarily be served by their communities (Miles 1999, 2003). One example from the early 1900s is a young Christian theology student, Ernst Christoffel, whose faith called him to leave his native Germany and work in the Middle East with blind children. Today his legacy is the mission group, the Christian Blind Mission, which has established more than 1,000 projects for disabled children in 108 developing nations throughout the world (Christian Blind Mission International 2004). An American minister also called by his faith was the Reverend Andrew Foster, who left for Africa in the 1950s and founded the Christian Mission for Deaf Africans. In his 30-year ministry, Foster founded 31 schools and 2 centers throughout Africa (Christian Mission for the Deaf 2004).

Whether missionaries in the 1800s felt called to spread their Christian faith or to help the most marginalized members of society,

European Christians were often closely allied with colonial powers while working overseas or perceived by indigenous people to be allied with these powers whether they were working in concert with them or not. An example is a retired British minister, the Reverend Gilby, who brought teachers and financial donations to the Caribbean and established schools for deaf people in Jamaica. At the time, most colonial powers believed that people with disabilities should not receive services from the colonized country, but donations from the colonizing country or from expatriate philanthropic groups living in the colonized country led to the idea of acting and behaving charitably toward people with disabilities. "Charity" removed the local government's obligation of offering services to the disabled and left the responsibility to church groups and nonprofit organizations (Ingstad 2001). The Jamaican government relied on the goodness of the foreign church to support deaf children on the island. To this day, donations and volunteers from American church groups and foreign nonprofit groups financially support most of the schools for the deaf in Jamaica (Wilson 2000).

Looking at people with disabilities as recipients of charity in the Christian church has been in existence for the past several hundred years. This dependency on foreign churches for social services for disabled people in developing countries continues today. Driedger, Enns and Regehr (1989) believe that the Christian church has seen disabled persons as cripples, beggars, and objects of sympathy. The Islamic and Hindu religions have tended to have the same point of view and have had a tradition of giving alms to poor and disabled people (Miles 1999). Missionaries who look at people with disabilities as objects of charity will work not necessarily to empower them, but would be more likely to follow a medical or rehabilitation model of support (Wilson 2000).

Deaf theologian Hannah Lewis has identified four models of charity: moral economy, liberal development, taking responsibility, and liberation. The impact of each of these models is evident in the history of Christian mission from the North to the global South as well. From ancient times until the late nineteenth century, the dominant construction of disabled people in Christian churches as social institutions was much like that of poor people. The division of the world into categories of privileged people and unfortunates was accepted as part and parcel of reality. Instead of any efforts to change the structural nature of the charitable relationship between these two classes of people, a *moral economy* was established whereby the privileged were expected to make voluntary contributions to the well-being and care of unfortunates among them. Such motivations formed a theological and social obligation to "care for the poor" in many religious communities without challenging the reasons why poverty and inequality occurred in societies (Lewis 2007). The moral economy model was a strong motivation in the establishment through missionary efforts of not only institutions to benefit disabled and deaf people in the global South but also the first public school for deaf children in the United States in 1816 (Lane 1984).

The advent of the Industrial Revolution in the West began to erode the societal connections between classes of people that religious teaching had provided and thus also devalued the sense of moral obligation motivating voluntary contributions in the moral economy model. Thus, a new model of charity arose that established charity as an industry of services in its own right. This *liberal development* model of charity saw the rise of social service agencies, government involvement in the welfare of "unfortunates," and the development of service professionals who were seen as "experts" in identifying and serving the needs of recipients of charity. Often, this model led to further disenfranchisement of deaf and disabled people by replacing their own knowledge of their struggles and needs with the expertise of highly educated professionals. Therefore, a system of continuing dependency was created by which recipients of charity were viewed as unaware of their own self-interests or unable to properly care for themselves (Lewis 2007). This shift in approaches was reflected in the establishment of other schools for the deaf in the United States as a growing number of deaf schools were supported by state governments using the rationale that if deaf people were to be functioning members of a democratic society, the state is responsible for their well-being and preparation for entry into that society (Lane 1984).

Concerns over the creation of classes dependent on the social welfare programs of governments ultimately gave rise to a third model of charity. This model of *taking responsibility* views the recipients of charity as being moral agents and in need of being responsible with their decisions and actions in life. Therefore, those who make poor choices in life resulting in poverty become undeserving of charitable aid as a consequence of their own choices. Alternatively, those who do receive charitable contributions are charged with a responsibility to use them in a manner that will be seen as fitting to advance their chances in society (Lewis 2007). Although this model is largely couched in the tradition of Western individualism, the concerns of created and ultimately enforced dependency are also echoed in missiological reflections. The controversial declaration of the 1974 All-African Council of Churches to place a moratorium on missionaries and mission funding from the West reflected a growing awareness of the detrimental effects of liberal development style mission programs as well as unease with the implicit control of how funds were to be used under a model that would enforce responsibility as defined by the donor bodies (Yates 1994).

The *liberation* model of understanding the relationship between privileged and disenfranchised classes in society is developed within various liberation theologies. This approach emphasizes the need for various disenfranchised classes to be the authors of their own stories and agents of change in society to alter their own circumstances. Such an approach assumes that a great deal of social and institutional structural change will take place as the issues that create poverty, inequality, and barriers to advancement are identified, addressed, and removed (Lewis 2007). The liberation model of charity seems to develop more equitable relationships between both missionary sending societies and those receiving them. Likewise, mission groups taking this approach are much more likely to see people with disabilities as equals in the eyes of God and in their churches and therefore have a tendency to develop projects that are self-sustaining and inclusive.

Strategies for Mission Work

There are three major ways foreign churches begin evangelizing to or working with people with disabilities overseas.

1. Some foreign churches "plant" new churches in developing countries for an entire community. Through experiencing a culturally more open attitude about including people with disabilities in church services by the foreign missionaries, native church members may be more inclined to bring disabled family members to church. A shift in attitude by the church community may occur, and the church membership becomes more inclusive. Or, it may be that a foreign missionary see a need to call another missionary to work specifically with the disabled members of their church for the purpose of evangelization or for managing special projects.
2. Churches may be founded specifically for people with disabilities by foreign missionaries. Most often this is seen when missionaries choose to establish churches specifically for deaf people.
3. Foreign churches may form social institutions such as clubs and workshops, and advocacy groups may be initiated with the goal of bringing people with disabilities together for solidarity, training, and mutual support.

The classic approach to missionary endeavors in relation to church planting is known as the *Three-Self* method. This method seeks to establish native churches that are self-governed, self-supported, and self-propagating. American Congregationalist Rufus Anderson and English Anglican Henry Venn developed these principles simultaneously in the mid-nineteenth century (Beaver 1967; Warren 1971). Although it appears that their initial thoughts on mission development and church planting were developed independently, they did come to know of one another's work and Anderson's emphasis on self-propagation may have influenced Venn's later work (Beaver 1967). The three-self movement's desire to see local churches become autonomous and nonreliant on the bodies funding their missionary origins is laudable. Anderson's admonishment that the foreign missionary should never be the pastor of a missionary church but instead identify and train local leadership to govern and manage the affairs of the congregation offers a stronger hedge against more colonizing influences in Christian mission (Beaver 1967). These local churches then are to become the center for Christian aid services throughout their societies rather than foreign missionary personnel and funding.

However, this model has some stumbling points when applied to missionary efforts with disabled and deaf people. As disabled and deaf people in most societies, and particularly in developing countries, find themselves severely economically marginalized as a result of unemployment and underemployment, the self-supporting nature of these ministries becomes problematic. If indigenous church bodies cannot absorb the cost of these missions inclusive of disabled people without external assistance from a missionary group, the inclusion of disabled people may wither or require a continuance of some semblance of charity relationship between all involved.

Similarly, the self-propagating aspect of this model can be problematic for those mission groups establishing churches specifically for deaf people. Whereas the emphasis on self-propagation as raised by Anderson was primarily an issue of evangelization, he also emphasized the importance of missionaries providing and teaching a model Christian home life that would propagate the church generationally as well (Beaver 1967). Because most deaf people are born into hearing families and are deaf as a result of prenatal or postnatal illness rather than any genetic cause, a church founded of deaf people will most likely not self-propagate generationally as their children will largely be born fully hearing. Despite these barriers, many deaf churches do continue for quite some time growing through evangelism but often remain one generation thick. Another limitation is the financial reality of sustaining and propagating an independent deaf church in a developing nation. Unless a deaf church is to be led by volunteer clergy with no physical meeting place of their own and little or no material goods, it will require financial support from its membership or other sources. The financial hardships faced by deaf people in developing nations often preclude them from being able to contribute anything but their time to church-planting efforts. Even the contribution of their time becomes a scarce commodity as the struggle for basic necessities consumes a large portion of their daily lives as aging parents and siblings with growing families of their own can no longer provide the security of support they did when a deaf family member was young. Thus, many deaf congregations become financially dependent either on local hearing congregations or overseas mission bodies. While such efforts can maintain a congregation, they undermine the self-sufficiency and independence of practice fostered by the three-self approach.

Despite these limitations, deaf congregations continue to be a vital and positive presence in the lives of deaf people in developing nations. Often they are the only gathering place for deaf people for not only spiritual care but also social interaction. They can play a vital role in deaf people supporting one another and building communities of mutual care and self-advocacy. Deaf churches in developing nations often also act as deaf clubs where crucial news about local politics, health care and preventative medicine efforts in the community, and survival strategies coincide with worship services, scripture studies, and recreational activities. Such holistic communities of deaf life that often develop around deaf church-planting efforts make significant positive contributions to the lives of deaf people in developing nations, which may outweigh the concerns created by financial dependency. However, care must be taken that funding bodies allow for local autonomy and develop as much self-sufficiency as possible as the breach of trust and effect of losing such a community because of a sudden lack of funding would be potentially devastating.

An alternative to the church-planting goal of Christian missions is reflected in the approach of James Dennis who wrote a comprehensive review of Christian missions and methods in 1896 after a series of lectures at Princeton University. While Dennis did not deny that the primary goal of many Christian missions was ultimately evangelization, he placed a stronger emphasis on the resulting social changes brought by Christian missionary work. Missionaries were to bring not only new ecclesial institutions into receiving societies but also educational, literary, commercial, industrial, and medical institutions. Thus, the overall impact of Christian missionary presence was as sociological as it was theological (Dennis 1897). The aim of this approach is to serve by example rather than proselytizing. The theological principles of Christian charity and solidarity become the foundation for assisting local communities in tasks and problems they have not yet found the resources to address rather than concern for personal conversion or the building of the institutional church. This approach is often the underpinning of mission groups seeking to establish clinics, clubs, work training projects, and schools to benefit disabled and deaf people in developing nations. The establishment of such institutions then becomes not only practical assistance for those who gain new skills and status through participation and services but also an example for local society of potential solutions to what is often seen as a societal problem in the lack of care shown for people with disabilities. However, this model often runs into the limitations of the liberal development model of charity discussed above. If careful consideration is not taken to ensure that disabled and/or deaf people are guiding these programs, they can create dependency on foreign or local nondisabled leadership.

In practice, these two approaches to missionary presence in the global South are often found working in tandem. A mission group from the North may initiate the founding of a congregation specifically for deaf people with the intention of developing local deaf leadership and governance. The deaf congregation could identify one of their major struggles as the inability to find meaningful work and income in order to survive economically. Seeing other international aid workshop projects designed to benefit marginalized people may inspire the deaf congregants to desire for such an opportunity to be available for their own benefit. Deaf congregants may approach foreign mission groups or aid agencies again to request funding to initiate such a workshop. This workshop then becomes another missionary effort of foreign aid, and although it may retain funding from the same financial backers as the church, it may receive funding from other donors or generate income on its own. In some cases, such a workshop may be a direct ministry of the deaf congregants in their efforts to provide meaningful support for their members. In other cases, these workshops may be structurally independent of local congregations and share only an organic relationship as they deal with the needs of the same community of deaf people. In either case, the presence of foreign funding to maintain the workshop is likely to maintain some necessary relationship between mission groups providing financial support and deaf congregants receiving it rather than establishing a church that is truly self-governed, self-supported, and self-propagated.

Missionaries may arrive overseas with the objective of evangelizing and converting natives to their religious beliefs to bring material and financial aid, and/or set up programs to educate, rehabilitate, or vocationally train church members, including those who are disabled or deaf. Missionaries also travel overseas to specifically minister to the deaf community.

In all cases, Yutta Fricke's strategies (Fricke 2003) for best practices by international development organizations can also be followed by mission groups. Consultation, capacity-building of disability organizations, community mainstreaming, and commitment are central for disability inclusion in mission work targeted for people with disabilities overseas. Because of the manner foreign church groups tend to work with and for people with disabilities overseas, some additional practices will also be suggested for missionaries and volunteers. Two organizations who have followed the four Cs and whose practices are noteworthy and replicable are the North American Christian Organization and the Mennonite Central Committee (MCC). Examples of their work will be interspersed throughout this chapter.

Consultation

1. *Listen to the people.* Ideally, mission work initially begins when people with disabilities approach a foreign church group. They may ask for assistance in building a church or a school. Perhaps they request that a volunteer or a missionary from a foreign church group come to work in an existing church, or fund a project targeted for people with disabilities. Some mission groups decide where they think a church should be planted, or what programs their disabled church members need without input from the people requesting assistance. The mission group must first sit with the disability group and work with them in discovering what their needs and desires are before any decisions are made. MCC sits with community leaders and writes a job description with the community before calling a North American volunteer to come work overseas. MCC plans new projects and programs with the people rather than for the people. As an example, whereas a Northern church without community input may think purchasing brailed hymn books as important, blind church members' priority may be aluminum canes and mobility training instead.

2. *No assumptions.* It is important not to assume that religious values and beliefs are replicated from one country to the next even though all people belong to the same faith. A religion's attitudes or beliefs concerning disabilities in the South may not be known or believed in the North. Although some members of the Catholic Church in northeast Brazil may believe the "evil eye" caused their child's disability, members of the Catholic Church in the North may find these beliefs unfounded. Do not discount or belittle their religious beliefs. Rather honor them while sharing your own.

3. *Collaboration.* Seek out any disability organizations that may exist in the area, and work with them, learn from them, and support them. They could be a mission group's best ally in achieving the church's goals, and collaboration will help the disability organization reach its goals. The church alienating or not recognizing their existence works at cross purposes for everyone.

4. *Learn from the past.* Ask people with disabilities about the history of churches and other domestic and international organizations that have worked and included them in their programs. If possible, build upon past trainings, learn from past successes and difficulties, review and revise what has been done. If a Bible study ground to a halt because the rainy season made roads impassable by cane users, adapt your strategy. Do not assume programs have never been attempted or you may be reinventing a wheel rather than just patching it.

Capacity Building of Church Members with Disabilities

1. *Exchanges.* Building partnerships between churches with people with disabilities in the North and South are beneficial. A Pennsylvanian Deaf Mennonite Church financially and spiritually supports other deaf churches in developing countries. Some of the church members from both the North and the South have done exchanges in order to share their stories and their faith, enriching the lives of their respective church communities. The Pennsylvanian Deaf community becomes educated about the social, economic, and political situation of a Deaf community in another country as well as learns how best to support their deaf brothers and sisters overseas. The group coming from the South may learn fresh approaches to sharing their faith as well as innovate strategies that they can bring home.

2. *Professional assistance.* If a missionary or volunteer is called to work in a developing country, it is essential that they be professionals in the field in which the disability community calls them. Missionaries are less effective and may be more of a hindrance than a support if they arrive overseas without a background in disabilities. It would be inappropriate for anyone lacking credentials in educating deaf children to open a school in the United States. The reverse is also true. Imagine missionaries going overseas, also without a background in deaf education, sign language, or Deaf culture, yet opening a school for deaf children. Some may rationalize that any school is better than no school, but more harm than good may happen if people are not properly prepared for the work they are to do overseas. Some mission groups have brought signed English from the United States and ignored their host country's native sign language. This is a kind of colonialization where a native people's language is influenced and changed by an outside influence. Mission groups can contact special education or disability study programs at Northern universities and in the developing countries themselves, which offer degrees in the specialized area to recruit volunteers and missionaries. Mennonite Central Committee sent trained teachers to Bolivia to work with children with cognitive disabilities and provided teachers to the St. Joseph's Mission in Swaziland to train those who taught children with physical disabilities.

Capacity Building

1. *Inclusive Church Council.* Sometimes donations intended to support a church's disabled members are sent from the foreign mission office to an overseas church whose financial expenditures are overseen by able-bodied church leaders. Fricke suggests that someone with a disability sit on the board of directors of international organizations. So, too, should Church Councils in the North include members with disabilities. Church Councils in the South should also include people with disabilities to hear what their needs are or inappropriate decisions could be made. As an example, a British church group sent money to support deaf members of a southern Brazilian Christian church whose church board was made up of all able-bodied people. Without deaf representation, the board decided to spend the money on white gloves and gowns for a hearing choir of 20 singers who signed hymns

into LIBRAS, Brazilian sign Language, which was beautiful, but did not resolve any of the deaf church members' needs. Councils could also establish a subcommittee consisting of disabled church members in order to make decisions for themselves since the church council itself may not be familiar with the issues facing their disabled members.

2. *Inclusive programs.* A church could find that a well-intentioned special project created for their disabled members may inadvertently alienate individuals from their church community. For example, opening participation in new projects or Bible studies to all members of the church instead of only for disabled church members will lessen any divisions that could occur. Instead of excluding any one group, or focusing only on one group, churches can model inclusiveness, unity, and cooperation.

3. *Take advantage of the mission group's unique position in the community.* Members of the disabled community who attend religious services do not all attend the same church. At times, foreign missionaries may be surprised at the strong divisions between different denominations in their neighborhood. Sometimes being a foreigner gives one license to move between the two (or three) groups much more easily than a native. Use this to your advantage, and offer development projects to disabled people nonchurch members. You may find that people who have never sat with one another because of their diverse religious beliefs may begin a dialogue with one another as they work together. They will learn from one another that they all face the same challenges and barriers. These common struggles could unite them in fighting for their rights locally.

4. *Freedom of choice.* The Jehovah Witnesses and the Church of Latter Day Saints are two churches that have adapted their religious materials into Braille and a multitude of sign languages from around the world. They are straightforward about their evangelizing and make it clear to disabled people that they want to convert them to their faith. Some churches have used donations from abroad such as food or clothing, as incentives to attract poor, disabled people to their churches in order to win them over. Dependency and mistrust can result when people are not respected and included in a church as a contributing, faithful member instead of a cajoled, bought "convert." Foreign incentives do not last forever, and a church would only have its faith left to share if its source of goods ends. It is best to build a strong

foundation of faith accompanied by sustainable programs based upon a church's statement of faith rather than have a church full of members dependent on material goods.

5. *Letting go.* If missionaries are accompanying a church (such as a Deaf church) as it becomes established, it is critical that the missionary assist and train the leadership and not take the church on as his or hers. The goal should be for the church members to eventually manage the church on their own so that the missionary can return home or move on to new work.

Commitment

1. *Review your church's statement of faith.* For those churches whose congregation includes people with disabilities, make it clear as to why those who have been traditionally marginalized from the church have been included in the church based upon its statement of faith. Read it together as a church community (along with your disabled members since they make up your church community, too), and discuss how looking at people with disabilities as recipients of charity or as a separate entity within your church does not contribute to your or their spiritual growth. Notice how the statement changes in meaning as disabled people read it *with* you as equals.

Community Mainstreaming

1. *Church role model.* Whereas a community may never have paid attention or given credence to people with disabilities in their community before, a church may be the first place in which the community sees people with disabilities treated as equals. An Mennonite Central Committee volunteer worked alongside the local Catholic Church and trained two hearing allies of the Deaf community how to interpret the mass into sign language. Initially, the hearing church members complained about the interpreters' presence on the altar and mocked their signing gestures, but with patience and perseverance, the interpreters and the Deaf community continued to attend mass. Within a year's time, because of the exposure at church, church members were taking sign language classes taught by deaf adults, more deaf people felt comfortable attending mass, and deaf people in the community (not only Catholics) felt more accepted and freer to use their sign language in public. Church

members then began to feel more comfortable to bring their disabled family members to church, too.

2. *Inclusion.* It is important not to keep the people marginalized by making them special and different from the community. Able-bodied community members could become jealous and frustrated that a marginalized group of people is now receiving large amounts of materials and funding that had never existed before. Include other church members, the disabled person's family members, and neighbors in programming. If students and their teachers are sponsored by an overseas Christian organization and regularly receive school supplies, share them with the rest of the school. The children with disabilities will be more accepted and appreciated.

3. *Missionaries/Volunteers with disabilities.* Mission groups should make a concerted effort to find missionaries and volunteers with disabilities. They are excellent role models for those who are disabled as well as means to change a community's attitudes and beliefs about what people with disabilities can do. Mennonite Central Committee sent two volunteers with disabilities to a rural town in northeast Brazil where the community was surprised at the work they could accomplish "despite" their disabilities. The townsfolk began to look at their own community members with disabilities in a new light.

Other Considerations

Material and Monetary Donations

1. *People are listening. Teach and change them.* Missionaries and volunteers need money to support themselves and their programs while overseas and will rely on assistance from their home churches. Many missionaries return home and raise funds from the pulpit or through periodic newsletters. Instead of showing photos meant to pull heartstrings or telling sad stories of people with disabilities living in abject poverty, a positive approach would be better. Tell success stories of those who have changed their lives and/or those in their communities for the better. Tell what can be done despite the circumstances people must live in. Sharing stories also affords the opportunity to discuss the reasons that people with disabilities are forced to live in poverty and the injustices that exist throughout the developing worlds.

Positive stories mobilize audiences to put their religious beliefs into action in stemming poverty at its root cause, not only through donations but also through their lifestyle and politics. The MCC-returned volunteers tell stories of hope and encouragement as well as how their Christian faith calls them to work for peace and justice.

2. *Accept only appropriate materials.* Before accepting material donations, be sure that they are materials your community will be able to use. For example, an American church donated hearing aids to deaf children in a rural community in Kenya. The batteries were prohibitively expensive. No technician was available to set or monitor the hearing aid frequencies nor to make new ear molds as the children's ears matured and changed. It is best to ask the disabled community what their material needs are. MCC sent materials to build a chicken co-op for Zimbabweans at the National Rehabilitation Center, and blacksmith tools, gardening tools, and sewing machines were provided to Laotians with leprosy to run businesses. Instead of sending unusable American wheelchairs to Brazil, an MCC volunteer returned to Brazil with specialized tools that a disability organization requested in order to adapt their wheelchairs to the harsh terrain.

3. *Use donations wisely.* Shipping donated materials from the North to the South can be expensive. It may make more sense to save the money on the shipping and send it to the disability organization so that they can purchase the materials in their home country. One MCC worker realized that it was cheaper to purchase school materials overseas than having her church send pencils, pens, and books to her through the mail.

4. *Work teams.* Many church groups in the North will send work teams to the South to construct buildings such as schools and churches, for two weeks or for several months. Usually each short-term volunteer will raise his or her own funding through his or her home churches. The trips can be quite costly as Atkins (1991) calculated the cost of a work team of 50-plus people who went to Nairobi. Transportation, housing, and feeding the volunteers cost more than $120,000. Perhaps that money could have been better spent giving the money directly to the church group overseas. If a work team does go overseas, the disabled natives should be working right alongside the Northern volunteers instead of as bystanders. The Jamaican deaf community was saddened and disappointed that they were not involved in

the building of some schools for deaf children and wondered why they were not included. Instead of working in a charitable mode, Northern volunteers could participate in empowering the recipients of their assistance and learn about the marginalization of disabled people in the country they are working and also appreciate the abilities and fortitude of the people they have come to assist. An alternative to a work team could be a study tour.

5. *Study tours.* Some churches arrange study tours where specific topics are the focus of their travel, such as visiting and fellowshipping with people with disabilities overseas. Northerners visit churches, organizations, institutions, and schools of and for people with disabilities. Time is arranged where all participants can fellowship and share their stories and their faith. MCC offers several study tours a year on various topics for Christians wishing to view life from a Southern perspective.

6. Instead of sending missionaries or volunteers overseas consider other ways to support people with disabilities in developing countries:

   a. *Support existing programs that empower people with disabilities.* MCC's Global Family Fund allows North Americans to send monthly financial support to existing schools and programs that include people with disabilities. An established Community-Based Rehabilitation Program run by Tanzanians with motor difficulties receives funds to convert tricycles into wheelchairs adapted for their special needs and to withstand dirt and sand paths in rural areas.

   b. *Sponsoring people with disabilities overseas to attend meetings or participate in exchanges.* MCC Thailand helped sponsor a participant to the World Congress of Disabled People International. MCC also sponsored a deaf Brazilian woman to work as an intern at the international office at Gallaudet University. Both returned to their home countries inspired by what they had learned and became leaders in their disability organizations. MCC sent two wheelchair users from Mexico and Nicaragua to a Thai refugee camp to learn how to make artificial limbs.

   c. *Support international and national disability organizations.* Instead of sending missionaries or volunteers overseas, use donations to directly support disability organizations who work with your church or that you know support your church's beliefs. MCC directly supported Disabled Peoples' International (DPI) for many years as one of DIP's leaders was a Mennonite and since DPI held the same human rights' vision as MCC.

Northern churches have worked for and with people with disabilities as long as missionaries have been traveling overseas. Their work has helped to inspire hope and transformation. Mission groups can continue to work alongside people with disabilities in sharing their beliefs and working for peace and justice.

References

Atkins, A. (1991). Work teams? No, "taste and see" teams. *EQ Quarterly* 27, 4.

Beaver, R. P. (Ed.) (1967). *To Advance the Gospel: Selections from the Writings of Rufus Anderson.* Grand Rapids, MI: Wm. B. Eerdmans Publishing Co.

Christian Blind Mission International. (2004). Retrieved from http://www .cbmi-usa.org

Christian Mission for the Deaf. (2004). Frequently asked questions. In *Christian Mission for the Deaf.* Retrieved June 8, 2011, from http://www.cmdeaf.org/faq. asp.

Dennis, J. S. (1897). *Christian Missions and Social Progress: A Sociological Study of Foreign Missions.* New York, NY: Fleming H. Revell Company.

Driedger, D., Enns, H., & Regehr, V. (1989). *Development and Disability: Occasional Papers, No. 9.* Retrieved from http://www.mcc.org/respub/occasional/9.html

Fricke, Y. (2003). *Planning for Success: Participatory Project Planning.* Helsinki: Abilis Foundation.

Ingstad, B. (2001). Disability in the developing world. In G. L. Albrecht, K. D. Seelman, & M. Bury (Eds), *Handbook of Disability Studies.* Thousand Oaks, CA: Sage.

Lane, H. (1984). *When the Mind Hears: A History of the Deaf.* New York, NY: Random House.

Lewis, H. (2007). *Deaf Liberation Theology.* Aldershot, England: Ashgate.

Mennonite Central Committee Home Page.www.mcc.org

Miles, M. (1999). *Educational and Social Responses to Disability in China, Japan & Korea, from Antiquity to 1950: A Bibliography of European-Language Materials, with Introduction and Some Annotation.* Retrieved November 22, 2009, from http://www.socsci.kun.nl/ped/whp/histeduc/mmiles/e-asiabib.html#int-4

Miles, M. (2003). *Disability & Social Responses in Some Southern African Nations: Angola, Botswana, Burundi, D.R. Congo (ex Zaire), Malawi, Mozambique, Namibia, Tanzania, Rwanda, Zambia, Zimbabwe. A Bibliography, with Introduction and Some Historical Items.* Retrieved November 22, 2009, from http://cirrie.buffalo.edu/bibliography/SAfrica1.html

Warren, M. (1971). *To Apply the Gospel: Selections from the Writings of Henry Venn.* Grand Rapids, MI: Wm. B. Eerdmans Publishing Co.

Wilson, A. (2000). Considerations for western educators working with deaf children in developing countries: Community development in a rural Brazilian town. In International Congress of Educators of the Deaf, Sydney, Australia, July 2000.

Yates, T. (1994). *Christian Mission in the Twentieth Century.* Cambridge: Cambridge University Press.

CHAPTER 11

Disability and the Love of Wisdom: De-forming, Re-forming, and Per-forming Philosophy of Religion[1]

Amos Yong

Introduction

My goal in this chapter is to interrogate traditional approaches to philosophy of religion and philosophical theology from a disability studies perspective, rethinking along the way issues in theodicy, religious epistemology, and questions of death and the afterlife that are commonly treated in traditional textbooks on philosophy of religion. This is a conversation whose time is long overdue, as disability perspectives have been noticeably absent in even the most recent discussions in the philosophy of religion.[2] Hence I refrain at this point in the Introduction from justifying this project, with the hope that its importance and timeliness will have emerged for readers at the end. Along the way, I will argue that when the human experience of disability interfaces with the philosophical discussion of religion, one of the results is a "performative philosophy of religion" whereby philosophical reflection does not exclude the speculative moment but is an activity that shapes human dispositions, activities, and political life.

I should add that my intended audiences are both those working in disability studies and those working in philosophy of religion.[3] While there are an increasing number of disability studies scholars who are trained philosophers as well as professional philosophers who have written on disability,[4] there has so far been no formal engagement with issues in the philosophy of religion. To be sure, theologians have spoken about issues in the philosophy of religion from disability perspectives,[5] but these have been taken up within a theological rather than philosophy of religion framework. On the other side, besides issues in biomedical and social ethics, philosophy of education, philosophy of law, and disability as a sociopolitical construct (these are vitally important topics that need to be continually addressed),[6] I also want to urge philosophers reflecting on disability to address topics in the philosophy of religion. This is an important task for philosophical approaches to disability since it often deals, as we shall see, with assumptions at the worldview level for other philosophical and nonphilosophical claims. In this chapter, I propose to inform discussions in the philosophy of religion from disability studies perspectives, and in the process also hope to pave the way for philosophy of religion contributions to disability scholarship.

Two caveats before proceeding: first, there is much in the philosophy of religion that we will not discuss directly, including the relationship between faith and reason, theistic arguments, natural theology, the attributes of God, miracles, religious language and religious truth, and religious diversity. Of course, because many of the topics in philosophy of religion are interrelated and because commitments made in any one arena will have implications for how to understand other contested matters, we will, in the process of dealing with issues in the problem of evil, religious epistemology, and death and the afterlife, touch on some of these matters. Yet we cannot pretend to present any exhaustive treatments in this context. If critical discussion is opened up, and others are motivated to bring other matters in philosophy of religion into dialogue with disability perspectives and vice versa, then I will consider the efforts invested in this project to have been a success.

Second, I will be working in this chapter with a broad definition of "disability" that is inclusive of both intellectual and physical impairments. In this view, the World Health Organization (WHO) defines a disability as "any restriction or lack (resulting from an impairment) of ability to perform an activity in a manner or within the range considered normal for a human being" (WHO 1980: 28). I would only note at present that while disabilities are inevitably individual experiences, WHO's definition opens up to include a social component inasmuch as the performance of activities is measured according to social—"within a range considered normal"—conventions. As we proceed, it should become evident that this social dimension is central to any substantive engagement between disability studies and philosophy.[7] I will also provide more specific examples of disability as they relate to particular issues in the philosophy of religion.[8]

Disability and the Problem of Evil:
Destabilizing Traditional Theodicies

Philosophy of religion texts all address questions related to the problem of evil. Insofar as many traditional approaches discuss theological doctrines related to divine attributes—for example, omniscience, omnipotence, omnibenevolence—these, in turn, have implications for the question, why does a good and all-powerful God allow bad things to happen to innocent people?[9] Now there is no consensus in philosophy of religion about the viability of any theodicy proposal; in fact, the consensus seems to be, rather, that there are a plurality of theodicies, each with its own strengths, but all with sufficiently glaring weaknesses that incline some to give up on the project of formulating theodicy merely as a theoretical enterprise.[10] As a theist, I do not think the task of constructing theodicies should be abandoned. At the same time, I agree that there are problems across the theodicy spectrum and that these are further intensified when assessed in disability perspective. In the following discussion, I briefly sketch four general types of theistic responses to the problem of evil and summarize unresolved questions from a disability point of view.[11]

First, there are what I call ontological and/or theological models designed to address the problem of evil. By this, I am referring to responses that understand evil as either intrinsically (ontologically) woven into the fabric of the universe or as being the result of God's (at least permissive) will for the world. In the former case, there are either cosmic dualist models such as Manicheanism or primordial chaos models such as that of E. S. Brightman and, more recently, Catherine Keller,[12] any of which would alleviate God from responsibility for evil. The latter might involve either privation models such as Augustine's in which evil has no ontological status of its own but is derivative from the lack of goodness, or more robust theological models such as that of Calvin wherein evil is allowed or even decreed (for high Calvinists) by God in order to achieve God's greater glory.

Besides the standard criticisms of each of these models, disability perspectives would add the following specific critical observations. Regarding dualist construals, there is the concern that disability is uncritically associated with evil, with the result that people with disabilities have been seen (historically) either to have in some way deserved the evil that has befallen them or to have personified the evils feared by (nondisabled) humanity.[13] Primordial chaos models fare a bit better, especially if disabilities are statistically distributed (randomly) across the population. This is more palatable both for the appearance of congenital disabilities related to unpredictable genetic mutations and for those that occur later in life because of accidental circumstances. However, if disability is the result of the cosmic chaos that can never be eradicated, will disability also be present in the afterlife? We will return to this question below.

Augustine's privation model was premised on the goodness of God and of God's creation of all things as good. Further, Augustine reasoned that if evil is the privation or lack of good, then insofar as anything exists, that in itself is good, whatever other lacks may be pertinent in that case. The result is that there is nothing existent that is wholly evil, since such would be nothing at all.[14] On the one hand, this view arms the humanity, dignity, and goodness of *people* with disabilities, without insisting that the disabilities are necessarily good. On the other hand, for some people with disabilities, their disabilities are neither merely the lack of ability nor the lack of something else; rather, their disabilities are palpable realities that cannot be explained away through the notion of privation. For them, the notion of evil as lack, while perhaps philosophically interesting, is neither phenomenologically nor existentially satisfying.[15]

Finally, perhaps the most challenging theological model for people with disabilities is that associated with or implied in the doctrine of divine sovereignty. Admittedly there are some who have come to terms with their disabilities as playing an important role in God's overall plan. The problem arises, however, when people with disabilities are told by the nondisabled that their disabilities are part of God's plan for their lives. It is one thing for an individual to come to accept his or her disability as the result of God's intentions, and embrace this as his or her own confession; it is quite another for others to be told by well-meaning and able-bodied people that God has basically chosen to inflict their disabilities for God's own reasons.[16] In the latter case, rather than conclude that God can indeed be trusted, God may instead become the one who, for no apparent reason at all, has arbitrarily chosen to wreck their lives. There are pastoral issues involved here, but the fundamental question remains theological: did or did not God choose to make me the way I am?

A second type of theistic response to the problem of evil is what is often called the freewill theodicy. This position involves a family of related views that suggest that the problem of evil either is the result of creaturely freedom unleashed by the fall of humankind or by the primordial fall of angels, or is related, for process theodicies, to the intrinsic freedom that pertains, in varying degrees of strength, to all creatures and even created things.[17] For advocates of the freewill defense, God is not ultimately responsible for evil; rather, God chose to create a world of free creatures because such a world is better than one without freedom. But free creatures can choose to commit evil acts, or to act in ways that bring about evil consequences. Thus, the freewill defense emphasizes creaturely responsibility for moral evil, but also suggests that natural evil is the result of a fallen world suffering the effects of actions perpetuated by rebellious spiritual beings known in the Christian tradition as Satan, the Devil, or demons (other fallen angels). For process theodicies, the suffering caused by natural disasters (natural evil) is an unavoidable outcome of the way that the world is, and in this regard overlaps with cosmic dualist or primordial chaos responses to the problem of evil (so I will say no more about process philosophical or theological theodicies here).

How might disability perspectives interact with freewill theodicies? I suggest that disability approaches may gravitate away from versions of the freewill defense involving spirit beings and toward those that emphasize human freedom. The chief concern with locating the blame for evil on a primordial fall of angels is that this kind of speculative theodicy does little to either motivate or inform our present engagement with disability and the issues it raises. The other side of this rationale is also why disability perspectives might be drawn toward the freewill defense: that it rightly focuses on all of the ways in which human freedom exacerbates the experience of disability. Yet disability advocates caution against the traditional association of freedom and evil in this case. This is because as traditionally articulated, the various amendments of the freewill defense have been called on to either justify why disabilities happen to people with them (i.e., because of their sin, carelessness, or irresponsibility) or to enable a sort of re-signed posture in the face of human evils (e.g., of wars and its consequences). However, a disability perspective would insist that the freewill defense should not be interpreted only at the level of if and how it may relate to *individuals* with disabilities. Rather there is a social dimension to disability, as signaled earlier in our working definition of disability. In this wider framework, the suffering experienced by people with intellectual or physical impairments is in some cases aggravated by and in other cases fully derived from the social, economic, and political structures that impinge on their lives.[18] Evil in this perspective originates systemically and structurally from the ableism that discriminates, excludes, and oppresses people with disabilities.[19] The freewill theodicy rightly calls attention to the role of creaturely freedom in causing and perpetuating evil, not in terms of people with disabilities receiving what is due for their sins, but in terms of identifying the social dynamics that cause harm and suffering in the lives of those with disabilities. When put in this way, however, evil is neither merely "explained" nor "justified"; rather, the sources of evil are named in order that the status quo can be addressed and dismantled. And this must be the collaborative work of both people with and without disabilities.

A third type of response to the problem of evil has been called the "soul-making theodicy." Given this label by John Hick (1966: part III), the basic outline actually is traced back to the early church father, Irenaeus of Lyons, and emphasizes that evil has been (at least) allowed by God because of its formative capacities for the development of moral virtues. Thus, within the divine scheme of things, evil is soul-shaping: it produces that kind of virtuous character that comes about only when people persevere through suffering and tragedy. The main questions with this Irenaean theodicy from a disability perspective are threefold. (1) Whose souls are being made and why? Why is it that in this model, it is first and foremost the souls of people with disabilities that are assumed to be in need of shaping? (2) Even if it is not assumed that disabilities are designed to shape the souls of people with them, nevertheless this model presumes an instrumental approach to disability; and in this case, the lives of people with disabilities become the means through which "nondisabled" souls can be bettered. Without denying the formative value of experiences of suffering, a disability perspective would caution against instrumentalizing the pain and suffering of a select group of people for the gains of others. Even if not specifically put this way, this is how the rhetoric of the soul-making theodicy is interpreted by people with disabilities.[20] (3) Finally, the question arises from a disability perspective that also plagues theodicies in general: are *all* experiences of disability (in particular) and evil (in general) soul-making? Are there not wholly gratuitous evils that defy any efforts to be rendered meaningful, even for those who believe that some experiences of disability and suffering can be virtue-forming?

The last type of response to the problem of evil is the recent articulation in specifically Christian theological circles of God as entering into the suffering of the world, especially but not only in the cross of Jesus Christ. Although with roots deep in the theological tradition, this "suffering God" view has been revived since the appearance of Jürgen Moltmann's *The Crucified God* (1974), and is currently gaining widespread adherence in theology-and-science circles.[21] What is attractive about this proposal is its admitting the intractability of the problem of evil, while yet insisting that God is not removed from our suffering but has entered into and embraced such in God's own life. On the one side, disability perspectives will welcome such a theodicy insofar as it neither stigmatizes the experiences of suffering connected with disability nor marginalizes people because of their disabilities. On the other side, as with theodicies of the primordial chaos (above) and even amidst the insistence that the "suffering God" is not a weak deity but a strong survivor, there are those who would question whether or not such a motif is sufficiently consoling for those who labor under the pain and tragedy that accompanies the experience of some disabilities.

Before proceeding, two summary comments are in order. First, as may be intuited from the foregoing, disability is difficult to categorize with regard to the problem of evil. On the one hand, the sufferings related to disability are in many cases classifiable under "natural evil" insofar as they may be results of the workings of nature; on the other hand, the social character of disability also means that much of its attendant sufferings come under the category of "moral evil." Beyond these, however, certain congenital disabilities—not fetal alcohol syndrome, which is clearly related to human responsibility, but genetically or chromosomally related syndromes such as trisomy 21 (Down syndrome)—are neither merely natural nor moral evils in terms of their etiologies. For theistic traditions, of course, this raises the theodicy question in earnest: how can an omnibenevolent and omnipotent God allow such evils in the world? Yet the answer cannot be simply saying that God will in the end "heal" such individuals of their genetic variation, as it is difficult to imagine how someone with trisomy-21 (for example) can be the same person without that chromosomal configuration. In these cases, for God not to allow the trisomic mutation may be for God not to allow the appearance of precisely that person. There may be no way, in this case, to eradicate the disability without eliminating the person.[22] I will return to this question in the Conclusion section.

The second observation is that, as is already clear, disability scholarship has long insisted on defining the experience of disability, including any suffering and evil that might be involved, in social terms. In this framework, disability perspectives highlight the social and political character of the nature of evil often absent in able-ist discussions of theodicy. Evil is neither a spiritual problem to be solved by a proper theology (or theodicy) nor an individual problem to be borne by people who embraced the soul-making character of their experiences. Rather, there is an irreducible social and relational aspect to all human experience, the experience of disability not exempted (Swinton 2002: 239–247).

If so, then any theodicy that disregards this social and relational dimension cannot speak convincingly into the disability community. It may be that when all is said and done, disability perspectives can point only toward an eschatological resolution for the unresolved challenges for theodicy (see further below). On the other hand, people with disabilities cannot only wait for God's eschatological response, and in that case, the questions and categories of traditional philosophy of religion need to be revised in order to take disability perspectives into account.

Disability and Religious Epistemology: Retrieving/Redeeming Subjugated Knowledges

At this point in our dialogue between disability studies and the philosophy of religion, it is worthwhile to focus more intentionally on the epistemological question of how and why disability perspectives make a difference in philosophy of religion. What justifies the argumentative force of disability experiences in this discussion? I suggest that disability perspectives contribute significantly to the chorus of postmodern voices resisting the Enlightenment and Eurocentric hegemony in traditional philosophy of religion. In contrast to the traditional emphases on the *if, how,* or *what* of religious experience,[23] postmodern and disability approaches focus instead on the *so what* and *so that* questions. To be more precise, building on the preceding discussion, I argue that the experiences of people with various sensory or mental limitations (a) call into question the conventional categories and assumptions of philosophy of religion; (b) supplement religious knowledge through insights largely unavailable to nondisabled epistemic viewpoints; and (c) engage other modes of knowing than those dominant in traditional philosophical reflection. The following discussion explicates each of these claims.

To begin this discussion, I note that the experience of disability brings to the fore new categories and assumptions to the task of philosophy of religion. We have already seen these movements at work in our discussion of the theodicy question above. To press home this point, I call attention to the work of Christian theologian Nancy Eiesland. Drawing from her lifelong experience of disability (with a form of degenerative bone disease), Eiesland (1994) suggests, for example, that what people with disabilities like hers need is not a miraculous cure or healing but a more just, inclusive, and hospitable world.[24] In contrast, then, to the traditional philosophy of religion's focus on the possibility (or not) of miracles, a disability approach to the topic highlights instead a liberating God (the central theme of Eiesland's theology and philosophy of disability). Whereas the traditional philosophy of religion has been perennially devoted to explicating the attribute of divine omnipotence, Eiesland's disability perspective identifies instead the "disabled God":

> ...I had waited for a mighty revelation of God. But my epiphany bore little resemblance to the God I was expecting or the God of my dreams. I saw God in a sip-puff wheelchair, that is, the chair used mostly by quadriplegics enabling them to maneuver by blowing and sucking on a strawlike device. Not an omnipotent, self-sufficient God, but neither a pitiable, suffering servant. In this moment, I beheld God as a survivor, unpitying and forthright. I recognized the incarnate Christ in the image of those judged "not feasible", "unemployable", with "questionable quality of life". Here was God for me. (Eiesland 1994: 89)

And finally, Eiesland's disability viewpoint brings the philosophy of beauty (aesthetics) back into dialogue with philosophy of religion, albeit through the most unexpected of sources: that of the disabled body:

> Most people with disabilities see our bodies not as signs of deviance or deformity, but as images of beauty and wholeness. We discern in our bodies, not only the ravages of injustice and pain, but also the reality of surviving with dignity. (Eiesland 1994: 115)

In each of these ways, the disability perspective re/introduces treasures old and new—justice, liberation, and beauty—to the task of philosophy of religion.

I suggest in addition that disability perspectives supplement religious knowledge through insights that are largely unavailable to the nondisabled. This is evident, for example, in the work of John Hull (2001), a British theologian who became totally blind. In learning to read the Bible again from a nonsighted perspective, Hull came to "see" that the Bible is written by sighted persons, and this explains why the majority of its readers do not question the sighted assumptions behind many of the metaphors that equate blindness with ignorance, unbelief, lostness, unworthiness, or despair. Furthermore, a nonsighted perspective is able to retrieve and reappropriate many of the blind characters in the biblical narrative and focus instead on the full range of human issues revealed through these lives rather than reduce them to flat identities dominated by their blindness. Last but not least, a nonsighted reading of the Bible recognizes Jesus' tactile or "hands-on" approach to people as well as his willingness to undergo blindness (through being blindfolded during the passion) for the sake of experiencing solidarity with the oppressed and marginalized. Hull concludes that God "himself" is beyond sighted-ness or blindness; rather, a close reading of the Bible from a nonsighted point of view reveals that God is not only at home in darkness but also is active amidst the darkness to accomplish God's purposes.

Hull's proposals are not easily verifiable except through the experience of nonsightedness. That is why I have identified his epistemic viewpoint as one that supplements insights otherwise unavailable to "normal" epistemic processes. This leads also to my third claim: that disability experiences engage other modes of knowing than those dominant in traditional philosophical reflection. Here, I am talking not only about how nonsighted perspectives can supplement sightedones; rather, I want to call attention to noncognitive and nonrational modes of knowing that are more or less absent in philosophy of religion discussions, but are prevalent in the lives of people with severe or profound intellectual disabilities.

My own interests in disability studies, motivated in part through growing up with a brother with a moderate form of intellectual disability, has focused on the religious knowing of people without even the "basic beliefs" identified by some philosophers of religion.[25] Here my interests are less in the epistemology associated with various savant syndromes, although the question of what difference such skills make in the religious knowledge of savants is an intriguing one.[26] Rather, I am more concerned with the connections between how people with intellectual disabilities know in general, and what that means for religious epistemology. In the case of those with severe or profound retardation, how can what they know even be determined, and who can or should speak on behalf of the intellectually disabled? Amidst this set of questions and others like them, time spent with people with intellectual disabilities soon reveals that there are modes of knowing in operation that may either precede or transcend the intellect, or both.[27] Rather than a rationalist epistemology or a propositionalist form of communication, people across the spectrum of intellectual disabilities engage the world and their significant others through affective, embodied, and relational forms of knowing. The difference in the cases of severe and profound disabilities is that these may be the only forms of knowing, but none of this is registered by ableist (or cognitivist) perspectives.

The result is not mysticism, as traditionally discussed in philosophy of religion texts—at least not in most cases—but simply the foregrounding of these basic modes of human knowing that have been generally overlooked in traditional philosophy of religion.[28] More specifically, then, if people with intellectual disabilities do not depend primarily on cognitive modes of knowing, then their religious knowing will also be similarly independent. In this framework, we come to see that the divine or transcendence is mediated through the "ordinary" forms of affective, embodied, and relational experiences that are operative in the background of all human knowing.[29] And whereas discussions of religious epistemology in traditional philosophy of religion may be pre-occupied with questions related to the evidential reliability of or jus-tification for truth claims, the religious epistemology of people with intellectual disabilities will be more focused instead on affective and embodied aspects of that which is good, beautiful, and even true. What emerges are divergent perspectives on received questions (and answers) that most traditional discussions in religious epistemology have not taken into account.

These examples drawn from the experiences of people with physi-cal, sensory, and intellectual disabilities lead to the following two sum-mary remarks. First, the religious knowledge of people with disabilities has been understandably marginalized in philosophy of religion simply because they have not been involved in such discussions. Now, although this situation is gradually changing, it remains true that the case needs to be made for securing rather than marginalizing disability perspec-tives from the philosophy of religion roundtable.[30] Ableist resistance will dismiss disability voices as just another politically correct imposi-tion on an existing conversation. Yet if all knowledge is political in some respect (and no knowledge is nonpolitical),[31] then such ableist assumptions need to be questioned and this can be done only from within the experience of disability that has traditionally been relegated to the underside of history. And the emphasis needs to be on disability *perspectives* (in the plural) since, as should be clear from the preced-ing, there is no one form of disability experience[32]; rather, there are various kinds of disabilities, and each voice needs to be heard on its own terms. Second, with the emergence of disability epistemologies in philosophy of religion, the focus shifts from the merits or demerits of religious beliefs and their evidential reliability to a discussion of the hope, attitudes, and affections related to religious life. Some religious epistemologists are being more sensitive to these matters,[33] although most discussions of religious epistemology remain absorbed with the traditional questions related to the cognitive and rational aspects of religious experience.[34] Far from rejecting the important discussions about faith and reason in philosophy of religion, disability perspectives require that faith be understood not just in terms of cognitively held beliefs, but as pervasive over the many domains of human experience.

This much wider epistemological spectrum means that disability perspectives suggest a third way between or beyond the debate between advocates of a pretheoretical (mystical) religious experience on the one side and proponents of a religious experience that is linguistically and textually mediated on the other.[35] While religious knowledge remains predominantly mediated by a tradition, yet in cases where such knowing is not cognitively dependent, there are alternative forms of engagement through which people can and do come to embody the true, the good, and the beautiful.

Disability, Death, and the Afterlife: Reappropriating Visions of Eternity

So far we have seen that disability perspectives can help retrieve subjugated epistemologies and reinvigorate the philosophical discussion. In this section, I wish to invoke disability viewpoints to explore discussions about death and the afterlife in philosophy of religion. From a disability perspective, Western discussions about the possibility and mode of the afterlife are just as problematic as Eastern religious and philosophical views regarding karmic reincarnation. Furthermore, traditional philosophical debates regarding the retention of personal identity in the afterlife are especially convoluted when viewed from the standpoints of the wide range of intellectual and physical disabilities, in terms of not only congenital conditions but also how human lives are shaped over time by capacities, environments, and relationships. Finally, traditional individualistic notions of heaven and hell, salvation and damnation, are also problematic when disability perspectives are factored into the conversation. In examining each of these issues briefly, I will argue that the human experience of disability upsets traditional formulations in philosophy of religion and encourages philosophers (and disabilities scholars) to look for other resources within the discourses of philosophy and religion to fashion alternative eschatological scenarios that will be, in turn, more inclusive of the experiences of persons with disability in the here and now.[36]

Traditionally, three major questions regarding the afterlife have received the bulk of the attention: First, is there or is there not an afterlife? This question has been especially persistent since the Enlightenment and its attendant materialistic, naturalistic, and positivistic worldviews. Second, if there is an afterlife, what is the relationship between what has traditionally been labeled the human soul and the body? On this question, the traditional Platonic dualism between soul and body has been more recently challenged by monistic, emergentist, and nonreductive physicalist construals of the mind-body relationship. This leads to the third question: what is the nature of the body in the afterlife? Especially in the Christian discussions in the philosophy of religion, the doctrine of the resurrection of the body has been the subject of extensive consideration. I will take up the first question before dealing with the latter two.

From a disability perspective, the question about whether or not there is an afterlife induces mixed responses. On the one hand, people with disabilities come from a wide spectrum of religious and philosophical positions, and for those who are drawn to materialism or naturalism in various respects, the idea of an afterlife is no more coherent than for nondisabled people with similar views. Then there are also those with disabilities who cannot bear the thought of "more of the same" in terms of "living" eternally with their disability conditions.[37] On the other hand, many people with disabilities, including most who are religious, have hoped for and believed in an afterlife in which they are free from their disabilities. For them, to even question the possibility of the afterlife is to question ultimate (cosmic and divine) justice. From this point of view, the injustice they have experienced in this life—whether it be the result of bad luck (chance mutations producing congenital disabilities) or moral irresponsibility—will be vindicated in the next. This same rationale renders less attractive notions of reincarnation derived from Eastern religious and philosophical traditions, the major alternative presented in traditional philosophy of religion discussions on the afterlife. If reincarnation is driven by karma, then either bad karma in a previous life has produced the present life with disability or the present life with disability puts one at a disadvantage of producing good karma for the next life, or both. The hope of people with disabilities in general, then, is dominated by visions of an afterlife in which the challenges associated with their conditions will be no more.

But if people desire an afterlife free from their disabilities, then the second and third questions regarding the nature of the afterlife in philosophy of religion become pertinent. For people with disabilities, however, these questions about personal identity expose a different set of concerns. For some people with physical disabilities, there is no question that the belief in the resurrection means nothing less than a fully capable and whole body. For others with various types of sensory and physical disabilities, things may not be so simple. For example, if people who are members of Deaf culture anticipate, "when we get to heaven, the signing will be tremendous!" what does that mean for hearing members in the afterlife?[38] How will the congenitally blind, who have learned to "see" with their hands and ears (Karlsson 1996: 303–330) be given the beatific vision? Will people who have lived most of their lives with prostheses be resurrected with what has become, for all intents and purposes, an integral aspect of their identity?[39] In fact, if Jesus's resurrected body retained the impairments in his hands, side, and feet, is that not suggestive that the resurrected bodies of people with disabilities will also retain signs of their impairments in the world to come?[40] These are questions about the continuity and discontinuity between the present life and the afterlife: if the discontinuity is too great, the sense of personal identity is threatened; if the continuity is too great, then the discontinuity posited between the present finite body and the anticipated resurrected body is undermined.

This question of continuity and discontinuity also presents itself, as already noted, with regard to people with intellectual disabilities. Parallel to the question about what happens to those who die as infants, with what bodies and what kind of personal identities will these people be resurrected in the afterlife? The major difference is that for the severely and profoundly disabled, some will die with adult bodies but undeveloped minds (Young 1990: 61–69). Another no less challenging scenario involves the resurrection of those who suffer brain damage and/ or the loss of memory and yet survive for many years before death.[41]

Finally, and perhaps most obviously, the question of personal identity relates to people with chromosomal variations that are what might be called identity-constitutive, such as trisomy 21 (Down syndrome). For these, "Could someone imagine their daughter with Down's syndrome as being her true self in the new heaven and new earth without some manifestation of her condition?" (Samuel and Sudgen 1998: 435) In each of these cases, and many others, personal identity is understood in terms of not only cognitive self-consciousness but (as seen in our earlier discussions on epistemology) also bodily structures, affective dispositions, and interpersonal relations. On these issues, reflections on the afterlife pose other questions than just those related to the mind-body problem, or *if* there will be an embodied existence.

But it is precisely the interpersonal and interrelational aspects of identity foregrounded by disability experiences that raise the final and perhaps most important set of questions for philosophical reflections on the afterlife. There are at least two aspects to the issues involved. On the one hand, there is the question about the deep interpersonal and intersubjective bonds that often develop between people with severe and profound disabilities and their caregivers.[42] To be sure, all people are interdependent on others in significant ways. However, the intense dependence in these specific cases form, shape, and irrevocably mark the identities of both those with disabilities and their caregivers. If such relationships are severed in the afterlife, it is difficult to conceive of how continuity is maintained for these persons.

On the other hand, we have already mentioned that the suffering of people with disabilities is often socially constructed. Beyond issues of social injustice, however, there are also issues related to the discrimination, marginalization, and exclusion perpetuated at the interpersonal level. From a disability perspective, eschatological vindication in the afterlife does not necessarily have to take the form of punitive assessments against their tormentors. At the same time, the experiences of persecution suffered by people with disabilities cannot be overlooked. This means that the final reconciliation will include a social dimension in which those with disabilities will be reconciled with their nondisabled oppressors.[43] Not coincidentally, I suggest, Jesus's parable of the eschatological banquet included the blind, lame, and crippled (Luke 14: 13, 21), just as they were, rather than only after they had been healed. Ultimately, justice, at least in the form of inclusion, must prevail if meaning is to be found in lives previously deemed unworthy of serious consideration. In this way, traditional discussions of heaven, hell, and the afterlife will factor in the complex webs of relationships that bind together people with disabilities and those who have wronged them.

During this discussion, I have refrained from postulating too many concrete proposals for thinking about the afterlife in disability perspective. Rather, my strategy has been to suggest questions derived from disability experiences that have not been posed in traditional discussions on the afterlife in philosophy of religion. In the end, asking the right questions about the afterlife has implications for how we conduct business in the present life. If we think that the afterlife is a "magical" fix for all the challenges posed by disability, then we may be more inclined to simply encourage people with disabilities (as has long been done) to bear up under their lot in life and await God's eschatological healing for their lives. Yet this assumes that the task of responding to the issues of disability belongs to God, and it also assumes that disability is primarily (perhaps only) an individual affair. I have maintained throughout this chapter, however, that there is an intractable social dimension to disability, and how we think about the afterlife shapes our vision for the present one. If life in the hereafter manifests the divine and cosmic justice we all hope for, and also includes people with disabilities in a sense just as they are—see, for example, the parable of the eschatological banquet at which the blind, lame, and deaf are included (Luke 14: 1–24)—then such notions of justice and inclusion should also guide our present efforts.

Conclusion: Enabling a Performative Philosophy of Religion

My goal in this chapter has been to interrogate traditional approaches to philosophy of religion from a disability studies perspective. We have focused our attention on issues in theodicy, religious epistemology, and questions of death and the afterlife, and used them as springboards to register disability perspectives on philosophy of religion topics. One of the most glaring issues has been the absence of disability perspectives in traditional philosophy of religion. It might even be said that one of the "evils" of theodicy has been the ignorance, neglect, and marginalization of disability voices. In this case, the first steps to any viable theodicy will need to retrieve and include such disability perspectives. As in the wider philosophical, political, and scholarly issues, the mantra of people with disabilities, "Nothing about us without us!" applies also to the philosophy of religion (Charlton 1998).

When disability perspectives are recorded, however, traditional theodicy is transformed into what some have called "anthropodicy" (Crenshaw 1983; Sontag 1981). But whereas others have coined this term to emphasize how human sinfulness and fallenness deflect divine responsibility, I wish to call attention to the task remaining before human beings who are confronted with the experience of disability in particular and of life itself in general. The foregoing discussion reveals that disability perspectives can help redirect discussion in the direction of what I call a praxis-oriented philosophy of religion (Swinton 2007). By this, I mean that even granting the speculative moment in philosophy of religion, disability perspectives will insist that such moments in the long run will need to invigorate the moral, social, and political practices that facilitate the healing of human life. Such healing is, arguably, the goal of all philosophical activity that loves wisdom and of religious activity that seeks to incarnate love. In other words, *philosophia*—the love of wisdom—in disability perspective cannot be neutral regarding bringing about the things of which wisdom speaks: goodness, truth, beauty, and justice. Put alternatively, in philosophy of religion perspective, philosophical reflection is sustained by that which religion in its own way seeks to realize: love—the love of God, the love for God, and the love of human beings for one another. When brought together in the disability perspective, wisdom and love are neither merely theoretical notions nor theological speculations; rather, they become the stuff by which philosophical reflection is supposed to be transformed so that the world might be changed.

This means that disability perspectives play an essential role in keeping philosophy and philosophy of religion out of its ivory tower and engaged with the concrete human experiences of life. Furthermore, a philosophy of religion informed by disability perspectives will be liberative for both philosophy and for religion insofar as both projects will be more deeply sensitized to the ultimate issues of human suffering, meaning-making, and hope. Hence disability perspectives will not only destabilize traditional formulations in philosophy of religion but also ultimately serve to rehabilitate philosophy of religion in ways that enable the proper performance of wisdom to manifest the good, true, and beautiful that is the stuff of authentic spirituality and piety.[44]

Notes

1. This chapter was previously published in 2009 in *ArsDisputandi*, *9*, and is reprinted here with permission.

2. In preparation for this chapter, I reviewed over a dozen recent textbooks in philosophy" of religion and not once did disability appear in the chapter or section titles or in the index. Even when there is an entire section on how "gender and ethnic diversity influence[s] our thinking about religion"—as there is in E. Stump & M. J. Murray (Eds.), *Philosophy of Religion: The Big Questions* (Malden, MA: Blackwell, 1999)—the perspective of dis/ability diversity is strikingly absent.

3. The field of disability studies is relatively new (in comparison with the philosophy of religion, only dating back to the disability movements that emerged out of the civil rights movement in the 1960s), but also quickly developing. It is interdisciplinary and multidisciplinary in scope, and is focused on bringing perspectives informed by the experience of disability to bear on other disciplinary and scholarly endeavors. For introductions, see D. Johnstone, *An Introduction to Disability Studies*, 2nd ed. (London, England: David Fulton, 2001); L. J. Davis (Ed.), *The Disability Studies Reader*, 2nd ed. (London, England: Routledge, 2006); and G. L. Albrecht (Gen. Ed.), *Encyclopedia of Disability*, 5 vols. (Thousand Oaks, CA: Sage, 2006). In this essay, I use ˜disability studies perspective" synonymously with "disability perspective".

4. E.g., Anita Silvers at San Francisco State University; Eva Feder Kittay at SUNY Stony Book; Licia Carlson at Seattle University; Roger S. Gottlieb at Worcester Polytechnic Institute; Martha Nussbaum at the University of Chicago; Jonathan Rée at Roehampton University; and Hans Reinders at the Free University of Amsterdam, just to name a few.

5. See, e.g., my *Theology and Down Syndrome: Reimagining Disability in Late Modernity* (Waco, TX: Baylor University Press, 2007); and T. E. Reynolds, *Vulnerable Communion: A Theology of Disability and Hospitality* (Grand Rapids, MI: Brazos Press, 2008).

6. E.g., D. Wasserman, J. Bickenbach, & R. Wachbroit (Eds.), *Quality of Life and Human Difference: Genetic Testing, Health Care, and Disability* (Cambridge: Cambridge University Press, 2005); P. Byrne, *Philosophical and Ethical Problems in Mental Handicap* (New York, NY: St. Martin's Press, 2005); D. Pothier & R. F. Devlin (Eds.), *Critical Disability Theory: Essays in Philosophy, Politics, Policy, and Law* (Vancouver, BC: University of British Columbia Press, 2006); and S. Tremain (Ed.), *Foucault and the Government of Disability* (Ann Arbor, MI: University of Michigan Press, 2005).

7. Both the individual and the social aspects of disability are emphasized in R. Hull, Defining disability—A philosophical approach. *Res Publica 4*(2) (1998), 199–210.

8. For the record, I write not as a person with any known disability, but as a brother of a man with Down syndrome; hence the motivation of my work in this area (see also Note 4 above).

9. As Joseph Runzo, *Global Philosophy of Religion: A Short Introduction* (Oxford, England: Oneworld, ch. 6, 2001) suggests, the "problem of evil" infects theistic traditions much more than others. This does not mean that there is no problem of evil in nontheistic traditions. Rather, the problem of evil in such traditions is unrelated to the task of theodicy, of justifying the reality of evil with the existence of a good and all-powerful God. For further discussion of evil in nontheistic traditions, see Bruce Reichenbach, Karma and the problem of evil. In G. E. Kessler (Ed.), *Philosophy of Religion: Toward a Global Perspective* (Belmont, CA: Wadsworth, pp. 248–255, 1999) and Wendy Doniger, Karma in Hindu thought. In D. Stewart (Ed.), *Exploring the Philosophy of Religion,* 6th ed. (Upper Saddle River, NJ: Pearson/Prentice-Hall, pp. 184–188, 2007).

10. For two critics of traditional theodicies along these lines, see T. W. Tilley, *The Evils of Theodicy* (Washington, DC: Georgetown University Press, 1991) and S. K. Pinnock, *Beyond Theodicy: Jewish and Christian Continental Thinkers Respond to the Holocaust* (Albany, NY: State University of New York Press, 2002); Pinnock's call is to supplement the theoretical task of theodicy with practical aspects that produce meaning and hope amidst suffering.

11. I realize that the following typologies are overgeneralized, and that nuances within various views might address disability concerns. However, the nuances are usually qualifications that are distinctive to particular revisions of an overall type, and these are often resisted by those who propose other qualifications to that type for their own purposes. Hence as part of my objective is to open up conversation between disability perspectives and philosophy of religion, my discussion of the various theodicies will remain at a general level.

12. E.g., E. S. Brightman, *Personality and Religion* (New York, NY: Abingdon Press, pp. 71–100, 1934) and C. Keller, *The Face of the Deep: A Theology of Becoming* (New York, NY: Routledge, 2003).

13. That disabilities, and people with them, are feared by nondisabled people is well documented—e.g., I. Katz, *Stigma: A Social Psychological Analysis* (Hillsdale, NJ: Erlbaum, 1981); M. Mitchell (Ed.), *Monsters: Human Freaks in America's Gilded Age* (Toronto, Canada: ECW Press, 2002); and M. Shildrick, *Embodying the Monster: Encounters with the Vulnerable Self* (London, England: Sage, 2002).

14. See the excellent summary selection of Augustine, Evil is Privation of Good In M. Peterson, W. Hasker, B. Reichenbach, & D. Basinger (Eds.), *Philosophy of Religion: Selected Readings* (New York, NY: Oxford University Press, pp. 231–235, 1996).

15. It is with great difficulty that the notion of evil as privation fits into auto-biographical accounts of disability—e.g., R. F. Murphy, *The Body Silent* (New York, NY: Henry Holt and Company, 1987); L. Kriegel, *Flying Solo: Reimagining Manhood, Courage, and Loss* (Boston, MA: Beacon Press, 1998); H. G. Gallagher, *Black Bird Fly Away: Disabled in an Able-bodied World* (Arlington, VA: Vandamere Press, 1998); and E. F. Kittay, *Love's Labor: Essays on Women, Equality, and Dependency* (New York, NY: Routledge, 1999)—especially against the rugged and honest portrayal of life with disabilities.

16. I discuss this issue in my *Theology and Down Syndrome*, pp. 167–169.

17. The most prominent advocate of process theodicy is David Ray Griffin; see his two books, *God, Power, and Evil: A Process Theodicy* (Philadelphia, PA: Westminster, 1967), and *Evil Revisited: Reponses and Reconsiderations* (Albany, NY: State University of New York Press, 1991).

18. For explication of these themes, see H. Livneh, On the origins of negative attitudes toward people with disabilities. In R. P. Marinelli & A. E. Dell Orto (Eds.), *The Psychological and Social Impact of Disability*, 3rd ed. (New York, NY: Springer, pp. 181–198, 1991); L. P. Francis, Disability. In R. G. Frey & C. H. Wellman (Eds.), *A Companion to Applied Ethics*. Blackwell Companions to Philosophy 26 (Malden, MA: Blackwell, pp. 424–438, 2003); and A. Mason et al., Prejudice toward people with disabilities. In J. L. Chin (Ed.), *The Psychology of Prejudice and Discrimination*, Vol. 4, *Disability, Religion, Physique, and Other Traits* (Westport, CT: Praeger, pp. 51–92, 2004).

19. Ableism is manifest in the belief of the majority nondisabled in their superiority, and it privileges the nondisabled. Society is culpable in discrimination against those with disabilities as ableism operates individually, culturally, and institutionally. For discussion, see M. Moore, S. Beazley, & J. Maelzer, *Researching Disability Issues* (Buckingham, UK: Open University Press, ch. 6, 1998); G. Hales, *Beyond Disability: Towards an Enabling Society* (Thousand Oaks, CA: Sage, 1996); and A. G. Johnson, *Privilege, Power, and Difference*, 2ded. (New York, NY: McGraw-Hill, 2006).

20. G. M. Jantzen, *Becoming Divine: Towards a Feminist Philosophy of Religion* (Bloomington, IN: Indiana University Press, p. 260, 1999) raises a parallel question about how the "we" who learns from suffering are often the "paradigmatically white, wealthy, highly privileged, and often male philosophers of religion." My point is to question how "we" nondisabled folk can so easily lay the burden of educating the human race on folk with disabilities.

21. J. Moltmann, *The Crucified God*. J. Bowden & R. A. Wilson (Trans.). (New York, NY: Harper & Row, 1974); for the appropriation of the "suffering God" thesis in science and theology discussions, see the various essays in J. Polkinghorne (Ed.), *The Work of Love: Creation as Kenosis* (Grand Rapids, MI: Eerdmans, 2005).

22. Stanley Hauerwas makes exactly this point in his Marginalizing the "Retarded." In Flavian Dougherty (Ed.), *The Deprived, the Disabled, and the Fullness of Life* (Wilmington, DE: Michael Glazier, Inc., pp. 67–105, esp. 69, 1984).

23. As evident in any chapter on "religious experience" found in standard texts on philosophy of religion.

24. In response to the idea that she would be made whole in heaven, Eiesland says, "Having been disabled from birth, I came to believe that in heaven I would be absolutely unknown to myself and perhaps to God. My disability has taught me who I am and who God is"; see N. Eiesland, Liberation, inclusion, and justice: A faith response to persons with disabilities. *Impact 14*(3) (2001–2002), 2–3 and 35, quotation from 2.

25. Here, I am referring, of course, to the school of Reformed epistemology; see, e.g., D. J. Hoitenga, Jr., *Faith and Reason from Plato to Plantinga: An Introduction to Reformed Epistemology* (Albany, NY: State University of New York Press, esp. ch. 7, 1991).

26. To my knowledge, no research on savant syndrome in relationship to religion has been conducted; I briefly discuss some of the literature on savant syndrome, although not specifically with regard to religious epistemology, in my *Theology and Down Syndrome*, p. 70.

27. Put in philosophical terms, Blaise Pascal said that "The heart has its reasons, of which reason knows nothing." Note also William Wainwright's argument that human cognition may actually track truth better when based properly conditioned by the passions, sentiments, and affections; see W. J. Wainwright, *Reason and the Heart: A Prolegomenon to a Critique of Passional Reason* (Ithaca, NY: Cornell University Press, 1995).

28. And these "other" modes of what I am calling affective, embodied, and relational knowing have more recently been highlighted in the broader philosophical conversation—e.g., A. R. Damasio, *Descartes' Error: Emotion, Reason, and the Human Brain* (New York, NY: Putnam, 1994); G. Lakoff & M. Johnson, *Philosophy in the Flesh: The Embodied Mind and Its Challenge to Western Thought* (New York, NY: Basic Books, 1999); J. Duran, *Toward a Feminist Epistemology* (Savage, MD: Rowman & Littlefield, 1991); J. I. M. Carpendale & U. Müller (Eds.), *Social Interaction and the Development of Knowledge* (Mahwah, NJ:

Erlbaum, 2004); and H. L. Edge, Individuality in a relational culture: A comparative study. In H. Wautischer (Ed.), *Tribal Epistemologies: Essays in the Philosophy of Anthropology* (Aldershot, UK: Ashgate, pp. 31–39, 1998).

29. I expand on this in my *Theology and Down Syndrome,* pp. 180–191; see also the literature cited there.

30. The same was true with the emergence of feminist philosophy and epistemology. Interestingly, feminists with disabilities have also had to defend their place in feminist philosophy circles. See the discussion by A. Silvers, Disability. In A. M. Jaggar & I. M. Young (Eds.), *A Companion to Feminist Philosophy* (Malden, MA: Blackwell, pp. 330–340, 1998).

31. As argued by M. Schillmeier, Othering blindness—On modern epistemological politics. *Disability and Society 21*(5) (2006), 471–484.

32. This pluralism applies to the spectrum of both physical and intellectual disabilities; see, e.g., K. Fiser, Philosophy, disability, and essentialism. In L. Foster & P. Herzog (Eds.), *Defending Diversity: Contemporary Philosophical Perspectives on Pluralism and Multiculturalism* (Amherst, MA: University of Massachusetts Press, pp. 83–101, 1994) and D. Goodley, Learning difficulties, the Social model of disability and impairment: Challenging epistemologies. *Disability & Society 16*(2) (2001), 207–231.

33. See N. Wolterstor, Religious epistemology. In W. J. Wainwright (Ed.), *The Oxford Handbook of Philosophy of Religion* (Oxford, England: Oxford University Press, pp. 245–271, esp. pp. 246–247, 2005).

34. These are the main issues in traditional philosophy of religion, as reflected by the essays in Part I: Religious Epistemology. In W. L. Craig (Ed.), *Philosophy of Religion: A Reader and Guide* (New Brunswick, NJ: Rutgers University Press, 2002).

35. For both sides to this debate, see W. L. Rowe, *Philosophy of Religion: An Introduction,* 4th ed. (Belmont, CA.: Thomson/Wadsworth, ch. 5, 2007) and M. L. Peterson & R. J. Van Arragon (Eds.), *Contemporary Debates in Philosophy of Religion* (Malden, MA: Blackwell, ch. 5, 2004).

36. The following expands my chapter on eschatology in *Theology and Down Syndrome,* ch. 9, and my essay, Disability, the human condition, and the spirit of the eschatological long run: Toward a pneumatological theology of disability. *Journal of Religion, Disability, and Health 11*(1) (2007), 5–25.

37. B. Davies, *An Introduction to the Philosophy of Religion,* 3rded. (Oxford, England: Oxford University Press, pp. 311–312, 2004) touches briefly on this matter. In response to the question "would immortality be a good thing?" A. Stairs & C. Bernard, *A Thinker's Guide to the Philosophy of Religion* (New York, NY: Pearson/Longman, pp. 307–309, 2006) also discuss that they call "the attractiveness condition," but fail to bring disability perspectives into their equation.

38. See R. Hitching, *The Church and Deaf People: A Study of Identity, Communication and Relationships with Special Reference to the Ecclesiology of Jürgen Moltmann* (Waynesboro, GA: Paternoster, passim, 2004).

39. E.g., as explored in M. Smith & J. Morra (Eds.), *The Prosthetic Impulse: From a Post Human Present to a Biocultural Future*(Cambridge, MA: MIT Press, 2006).

40. This is how some people with disabilities think they will recognize their patron saints, through the presence of impairments through which they "earned" their sainthood; see the discussion of Saint Margaret of Castello, a limped, hunched, blind, and dwarfed woman who accomplished over 200 miracles and was beatified in 1609, as reflected on through the life of a man with cerebral palsy, in R. Orsi, Mildred, is it fun to be a cripple?: The culture of suffering in mid-twentieth-century American Catholicism. In T. J. Ferraro (Ed.), *Catholic Lives, Contemporary America* (Durham, NC: Duke University Press, pp. 19–64, 1997).

41. The most highlighted case, although by no means the only type of memory loss situation, is Alzheimer's disease. D. Keck, *Forgetting Whose We are: Alzheimer's Disease and the Love of God* (Nashville: Abingdon, 1996), suggests that God is the rememberer or historian whose eschatological salvation consists in preserving and restoring to creatures our memories of being the beloved people of God.

42. This involves parents and children, as well as spouses. But they could also emerge in professional relationships between caregivers and their clients. For philosophical reflection from the caregiver point of view, see B. Hillyer, *Feminism and Disability* (Norman, OK: University of Oklahoma Press, 1993).

43. For a discussion of the many layers of justice in disability perspective, see J. C. Kirby, Disability and justice: A pluralistic account. *Social Theory and Practice 30* (2) (2004), 229–246; for consideration of the social dimension of justice in eschatological perspective, see M. Volf, The final reconciliation: Reflections on the social dimension of the eschatological transition. *Modern Theology 16*(1) (2000), 91–113.

44. Research for this chapter was funded in part by a Louisville Institute Faith and Life sabbatical grant for 2005–2006. An earlier version of this chapter was presented to the Disability and Religion section of the American Academy of Religion annual meeting, 18 November 2007, in San Diego, CA. Thanks to Kent A. Eaton (Bethel Seminary) for his response to the papers at this event, and to Thomas R. Reynolds, James K. A. Smith, Kristin Herzog, and Bradford McCall for their feedback on earlier versions of this chapter. Yet I remain fully responsible for the shortcomings herein.

References

Charlton, J. I. (1998). *Nothing About Us Without Us: Disability, Oppression and Empowerment.* Berkeley, CA: University of California Press.

Crenshaw, J. L. (1983). Introduction: The shift from theodicy to anthropodicy. In James L. Crenshaw (Ed.), *Theodicy in the Old Testament* (1–16). Philadelphia, PA: Fortress.

Eiesland, N. L. (1994). *The Disabled God: Toward a Liberatory Theology of Disability.* Nashville, TN: Abingdon.

Hick, J. (1966). *Evil and the God of Love.* Reprint, London, England: Fontana, 1968.

Hull, J. M. (2001). *In the Beginning There was Darkness: A Blind Person's Conversations with the Bible.* Harrisburg, PA: Trinity Press International.

Karlsson, G. (1996). The experience of spatiality for congenitally blind people: A phenomenological-psychological study, *Human Studies 19,* 303–330.

Samuel, V., & Sugden, C. (Eds.) (1998). Biblical and theological reflections on disability. In *Mission as Transformation: A Theology of the Whole Gospel* (pp. 429–437). Oxford, England: Regnum.

Sontag, F. (1981) Anthropodicy and the return of God'. In Stephen T. Davis (Ed.), *En-countering Evil: Live Options in Theodicy* (pp. 137–151). Atlanta, GA: John Knox.

Swinton, J. (2002). Constructing persons: Macmurray and the social construction of disability. In David Fergusson & Nigel Power (Eds.), *John Macmurray: Critical Perspectives* (239–247). New York, NY: Peter Lang.

Swinton, J. (2007). *Raging with Compassion: Pastoral Responses to the Problem of Evil.* Grad Rapids, MI: Eerdmans.

World Health Organization. (1980). *International Classification of Impairments, Disabilities, and Handicaps.* Reprint, Geneva, Switzerland: World Health Organization, 1993.

Young, F. (1990). *Face to Face: A Narrative Essay in the Theology of Suffering* (pp. 61–69). Edinburgh, Scotland: T and T Clark.

Notes on Contributors

Julia Watts Belser is Assistant Professor of Judaism at Missouri State University, where she focuses on the cultural study of rabbinic literature. She earned her PhD in Jewish Studies at the University of California, Berkeley, and the Graduate Theological Union, and received rabbinic ordination from the Academy for Jewish Religion, CA. She currently serves as cochair of the Disability and Religion group at the American Academy of Religion.

Arseli Dokumaci is pursuing a PhD in Performance Studies at Aberystwyth University. Her practice-based project is focused on subtle disabilities and performativity. Her research interests include disability, materiality, and performance in everyday life.

Bonnie L. Gracer received a Master of Arts degree in Jewish Studies from Baltimore Hebrew University, a Master of Social Work degree from Catholic University, and a Bachelor of Arts degree from Brandeis University. Currently she works at the U.S. Department of Education, National Institute on Disability and Rehabilitation Research.

Christine James is an Associate Professor of Philosophy and Religious Studies at Valdosta State University. She has published a variety of articles and book chapters in scholarly journals such as the *Journal for Philosophical Practice, The Journal for the Study of Religions and Ideologies, The International Journal of Sociology and Social Policy, Essays in Philosophy, The Southwest Philosophy Review, The Journal of Consciousness Studies, and Biosemiotics*. She has presented her research at conferences throughout the United States, Canada, Austria, Spain, and the United Kingdom.

Jennifer L. Koosed is Associate Professor and Chair of Religious Studies at Albright College in Reading, PA. In addition to numerous articles, she is the author of the books *(Per)mutations of Qohelet: Reading the*

Body in the Book (2006) and *Gleaning Ruth: A Biblical Heroine and Her Afterlives* (2011). Her research interests include Persian Period literature, feminist interpretation, and the intersections of Bible and popular culture.

Matthew L. Long received his MA in Religious Studies focusing on Islamic studies from the University of Georgia in 2007. His specialties include Qur'an, Hadith, Early Islamic History, and Comparative Religious studies. He has published a number of chapters and articles since receiving his MA and currently teaches the Islamic studies section of World Religions at Chatfield College in Cincinnati, OH.

Autumn Molinari holds a Master's Degree in Social Work from Southern Illinois University Edwardsville. Autumn is a Licensed Clinical Social Worker currently working for Southern Illinois Healthcare Foundation. She provides outpatient mental health therapy for the underprivileged including those who are chronically mentally ill, homeless, jobless, in poverty, and who are experiencing a number of major life stressors.

Gerald V. O'Brien is a tenured Professor of Social Work at Southern Illinois University Edwardsville. His primary research interest relates to disability ethics, policies related to persons with disabilities, disability history, particularly the American eugenics movement, and metaphor analysis pertaining to the framing of minority groups within the context of alarm periods.

Darla Schumm is an Associate Professor of Religion at Hollins University—a small liberal arts women's college nestled in the midst of the Blue Ridge Mountains. Darla received her BA in interdisciplinary studies with concentrations in history, psychology, and women's studies from Goshen College, her MA in Social Ethics from the Pacific School of Religion in Berkeley, CA, and her PhD in Religion, Ethics, and Society from Vanderbilt University. Darla's current research focuses on intersections between religious studies and disability studies. She has several published articles in this area and is the coeditor of this volume and its companion *Disability and Religious Diversity: Cross-Cultural and Interreligious Perspectives.* She enjoys running, knitting, reading, and playing with her son in her free time.

Elizabeth R. Sierra recently completed her doctorate in philosophy at SUNY Binghamton University. She is presently an Assistant Professor of Psychology for the University of Alaska – Anchorage, Prince William Sound Community College. Prior to this she was the Student Support

Service Coordinator and Counselor for the Title V STEM Learning Communities at the University of Texas at Brownsville. Her research examines the ambiguities of whiteness and nonwhiteness at the disciplinary intersections of existential philosophy, Chicana studies, gender and sexuality studies, critical race theory, disability studies, medical anthropology, critical media studies, and counseling practice.

Michael Stoltzfus is Professor of Philosophy and Religious Studies at Valdosta State University in Valdosta, GA. In addition to numerous articles, he is contributing editor of this volume and its companion *Disability and Religious Diversity: Cross-Cultural and Interreligious Perspectives* (2011). He teaches courses in the areas of comparative religious ethics, religious pluralism and interreligious dialogue, world religions, and the intersections of religion and popular culture. His PhD in religion, ethics, and society is from Vanderbilt University (1998). Email: mjstoltz@valdosta.edu.

Kristi Upson-Saia is Assistant Professor in the Department of Religious Studies at Occidental College. Her research focuses on representations and performances of the body in the late antique Mediterranean world, specifically on the ways in which early Christians' clothing broadcasted their identity and cultural superiority (*Early Christian Dress: Gender, Virtue, and Authority*, 2011), how members of Syriac congregations embodied orthodoxy through the singing of hymns, and, most recently, how wounds and deformities were imagined to symbolize piety and to facilitate community.

Kirk Van Gilder, PhD, is an instructor at Gallaudet University in the Department of Philosophy and Religion. Kirk was born hard-of-hearing before losing more hearing in late adolescence and transitioning into the Deaf world. He is an ordained United Methodist clergyperson and has served as a minister in Deaf churches in Baltimore and Pasadena, MD, as well as campus minister to Gallaudet University from 1997 to 2002. Kirk has also traveled to Kenya, Zimbabwe, and Turkey to work with Deaf community development and support. Kirk hopes to continue his travels and research in other countries as well as present his findings and experiences to a wide variety of scholarly and nonscholarly audiences.

Amy T. Wilson is the Program Director for the Master of Arts Degree in International Development at Gallaudet University in Washington, DC. Amy's research and teaching interests are grounded in an interdisciplinary tradition and examines issues at the intersection of development assistance, disability/deafness, gender, and program evaluation. Her research, writing, and consulting center on the effectiveness of northern development assistance from federal agencies, nongovernment organizations, and faith-based groups to people with disabilities and deaf communities in resource-poor countries. Her publications also cover global health care issues for women, adolescents, and children with disabilities in developing countries, human rights of persons with disabilities, and a transformative sociocultural participatory model of program evaluation.

Amos Yong is J. Rodman Williams Professor of Theology at Regent University School of Divinity in Virginia Beach, VA, where he also is director of the PhD in Renewal Studies program. His graduate education includes degrees in theology, history, and religious studies from Western Evangelical Seminary and Portland State University, Portland, OR, and Boston University, Boston, MA, and an undergraduate degree from Bethany University of the Assemblies of God. He has authored or edited over a dozen volumes through 2010. Books forthcoming in 2011 include *Afro-Pentecostalism: Black Pentecostal and Charismatic Christianity in History and Culture* (New York University Press), *Who is the Holy Spirit: The Acts of the Spirit, the Apostles, and Empire* (Paraclete Press), *The Spirit of Creation: Modern Science and Divine Action in the Pentecostal-Charismatic Imagination* (Eerdmans), and *The Bible, Disability, and the Church: A New Vision of the People of God* (Eerdmans). For a full list of publications, see http://www.regent.edu/acad/schdiv/faculty_staff/faculty/yong.cfm. He and his wife, Alma, have three children—Aizaiah (20), a junior at Regent University, Alyssa (17), a freshman at Northwest University of the Assemblies of God, and Annalisa (15), a sophomore in high school in Chesapeake, VA.

Index